"21世纪多维英语规划教材" 专家委员会

顾　问：何自然　梁锦祥
总主编：陆道夫　肖坤学
专家委员会成员：（按姓氏音序排列）

陈建平（广东外语外贸大学）　　　牛保义（河南大学）

陈晓茹（广东工业大学）　　　　　彭建武（山东科技大学）

董金伟（广东外语外贸大学）　　　沈素萍（对外经济贸易大学）

范武邱（中南大学）　　　　　　　王东风（中山大学）

宫　琪（暨南大学）　　　　　　　王丽丽（福建师范大学）

郭　雷（华北电力大学）　　　　　王　哲（中山大学）

郭英剑（中央民族大学）　　　　　肖坤学（广州大学）

何高大（华南农业大学）　　　　　谢江南（中国人民大学）

黄运亭（华南理工大学）　　　　　辛铜川（广州医科大学）

李　月（桂林电子科技大学）　　　张国申（中国药科大学）

凌海衡（华南师范大学）　　　　　张晓红（深圳大学）

刘涛波（华南理工大学）　　　　　张广奎（广东财经大学）

陆道夫（广州大学）　　　　　　　赵德玉（中国海洋大学）

陆国飞（浙江海洋学院）　　　　　朱　跃（安徽大学）

IIIE 21世纪多维英语规划教材

总主编　陆道夫　肖坤学

英译
中国文化经典精读教程

陆道夫　粟孝君　主编

A READING COURSE FOR CHINESE CULTURE
CLASSICS IN ENGLISH TRANSLATION

暨南大学出版社
JINAN UNIVERSITY PRESS

中国·广州

ENGLISH

21 世纪多维英语规划教材

《英译中国文化经典精读教程》编委会

主　编　陆道夫　粟孝君

副主编　陈　姝　李涤非　刘真延

编　者　（按姓氏音序排列）

陈　姝　韩　东　陆道夫　李涤非

刘真延　刘玉婷　粟孝君　王　璐

许　瑾　叶　青

Foreword （总序）

何莲珍

　　中国的英语教学近年来取得了骄人的成绩，这是不争的事实。但回溯历史，我国的外语教学即便从清代最早培养译员的京师同文馆算起，也不过100多年。期间受西方语言教学理论与实践的影响，我国的外语教学经历了从传统语言教学到结构主义教学到交际法教学的转变，教学的重点也经历了从知识的传授到技能的培养到交际能力的培养的转变。

　　进入21世纪，我国教育部颁布了《大学英语课程教学要求》（以下简称《课程要求》），对高等学校非英语专业本科生大学英语课程教学提出了一般要求、较高要求和更高要求。一般要求是高等学校非英语专业本科毕业生应达到的基本要求，较高要求或更高要求是为有条件的学校根据自己的办学定位、类型和人才培养目标所选择的标准而推荐的。按照《课程要求》，大学英语课程体系应该将综合英语类、语言技能类、语言应用类、语言文化类和专业英语类等必修课程和选修课程有机结合起来，以确保不同层次的学生在英语应用能力方面得到全面的训练和充分的提高。《国家中长期教育改革发展规划纲要（2010—2020年）》也对我国今后十年的高等教育发展提出了明确的目标：完成从数量到质量的转变，进而提高我国高等教育的国际化办学水平，培养大批具有国际视野的跨学科、复合型创新人才。

　　现任美国耶鲁大学校长的理查德·乐文（Richard Levin）教授对我国

高校本科教育创新型人才的培养提出了两条有益的建议，令人深思。乐文教授强调要拓宽跨学科的广度，培养批判性思维。前者是要开展通识教育（General Education），后者是要打破思维定式（Thinking Set），这两者是中国学生创新能力持续发展的基础。

无独有偶，早在 1928 年，同样是在美国的耶鲁大学，著名的耶鲁大学报告提出了"头脑的纪律"和"头脑的家具"的惊人之说。专业知识就像脑袋里面装进的家具，在迅速变革的世界中，从长远来讲并没有太多的价值；学生需要的是头脑的纪律或者说思考的框架，让他们适应不断变化的环境，找到解决问题的各种方案，成为主动学习或自觉学习的独立思考者，而不再是被动机械的接受者。

在国内外这种教育背景之下，"怎样学习英语"这个古老的话题似乎又有了新的含义。在我看来，学习英语至少有以下两大要素是要铭记在心的。

打好语言基本功是英语学习的第一要素。扎实的语言基本功是成为国际化人才的关键。语言基本功包括语言知识和语言技能。语言知识包括语音知识、语法知识、词汇知识等。在大学英语学习阶段，我认为词汇学习不仅要在广度上下功夫，更要在深度上下功夫。语言技能包括领会式技能和复用式技能，两者缺一不可。除此之外，语言基本功还包括交际能力。交际能力包括语言能力，但不仅仅是语言能力，还包括语篇能力、语用能力，一个具有交际能力的学习者不仅能按照语法规则组成语法正确的句子，而且知道何时何地对何人使用这些句子。

扩大知识面是英语学习的第二要素。英语中有句俗语："A jack of all trades and master of none." 中文意思是"样样通一点，样样不精通"，也就是我们中国人所说的"万金油"。作为一个英语学习者，我认为需要有一种成为"万金油"的精神。英语学习者要扩大知识面，千万不要为学英语而英语，要多方面、多途径地涉猎各方面的知识。学习者不仅要了解目标语国家的历史、地理、政治、经济、文化、风俗和科技等方面的情况，更要深入了解本国的历史、文化等方面的情况，从而让自己成为中外文化交流的使者和桥梁，让中国更好地了解世界，让世界更好地了解中国。

恐怕没有人会否认，成功的英语学习者除了语言天赋之外，良师的指导和教材的辅助也是功不可没的。随着我国大学英语教学改革的不断深入，英语教学理念也发生了很大的变化。现代英语教学已实现了从"单纯掌握英语语言工具"到"获取信息、有效交流，甚至抢占知识资本和信息资本"的转变，许多英语新课程也都注入了"以人为本"的教育理念，从过去单纯注重知识传授，转变为引导学生学会学习、学会分析、学会思辨、学会批判、学会合作、学会生存、学会做人，打破了过于狭窄的课程设计和教学定位，转而关注通才教育和素质教育。这几年国内的英语教材在国际化视野下实现了内容的优化与整合，从单一到多维，从单项到立体，从语言知识到文化意识，从语言技能的输入到专业案例的实操，教材的多元化可谓精彩纷呈，势在必行。

暨南大学出版社与时俱进地研发并精心策划了这套由广州大学陆道夫教授、肖坤学教授总主编的"21 世纪多维英语规划教材"，就是在上述这种新的教学理念基础之上，经过多位英语专家教授把关、一线教师教学实践体验、多轮课堂教学检验的一次大胆尝试。

"21 世纪多维英语规划教材"试图建立一个多维度、跨学科、宽视野的立体化教材资源库。本套教材包括《商务英语跨文化交际》、《新编会展英语实务》、《医学英语视听说教程新编》、《医学英语 SCI 论文写作教程》、《法律英语翻译教程》、《西方文化英文经典选读》、《英译中国文化经典精读教程》、《英美经典短篇小说阅读教程》、《大学英语人文通识读本》、《大学英语通用翻译教程》、《英语专业学士论文写作教程》等。编写过程中充分考虑到英语学习者输入与输出、语言与文化、知识与能力、个人与社会、历史与现实、理科与人文的多维交叉和相互渗透。整套教材不仅蕴含了丰富的英语语言资源与文化信息，还精选了当代经济生活中的医学英语、商务英语、会展英语、法律英语、涉外翻译等各类真实语境材料，克服了传统英语教材中务虚避实的形式主义流弊，体现了编者们丰厚的教学积累和温馨的人文关怀。能力培养与人格塑造并重，语言运用与思维训练齐举，应该说是本套教材的一大亮点。我相信，暨南大学出版社这套"21世纪多维英语规划教材"，将会给我国21世纪复合型创新英语人才的培养带来新的启迪，做出新的贡献。

教育部高等院校大学外语教学指导委员会副主任委员
全国高等院校研究生外语教学研究会会长
浙江省高等学校外语类教学指导委员会主任委员
浙江大学外国语学院院长，博士生导师

Preface （前言）

  随着 400 多所孔子学院近十年来在海外的兴办与发展，中国文化越来越引起国外专家学者、平民百姓的浓厚兴趣。然而，与之相应的中国文化英语教材建设似乎没能实现同步发展。在国内的许多大、中小学，用英语开设中国文化课程的更是少之又少，以至于不少人虽然谈起西方文化如数家珍，可一旦用英语谈起中国文化，就会因为语言障碍和知识匮乏而捉襟见肘。更有甚者，北京大学和清华大学的两位教授竟然把孟子（Mencius）译为"门修斯"或"孟修斯"，把蒋介石（Chiang Kai-shek）译成"常凯申"，令人啼笑皆非。不少大学生或老师对那些诸如"拜年"（a-happy-new-year-wish）、"对联"（couplets）、"科举制"（imperial civil examination system）以及"三纲五常"（three cardinal guides and five constant virtues）之类富有历史内涵的中国文化术语，不知如何用英语表达（见本书附录二"常用中国文化专有术语汉英对照精选"）。在 2013 年 12 月新启动的大学英语四级考试的"段落汉译"中，许多考生对"丝绸之路"、"中秋节"、"福、寿、禄"、"中国结"等中国文化专有词汇无从下笔，直呼"坑爹"，有不少考生甚至干脆用汉语拼音代替英译。这无疑暴露了目前我国英语教学对中国文化的漠视和短见。针对这一情况，我们组织了国内几所大学的一线骨干老师，在近几年开设大学英语拓展课"中国文化英语阅读"的基础上，编写了这本《英译中国文化经典精读教程》，试图通过对先哲圣贤们的经典著作的译本选读，挖掘中国文化的精髓，把握中国文化的精神，为中国文化在海外的传播做些力所能及的贡献。

　　《英译中国文化经典精读教程》选择了能够代表中国传统文化的 17 本经典著作——《诗经》、《大学》、《中庸》、《论语》、《孟子》、《易经》、《道德经》、《庄子》、《文心雕龙》、《战国策》、《史记》、《孙子兵法》、《三国志》与《三国演义》、《金刚经》、《黄帝内经》、《茶经》等，几乎涵盖了中国传统文化能够涉及的文学、哲学、史学、医学、农学、宗教、军事等重要领域。每一单元分为"背景简介"、"文本选读"、"难点释义"、"问题思考"、"经典导读"、"译本链接"等 6 大板块。

　　作为"21 世纪多维英语规划教材"的一种，《英译中国文化经典精读教程》可与已经出版的《西方文化英文经典选读》配套使用，作为本科生大学英语拓展课程、英语专业高年级选修课程、海外孔子学院中国文化专修课程等的教材。

　　根据我们近三年在广州大学和南方医科大学开设该课程的教学实践，通常情况下，作为大学英语拓展课程，"英译中国文化经典阅读"课程可安排在大学二年级第二学期或大学三年级第一学期开设，英语专业可根据学生的实际英语水平，在大一下学期或大二上学期开设。阅读经典原文是实现本课程教学目标的根本保障，因此教师应严格要求学生按时、按质、按量完成阅读任务。不同的学校可以根据学生的实际水平酌情增减阅读量。为了加深学生对经典的理解，进一步训练学生的思辨能力和独立思考能力，使之能够主动进行立论、辩论或对自己的论点进行修正，主讲教师可以每 3 ~ 4 周集中开展一次讨论课，或者就同一单元的同类主题，或者就不同单元的同类主题展开课堂讨论，或者安排 4 ~ 5 名学生选择本单元中的名家名篇，围绕"问题思考"中提出的问题，作 10 ~ 15 分钟的拓展性学术报告，并展开质疑、反诘、辩驳等形式的小组讨论。

　　该课程的考核不妨以形成性评估为主，终结性评估为辅。形成性评估包括学术报告、学期论文、小组讨论、读书笔记、阅读摘要等。形成性评估旨在考查学生的组织能力、思辨能力和学术写作能力；终结性评估主要以闭卷考试为主，考查学生对中国文化著名思想家、思想名著和相关文化背景的了解和熟悉程度。

《英译中国文化经典精读教程》是广州大学、上海外国语大学、广东财经大学、南方医科大学、华南农业大学、安徽工业大学、安徽外国语学院等高校一线老师历时三年通力合作的结果。全书的编写提纲、基本框架、文字修改均由陆道夫负责。全书的篇目选择、稿件统筹和校正则由陆道夫、粟孝君共同负责。附录二、附录三由叶青协助陆道夫整理完成。具体分工如下：

Unit One： 陈姝

Unit Two： 刘真延 、王璐

Unit Three： 刘真延

Unit Four： 粟孝君

Unit Five： 陆道夫、刘玉婷

Unit Six： 李涤非

Unit Seven： 粟孝君

Unit Eight： 陆道夫、粟孝君

Unit Nine： 陆道夫

Unit Ten： 粟孝君、韩东

Unit Eleven： 李涤非、叶青

Unit Twelve： 陈姝

Unit Thirteen：陈姝、陆道夫

Unit Fourteen：粟孝君

Unit Fifteen： 陆道夫、许瑾

Unit Sixteen： 陆道夫

本书在编写过程中参考了大量的文献典籍和现有的学术成果，参考文献已附在书后，恕不一一列出，谨致歉意和谢意。特别要感谢"大中华文库·汉英对照"编委会为我们提供的资料帮助；感谢国内及海外各位英译作者提供的优质译文；感谢浙江大学外国语学院院长何莲珍教授百忙之中

拨冗赐序；感谢西安外国语大学老校长，著名英语教育家杜瑞清教授的鼓励与支持。感谢广州大学国际交流处处长梁碧茹女士，美国卫斯理安学院副校长 Vivia L. Fowler 博士为我们提供的经费资助和资料援助。感谢暨南大学出版社人文分社社长杜小陆先生一以贯之的理解、尊重、支持、奉献与帮助。感谢广州大学、南方医科大学选修"中国文化英语"课程的近600名本科生。

我在《羊城晚报》上读过一篇随笔，大意是谈信息碎片化的微博浅阅读与文化经典的深阅读之间的差异，并由此而带来的思维方式和内心感受的不同之处。微博浅阅读只要求读者能在海量的信息碎片中作快速筛查，然后在两个原本没有关联的碎片中去建立联系，并把这种联系以巧妙漂亮的手法呈现出来即可。如此就可以赢得观众的欢呼和掌声。通常情况下，读者无须知道"为什么"，只需判断"是什么"，然后把一系列的"是什么"组合起来便大功告成。然而，文化经典的深度阅读则需要读者能够持续专注在书本上，集中全部精力，在阅读的同时必须深度思考。这种深度阅读的过程漫长而连续，且常常伴随着静思和默想。

令人遗憾的是，碎片化的微博浅阅读在当下却大行其道，越来越多的手机或 iPad "低头族"们其实与一台自动机器并无二致：他（她）们用眼睛读取一条信息碎片，用机械式的手指不断刷屏，作出转发、回复、跳过三种选择。这种过程周而复始，无穷无尽。在此，我禁不住想套用英国小说家狄更斯在其小说《双城记》中的开头几句来勾勒当下的某些时代特征：这是一个物质泛滥的时代，又是一个精神匮乏的时代；这是一个欲望蒸腾的时代，又是一个奢华浮躁的时代；这是一个信息超载的时代，又是一个心灵闭塞的时代；这是一个娱乐至死的流行文化时代，又是一个细品慢咽的高雅文化时代。匆匆的时代步伐，疾风暴雨式的全球化浪潮，每个人的内心和自我因此而受到不同方向的牵引，或离散，或纷乱，终至信仰缺失。不少人拜金、拜物、拜权势，甚至愚昧拜神仙，结果丢掉了"独立之精神，自由之思想"，不仅"奴在身"，而且"奴在心"，一味追名逐利，罔顾人格，贪慕虚荣，尽失尊严。所幸的是，在这样的时代，我们仍然有幸能够沉寂片刻，真真切切地去品读中国先哲圣贤们留下的文化经典之优、之美、之智、之深，这不仅是一种奢侈，而是一种福气。因为老祖宗给我们留下的这些文化经典，经过历史长河的洗涤和冲刷，是一种超越物质流俗的性灵之说、感悟之言和生命呐喊。对于那些每每徘徊、恍惚甚至有些迷惘的当下人来说，阅读这些圣贤经典，在某种程度上算是驳杂之中的单纯、重压之下的逃逸、欲望沟壑的真理；在很大程度上可以给我们带来人文的温暖、乡愁的慰藉、现实的观照和历史的反思。

鲁迅先生曾经说过："惟有民魂是值得宝贵的，惟有它发扬起来，中国才有真进步。"何谓民魂？传统文化经典无疑是其核心之一。我也深信，"腹有诗书气自华"，"红袖添香夜读书"。阅读经典，"会晤"大师；品味经典，领悟大师；阐粹经典，效仿大师。身处 21 世纪的我们这一代人，应该从中国文化经典中摄取精粹，让科学和理性在生命中绽放，让现实生活中的平庸、枯燥、无奇、丑陋和虚伪遁无去处，让人生旅程中的迷茫、彷徨、孤独、消沉、苦闷、恐惧等全都远离我们的心灵家园。阅读文化经典，应该是一个民族灵魂的核心所在，是一个民族精神的支撑载体，是一个民族文化的本质彰显，是一个民族热情力量的释放。一个民族固然需要时尚阅读、娱乐阅读、消费阅读、功利阅读、实用阅读，但是，深度的文化经典阅读之美、之乐、之智其实更能持久地或潜移默化地影响我们日渐空虚的精神世界，净化我们欲望蒸腾的心灵空间。衷心期望这本《英译中国文化经典精读教程》能够达到这样的编写目的。衷心期盼来自各位专家和读者的批评指正。

陆道夫

2013 年秋于小谷围岛广州大学城

A Reading Course for Chinese Culture Classics in English Translation

·

·

·

·

·

·

001 Foreword（总序）

001 Preface（前言）

001 Unit One   *The Book of Poetry*（《诗经》）

016 Unit Two   *The Great Learning*（《大学》）

031 Unit Three   *The Doctrine of the Mean*（《中庸》）

042 Unit Four   *The Analects*（《论语》）

061 Unit Five   *Mencius*（《孟子》）

079 Unit Six   *The Book of Changes*（《易经》）

093 Unit Seven   *Dao De Jing*（《道德经》）

105 Unit Eight   *Zhuang Zi*（《庄子》）

121 Unit Nine   *Wenxin Diaolong*（《文心雕龙》）

136 Unit Ten   *Records on the Warring States Period*（《战国策》）

152 Unit Eleven *Records of the Historian*（《史记》）

182 Unit Twelve *Sun Zi: The Art of War*（《孙子兵法》）

194 Unit Thirteen *Records of the Three Kingdoms & Romance of the Three Kingdoms*（《三国志》与《三国演义》）

206 Unit Fourteen *The Diamond Sutra*（《金刚经》）

216 Unit Fifteen   *Huangdi Neijing*（《黄帝内经》）

目录

ENG

A Reading Course
Classics in English

227   Unit Sixteen *The Classic of Tea* （《茶经》）

239   Appendix 1   Chinese Text（汉语文本原文）

290   Appendix 2   Bilingual Glossary of Chinese Culture（常用中国文化专有术语汉英对照精选）

305   Appendix 3   Booklists of "Library of Chinese Classics (Chinese-□ English)"《大中华文库》（汉英对照）部分书目

308   References（参考文献）

Unit One
The Book of Poetry（《诗经》）

I. 背景简介

The Book of Poetry（*Shijing*）, the first anthology of Chinese poems, was written by some anonymous authors dating from 10th to 7th centuries B. C. It was popular around the region from the north of the Yellow River basin to the Jianghan Drainage Area during the period from the early Western Zhou Dynasty to the mid Spring and Autumn Period. It comprises 305 poems and is said to have been complied by Confucius. There were four earliest versions of *The Book of Poetry*: in the states of Lu（by Shen Gong,）, Qi（by Hou Cang and Master Sun）and Han（by Han Ying）, and Duke Mao. Only the Mao version has survived until now, and the commentaries to the Han version have survived in the collection *Hanshi Waizhuan*（《韩诗外传》）. As early

the antiquated edition in 1920's

as in the Western Han Dynasty, it became one of "Five Classics" with other four books which are *Book of Documents*（《尚书》）, *Book of Rites*（《礼记》）, *I Ching*（《易经》）, *Spring and Autumn Annals*（《春秋》）as some of the Western Han Dynasty officials adopted Confucianism as the guiding principles of Chinese society.

The Book of Poetry has four divisions: Feng (Airs of the States), Xiao Ya (the Minor Odes), Da Ya (the Major Odes) and Song (Hymns). Feng is the collection of 160 short lyrics generally recording the love and emotions of the common people. Xiao Ya and Da Ya, both sung at courts or banquets, respectively comprises 74 social critical odes and 31 odes praising the Zhou Dynasty. Song, including 40 hymns in the three parts of the Hymns of Zhou, the Hymns of Lu, and the Hymns of Shang, was used by the upper class during their sacrifices to the gods and ancestors. Each poem in *The Book of Poetry* is framed in a Small Preface (Xiao Xu), and the first poem of each division has a Great Preface (Da Xu). The Small Prefaces introduce some general background on authors and society, and the Great Prefaces serve a moral or political interpretation of the poems.

The Book of Poetry had a very profound influence on ancient China in terms of culture, language, politics and thinking. Since it received the high praise of Confucius, a sage of China in Spring and Autumn Period, it has played an important part in the daily life of Chinese people. It is believed that through the study of *The Book of Poetry* people could highly promote the capabilities of observation and personal cultivation. And most importantly, it has exerted a great effect on Chinese literature. As the oldest extant collection of Chinese poetry, it is the onset of Chinese classical poetry. Its poetry style and measure have also been used in the study of Old Chinese phonology since the Qing Dynasty. Its spirit of realism paved a new way for the development of the Chinese literature of later times. Until now, it has been studied and memorized by scholars from all over the world over two millennia. It is a precious cultural heritage the people of ancient China left to the world.

II. 文本选读
Cooing and Wooing (Songs of Zhou)

By riverside are cooing
A pair of turtledoves[①];
A good young man[②] is wooing

A fair maiden he loves.

Water flows left and right
Of cresses③ here and there;
The youth yearns day and night
For the good maiden fair.

His yearning grows so strong,
He cannot fall sleep.
He tosses all night long,
So deep in love, so deep.

Now gather left and right
The cresses sweet and tender!
O lute, play music bright
For the bride sweet and slender!

Feast friends at left and right
With cresses cooked tender!
O bells and drums, delight
The bride so fair and slender!

(Translated by Xu Yuanchong)

Dense Millets④

Dense millets grow in all the fields,
Green sorghum⑤seedlings wave in wind.
For a long walk I can hardly take,
Past events make my heart⑥sink.

Intimate persons say I am worried,

But outsiders complain what else I want.

Oh! The distant heaven is there,

Who has done such evil thing?

Dense millets grow in all the fields,

Red sorghum spikes drop down.

For a long walk I can hardly take,

Past events like wine make me drunk.

Intimate persons say I am worried,

But outsiders complain what else I want.

Oh! The distant heaven is there,

Who has done such evil thing?

Dense millets grow in all the fields,

Ripe sorghum grains⑦pile up.

For a long walk I can hardly take,

Many past events make me choked.

Intimate persons say I am worried,

But outsiders complain what else I want.

Oh! The distant heaven is there,

Who has done such evil thing?

(Translated by Wang Fanglu)

Tsze⑧ K'in⑨

O you, with the blue collar,

Prolonged is the anxiety of my heart.

Although I do not go (to you),

Why do you not continue your messages⑩ (to me)?

O you, with the blue (strings to your) girdle-gems,

Long, long do I think of you.

Although I do not go (to you).

Why do you not come (to me)?

How volatile are you and dissipated,

By the look-out tower⑪ on the wall!

One day without the sight of you,

Is like three months.

(Translated by James Legge)

A Wood Cutter's Song (Songs of Wei)

Chop, chop our blows on the trees go;

On riverside⑫ we pile up wood.

See clear and rippling water flow.

How can those who nor reap⑬ nor sow⑭

Have three hundred sheaves⑮ of corn in their place?

How can those who nor hunt nor chase⑯

Have in their courtyard badgers of each race?

Those lords are good

Who need not work for good.

Chop, chop our blows for wheel-spokes go;

On river shore we pile up wood.

See clear water straightforward flow.

How can those who nor reap nor sow

Have three millions of sheaves in their place?

How can those who nor hunt nor chase

Have in their courtyard games of each race?

Those lords are good

Who need not work to eat their food.

Chop, chop our blows for the wheels go；

At river brink we pile up wood.

See clear and dimpling water flow.

How can those who nor reap nor sow

Have three hundred ricks⑰ of corn in their place?

How can those who nor hunt nor chase

Have in their courtyard winged games of each race?

Those lords are good

Who do not have to work for food.

(Translated by Xu Yuanchong)

The Reed⑱ (Songs of Qin)

Green, green the reed,

Dew and frost gleam.

Where's she I need?

Beyond the stream.

Upstream I go⑲,

The way is long；

Downstream I go.

She's thereamong；

White, white the reed,

Dew not yet dried.

Where's she I need?

On the other side⑳.

Upstream I go;

Hard is the way.

Downstream I go;

She's far away.

Bright, bright the reed,

Dew and frost blend.

Where's she I need?

At river's end.

Upstream I go;

The way does wind㉑.

Downstream I go;

She's far behind.

(Translated by Xu Yuanchong)

Gather the Thorn-ferns㉒

Let us gather the thorn-ferns, let us gather the thorn-ferns;

The thorn-ferns are now springing up㉓.

When shall we return? When shall we return?

It will be late in the (next) year.

Wife and husband will be separated㉔,

Because of the Xian-yun㉕.

We shall have no leisure to rest㉖,

Because of the Xian-yun.

Let us gather the thorn-ferns, let us gather the thorn-ferns;

The thorn-ferns are now tender[27].

When shall we return? When shall we return?

Our hearts are sorrowful;

Our hearts are sad and sorrowful;

We shall hunger, we shall thirst.

While our service on guard is not finished,

We can send no one home to enquire about[28] our families.

Let us gather the thorn-ferns, let us gather the thorn-ferns;

The thorn-ferns are now hard.

When shall we return? When shall we return?

The year will be in the tenth month[29].

But the king's business must not be slackly performed;

We shall have no leisure to rest.

Our sorrowing hearts are in great distress;

But we shall not return from our expedition.

What is that so gorgeous?

It is the flowers of the cherry tree.

What carriage is that?

It is the carriage of our general.

His war carriage is yoked;

The four steeds are strong.

Dare we remain inactive?

In one month we shall have three victories[30].

The four steeds are yoked,

The four steeds, eager and strong;

The confidence of the general,

The protection of the men.

The four steeds move regularly, like wings;

There are the bow with its ivory ends[3], and the seal-skin quiver[32].

Shall we not daily warn one another?

The business of the Xian-yun is very urgent.

At first, when we set out,

The willows were fresh and green,

Now, when we shall be returning,

The snow will be falling in clouds.

Long and tedious will be our marching;

We shall hunger; we shall thirst.

Our hearts are wounded with grief,

And no one knows our sadness.

(Translated by James Legge)

Ⅲ. 难点释义

① turtledoves, "雎鸠", 一种水鸟名。

② A good young man, "君子",《诗经》中对贵族男子的通称。

③ cresses, "荇菜", 草本植物, 叶浮于水面。

④ millets, "黍", 一种农作物, 即糜子, 籽实去皮后叫黄米, 有黏性, 可以酿酒、做糕等。

⑤ sorghum, "稷", 谷子, 一说高粱。黍的一个变种, 散穗, 籽实不黏或黏性不及黍者为稷。

⑥ my heart，"中心"，指内心。

⑦ grains，"实"，籽粒。

⑧ Tsze，"子"，古代对男子的美称。

⑨ K'in，"衿"，衣领。

⑩ continue your messages，"嗣音"，传音讯。嗣，通"贻"，音 yí。

⑪ the look-out tower，"城阙"，城门楼。

⑫ riverside，"干（àn）"，通"岸"，水边。

⑬ reap，"稼"，播种。

⑭ sow，"穑"，收获。

⑮ sheaves，"廛（chán）"，古制百亩。三百廛，三百户。

⑯ nor hunt nor chase，"不狩不猎"，不打猎。狩，冬猎；猎，夜猎。诗中皆泛指打猎。

⑰ ricks，"囷（qūn）"，束。一说圆形的谷仓。

⑱ the reed，"蒹葭（jiān jiā）"，芦荻，芦苇。

⑲ upstream I go，"溯洄（sù huí）"，逆流而上。

⑳ on the other side，"湄（méi）"，岸边，水与草交接之处。

㉑ wind，"右"，迂回曲折。

㉒ thorn-ferns，"薇"，豆科野豌豆属的一种，学名叫荒野豌豆，现在称作大巢菜，种子、茎、叶均可食用。

㉓ springing up，"作"，指薇菜冒出地面。

㉔ wife and husband will be separated，"靡（mǐ）室靡家"，没有正常的家庭生活。靡，无。室，与"家"义同。

㉕ Xian-yun，"玁狁（xiǎn yǔn）"，中国北方古代少数民族名，即北狄、匈奴。

㉖ no leisure to rest，"启居"，跪、坐，指休息、休整。启，跪、跪坐。居，安坐、安居。古人席地而坐，两膝着席，危坐时腰部伸直，臀部与足离开；安坐时臀部贴在足跟上。

㉗ tender，"柔"，柔嫩。"柔"指比"作"更进一步的生长，形容刚长出来的薇菜柔嫩的样子。

㉘ enquire about，"聘（pìn）"，问，谓问候。

㉙ the tenth month，"阳"，此处指农历十月，小阳春季节。

㉚ three victories，"三捷"，三次胜利。谓接战、交战。一说，捷，邪出，指改道行军。此句意为一月多次行军。

㉛ ivory ends，"象弭（mǐ）"，"弭"为弓的一种，其两端饰以骨角。象弭，以象牙装饰弓端的弭。

㉜ seal-skin quiver，"鱼服"，鱼皮制的箭袋。

IV. 问题思考

1. Why the onomatopoeic *Cooing and Wooing*, in your opinion, is put at the beginning of *The Book of Poetry*?

2. What is the relationship between the collecting cresses and courting the lover in the poem of *Cooing and Wooing*? What kind of spirits could be reflected in *Cooing and Wooing*?

3. What is the metaphorical meaning of *Dense Millets* in the poem?

4. What, in you opinion, does the "past events" refer to in the poem? How many figurative speeches has the poet applied to developing the theme of *Dense Millets*?

5. Why the poet repeatedly mentioned the collar and accessory of her lover in the poem *Tsze K'in*? How does the poet express the love and missing in the poem *Tsze K'im*? Discuss with your classmates by giving more examples.

6. According to the verses "How can those who nor hunt nor chase/Have in their courtyard winged games of each race? /Those lords are good/Who do not have to work for food", what issue is raised in the poem *The Reed*?

7. Apparently "cutting woods" is a symbolized action in the poem *A Wood Cutter's Song*. What do you think of its function in developing the theme?

8. What is the function of depicting "reeds" in the poem *The Reed*? Is the tone of the poem happy, ironic, sad, humorous, or detached? How is the tone established and revealed?

9. What is the relationship between the homesickness and "gathering the thorn-ferns" in

the poem *Gather the Thorn-ferns*? What kind of spirits could be reflected in the poem *Gather the Thorn-ferns*?

V. 经典导读

《诗经》是我国第一部诗歌总集，先秦时称为"诗"，西汉时被奉为儒家经典，始称"诗经"，其创作年代，距今大约 2 500 年。

《诗经》共收录诗歌 305 首，因此又被称为"诗三百"。诗集中所有的诗歌都按照"风、雅、颂"的标准进行分类。历来对"风、雅、颂"的解释各有不同，比较广泛的是"题材说"、"用途说"和"曲调说"，即分别认为"风、雅、颂"是《诗经》中的诗歌在题材上、用途上或音乐曲调上的一种划分。"风"在《诗经》中又名"国风"，共 160 首，包括当时周南、召南、郑、齐、魏等十五国在内的民间乐谣。"雅"分"大雅"和"小雅"，共 105 篇，其中"大雅"31 篇，多作于西周初期，"小雅"74 篇，多作于西周末期；"雅"意为"正"，雅乐即为正乐，正乐之歌乃宫廷乐歌，也就是说，雅是周代朝廷的正乐。"颂"共 40 篇，分"周颂"、"鲁颂"、"商颂"，乃庙堂之音，是王侯举行祭祀或其他重大典礼时专用的乐歌。

《诗经》在表现手法上大量运用了"赋、比、兴"，它们与"风、雅、颂"合称"六义"。"赋"的特点是直接叙事，通过铺陈情节来抒发感情，"比"就是在文中运用比喻和比拟，"兴"即"起"，在诗歌创作中常常表现为托物言情。《诗经》中赋中有比，比中起兴，兴中再转赋，"赋、比、兴"的运用娴熟自然，是构成《诗经》民歌中浓郁风土气息的重要原因。

《诗经》中的绝大多数篇目都是反映普通百姓的现实生活和日常经验的抒情诗，其主要内容可分为以下七类：

（1）反映婚姻和爱情，如《周南·关雎》、《邶风·静女》、《秦风·蒹葭》，等等。

（2）反映战争和徭役，如《齐风·东方未明》、《小雅·何草不黄》、《小雅·采薇》，等等。

（3）反映生产劳动，如《周南·芣苢》、《魏风·十亩之间》、《小雅·大田》，等等。

（4）反映阶级压迫和社会不平，如《魏风·伐檀》、《魏风·硕鼠》，等等。

（5）反映周民族兴起，如《大雅》中的《生民》、《皇矣》、《大明》，等等。

（6）揭露不公、讽喻时政，如《齐风》中的《南山》、《载驱》和《秦风·黄鸟》，等等。

（7）尊天敬祖的宗教性祭歌，如《维天之命》、《文王》，等等。

《诗经》中的诗歌大多由韵律整齐的四言写成，间或杂有二言至八言不等，结构中较多采用重章叠字的形式，每章只换少数几个字，造成一咏三叹、强化感情的艺术效果。《诗经》中的诗歌大多隔句押韵，采用韵脚押在偶句尾部的押韵方式。这种押韵方式既增加了语言上的节奏之美，又间接起到了层层推进主题的作用。

《诗经》在总体上是一部富含现实主义精神的诗歌总集，带有鲜明的政治与道德色彩，它揭示了奴隶制社会中被剥削者和剥削者之间不可调和的阶级矛盾，表达了当时劳动人民对统治阶层的抗争和怨恨，预示了整个奴隶制社会行将崩溃与覆灭。作为中国文学的主要源头之一，《诗经》无论在诗歌形式还是思想内容上，都为我国后世的诗歌创作奠定了深厚的基础，并对我国的文学发展产生了深远的影响。

《关雎》是《诗经》的首篇，古人把它冠于三百篇之首，说明它在《诗经》中具有不言而喻的重要地位。孔子认为，《关雎》中男主人公在情感表达上的含蓄内敛与自我克制是表现"中庸"（the doctrine of the Mean）之德的典范，谓之"乐而不淫，哀而不伤"（Joyous but not indecent, mournful but not distressing）；《毛诗序》则赋予该诗在道德意义上的另一层解读，认为其表现的是典范意义上的夫妇伦理思想，而夫妻为人伦之始，夫妇之德乃天下一切道德纲常的基础。然而后世的很多学者却认为，《关雎》的主题并非如此大义，它的内容其实很单纯，就是描写一位男子追求自己的心上人，从求之不得到求而得之的情绪转换过程。一个"求"字贯穿通篇，男子追求女子过程中的微妙心态纤毫毕现，有首有尾，心理刻画曲折入微，是一篇极传神的男女言情佳作。

《黍离》一诗采用典型的比兴手法。诗人运用黍的散穗向四周分开下垂的姿态来喻指亲人的离散和国家的衰亡。全诗层次分明，共三章，每章十句，三章的结构相同，每章只换两个词，一唱三叹，采用层层递进的方式，迂回往复地表现出主人公的无限忧思。

《子衿》是一首郑国民歌，全诗共三章，只有四十九个字，采用倒叙的手法，描写了一位女子因思念爱人而产生的既焦灼又责怨的微妙心理。"赋、比、兴"三种手法的交相使用，彼此融合，赋中用比，比中有兴，或起兴后再用赋。"子衿"、"子佩"与爱人的类比，"挑兮达兮，在城阙兮"的平铺直叙，"一日不见，如三月兮"（one day

所谓伊人，在水一方

without the sight of you, is like three mouths）的赋中起兴，共同创造了一个痴情女子的艺术形象，使《子衿》成为中国两千年来爱情诗作中永恒不朽的千古绝唱。

《伐檀》是《诗经》中表现反剥削、反压迫主题最有代表性的诗篇之一。诗中运用的"赋、比、兴"的写作手法及回旋重沓的方式非常有特点。句式变化丰富，长短不一，参差灵活，富有感染力，有四言、五言、六言、七言乃至八言，或叙事，或抒情，生动的语言使得主题得到充分表现。

《蒹葭》总共三章，全诗采用重章的形式，一咏三叹，每章八句，每一章的前两句都以"蒹葭"发端起兴，后六句则借景叙事抒情。融实景和幻境于一体，将实情与幻想相结合，是该诗最大的艺术特色。正如王国维《人间词话》所言，"《诗·蒹葭》一篇，最得风人深致"，"以我观物，故物皆着我之色彩"。虚与实的相互生发，景与情的彼此交合，让诗篇充满了韵味无穷的艺术感染力。

在《采薇》中，诗人以一位当时戍边士兵的口吻自述，他长年转战边陲，受尽思乡之苦。在一个大雪纷飞的冬日里，他终于解甲归里，独行在寒冷、泥泞的返乡路上，心中充满了对战争、家乡、祖国的种种忧思和怀想。《采薇》全诗六章，按其主题内容又可分为三层。整首诗歌采用自述和倒叙的手法，从对战争的追忆写起。诗歌的第一层为前三章，采用句式重叠的手法一咏三叹，表现戍兵在征战期间生活的艰难和对故乡深切的思念之情，并叙述了迟迟难归的原因。

VI. 译本链接

1. James Legge, *The Shi King*, Taipei：SMC Publishing Inc., 1991.

2. William Jennings，*The Shi King*，London & New York：George Routledge and Sons Limited，1891.

3. Arthur Waley，*The Book of Songs*，New York：Grove Press，1987.

4. 许渊冲：《许渊冲经典英译古代诗歌 1,000 首·诗经》，北京：海豚出版社，2013 年版。

5. 汪榕培、任秀桦译注：《诗经》（中英文版），沈阳：辽宁教育出版社，1995 年版。

Unit Two
*The Great Learning*① (《大学》)

Ⅰ. 背景简介

Zeng Zi (505 B. C. –435 B. C.), whose given name was Shen, and styled Zi Yu, was a native of Nanwu City in Lu in the late Warring States (now Jiaxiang County, Shandong Province). He was one of the main representatives in Confucianism and was traditionally called Zeng Zi. He took Confucius as his teacher at the age of sixteen. He studied very hard and got the true mass of the Master. Zeng Zi was the teacher of Confucius' grandson Kong Ji who later became the teacher of Mencius, another great philosopher in the Warring States Period. Thus, Zeng Zi was regarded as not only the principal inheritor and prophet of Confucianism, but also an initiator of the Simeng (Zi Si – Mencius) School. He was called Zong Sheng among the Confucianists. He was known as one of the five sages, as renowned as Confucius, Mencius, Yan Hui and Zi Si.

Zeng Zi (505 **B. C.** –435 **B. C.**)

Zeng Zi actively carried forward and developed Confucianism. He made his contributions to Confucianism by putting forward his thought in political conception, self-cultivation and filial piety. Zeng Zi held the political notion that "the cultivation of the person depends on rectifying the mind; the regulation of one's family depends on the cultivation of his person; the government of his kingdom depends on his regulation of the family; and the making the whole empire peaceful and happy depends on the government of his state". He believed "a superior man must be watchful over himself when he is alone". He proposed the idea of introspection and self-discipline for one's cultivation. He said "I reflect on myself three times a day", which was developed to be a popular way of self-cultivation. He also maintained that filial piety was the root of the regulation of family and the priority of family value. All his notions have profound impacts for twenty centuries on Chinese culture, and still influence the construction of the harmonious modern society.

Zeng Zi wrote two books, *the Great Learning* and *Filial Piety*, both of which are the Confucian classics.

Ⅱ. 文本选读
THE GREAT LEARNING

My master, the philosopher Cheng, says "*The Great Learning* is a book left by Confucius, and forms the gate by which first learners enter into virtue. That we can now perceive the order in which the ancients pursued their learning, is solely owing to the preservation of this work, the Analects and Mencius coming after it. Learners must commence their course with this and then it may be hoped that they will be kept from error."

THE TEXT OF CONFUCIUS

What *the Great Learning* teaches is to illustrate illustrious[2] virtue; to renovate the people; and to rest in the highest excellence. The point where to rest being known, the object of pursuit is then determined; and, that being determined, a calm unperturbedness[3] may be attained. To that calmness there will succeed a tranquil repose[4]. In that repose there may be careful deliberation, and that deliberation will be followed by the attainment of the desired end. Things have their root and their completion. Affairs have their end and their beginning. To know what is first and what is last will lead near to what is taught in *the Great Learning*. The ancients, who wished to illustrate illustrious virtue throughout the empire, first ordered well their own States. Wishing to order well their States, they first regulated their families. Wishing to regulate their families, they first cultivated their persons. Wishing to cultivate their persons, they first rectified[5] their hearts. Wishing to rectify their hearts, they first sought to be sincere in their thoughts. Wishing to be sincere in their thoughts, they first extended to the utmost their knowledge. Such extension of knowledge lay in the investigation of things. Things being investigated, knowledge became complete. Their knowledge being complete, their thoughts were sincere. Their thoughts being sincere, their hearts were then rectified. Their hearts being rectified, their persons were cultivated. Their persons being cultivated, their families were regulated. Their families being regulated, their states were rightly governed. Their states being rightly governed, the whole empire was made tranquil and happy. From the emperor down to the mass of the people, all must consider the cultivation of the person the root of every thing besides. It cannot be, when the root is neglected, that what should spring from it will be well ordered. It never has been the case that what was of great importance has been slightly cared for, and, at the same time, that what was of slight importance has been greatly cared for.

COMMENTARY OF THE PHILOSOPHER ZENG

In *the Announcement to Kang*[6], it is said, "He was able to make his virtue illustrious." In *the Tai Jia*[7], it is said, "He contemplated and studied the illustrious decrees of Heaven[8]." In *the Canon of the Emperor Yao*[9], it is said, "He was able to make illustrious his lofty virtue." These passages all show how those sovereigns made themselves illustrious.

On *the Bathing-tub of Tang*[10], the following words were engraved: "If your can one day renovate yourself, do so from day to day. Yea, let there be daily renovation." In *the Announcement to Kang*, it is said, "To stir up the new people." In *The Book of Poetry*[11], it is said, "Although Zhou was an ancient state, and the ordinance which lighted on it was new. " Therefore, the superior man in every thing uses his utmost endeavors.

In *The Book of Poetry*, it is said, "The imperial domain of a thousand *li*[12] is where the people rest. " It is also said, "The twittering yellow bird rests on a corner of the mound. " The Master[13] said, "When it rests, it knows where to rest. Is it possible that a man should not be equal to this bird?" In *The Book of Poetry*, it is said, "Profound was King Wen. With how bright and unceasing a feeling of reverence did he regard his resting place!" As a sovereign[14], he rested in benevolence. As a minister, he rested in reverence. As a son, he rested in filial piety. As a father, he rested in kindness. In communication with his subjects, he rested in good faith. In *The Book of Poetry*, it is said, "Look at that winding course of the Qi[15], with the green bamboos so luxuriant! Here is our elegant and accomplished prince[16]! As we cut and then file; as we chisel and then grind[17]: so has he cultivated himself. How grave is he and dignified! How majestic and distinguished! Our elegant and accomplished prince never can be forgotten. " That expression— "as we cut and then file" indicates the work of learning. "As we chisel and then grind" indicates that of self-culture. "How grave is he and dignified" indicates the feeling of cautious reverence. "How majestic and distinguished" indicates an awe-inspiring deportment[18]. "Our elegant and accomplished prince never can be forgotten," indicates how, when virtue is complete and excellence extreme, the people cannot forget them. In *The Book of Poetry*, it is said, "Ah! the former kings are not forgotten. " Future princes deem worthy what they deemed worthy, and love what they loved. The common people delight in what they delighted, and are benefited by their beneficial arrangements. It is on this account that the former kings, after they have quitted the world, are not forgotten.

The Master said, "In hearing litigations[19], I am like any other body. What is necessary is to cause the people to have no litigations?" So, those who are devoid of principle[20] find it impossible to carry out their speeches, and a great awe would be struck into men's minds; this is called knowing the root.

The above fifth chapter of commentary explained the meaning of "investigating things and carrying knowledge to the utmost extent," but it is now lost. I have ventured to take the views of the scholar Cheng to supply it as follows: The meaning of the expression, "The perfecting of knowledge depends on the investigation of things" is this: If we wish to carry our knowledge to the utmost, we must investigate the principles of all things we come into contact with, for the intelligent mind of man is certainly formed to know, and there is not a single thing in which its principles do not inhere. But so long as all principles are not investigated, man's knowledge is incomplete. On this account, *the Great Learning* for adults, at the outset of its lessons, instructs the learner, in regard to all things in the world, to proceed from what knowledge he has of their principles, and pursue his investigation of them, till he reaches the extreme point. After exerting himself in this way for a long time, he will suddenly find himself possessed of a wide and far-reaching penetration. Then, the qualities of all things, whether external or internal, the subtle or the coarse, will all be apprehended, and the mind, in its entire substance and its relations to things, will be perfectly intelligent. This is called the investigation of things. This is called the perfection of knowledge.

What is meant by "making the thoughts sincere" is the allowing no self-deception[21], as when we hate a bad smell, and as when we love what is beautiful. This is called self-enjoyment. Therefore, the superior man[22] must be watchful over himself when he is alone. There is no evil to which the mean man, dwelling retired, will not proceed[23], but when he sees a superior man, he instantly tries to disguise himself, concealing his evil, and displaying what is good. The other beholds him, as if he saw his heart and veins; of what use is his disguise? This is an instance of the saying "What truly is within will be manifested without". Therefore, the superior man must be watchful over himself when he is alone. The disciple Zeng[24] said, "What ten eyes behold, what ten hands point to, is to be regarded with reverence!" Riches adorn a house, and virtue adorns the person. The mind is expanded, and the body is at ease. Therefore, the superior man must make his thoughts sincere.

What is meant by "The cultivation of the person depends on rectifying the mind," may be thus illustrated: if a man be under the influence of passion, he will be incorrect in his conduct. He will be the same, if he is under the influence of terror, or under the influence of fond regard, or under that of sorrow and distress. When the mind is not present, we look and do not see; we hear and do not understand; we eat and do not know the taste of what we eat. This is what is meant by saying that the cultivation of the person depends on the rectifying of the mind.

What is meant by "The regulation of one's family depends on the cultivation of his person," is this: Men are partial where they feel affection and love; partial where they despise[25] and dislike; partial where they stand in awe and reverence; partial where they feel sorrow and compassion; partial where they are arrogant and rude. Thus it is that there are few men in the world, who love, and at the same time know the bad qualities of the object of[26] their love, or who hate, and yet know the excellences of the object of their hatred. Hence it is said, in the common adage[27], "A man does not know the wickedness of his son; he does not know the richness of his growing corn." This is what is meant by saying that if the person be not cultivated, a man cannot regulate his family.

What is meant by "In order rightly to govern his state, it is necessary first to regulate his family," is this: It is not possible for one to teach others, while he cannot teach his own family. Therefore, the ruler, without going beyond his family, completes the lessons for the State. There is filial piety: therewith[28] the sovereign should be served. There is fraternal submission[29]: therewith elders and superiors should be served. There is kindness: therewith the multitude should be treated. In *the Announcement to Kang*, it is said, "Act as if you were watching over an infant." If a mother is really anxious about it, though she may not hit exactly the wants of her infant, she will not be far from doing so. There never has been a girl who learned to bring up a child that she might afterwards marry. From the loving example[30] of one family, a whole state becomes loving, and from its courtesies, the whole state becomes courteous, while, from the ambition and perverseness of the one man, the whole state may be led to rebellious disorder—such is the nature of the influence. This verifies the saying, "Affairs may be ruined by a single sentence; a kingdom may be settled by its one man." Yao and Shun led on the empire with benevolence and the people followed them. Jie and

Zhou led on the empire with violence, and the people followed them. The orders which these issued were contrary to the practices, which they loved, and so the people did not follow them. On this account, the ruler must himself be possessed of the good qualities, and then he may require them in the people. He must not have the bad qualities in himself, and then he may require that they shall not be in the people. Never has there been a man, who, not having reference to his own character and wishes in dealing with others was able effectually to instruct them[③]. Thus we see how the government of the State depends on the regulation of the family. In *The Book of Poetry*, it is said, "That peach tree, so delicate and elegant! How luxuriant is its foliage[②]! This girl is going to get married. She will rightly order her household." Let the household be rightly ordered, and then the people of the state may be taught. In *The Book of Poetry*, it is said, "They can discharge their duties to their elder brothers. They can discharge their duties to their younger brothers." Let the ruler discharge his duties to his elder and younger brothers, and then he may teach the people of the state. In *The Book of Poetry*, it is said, "In his deportment there is nothing wrong; he rectifies all the people of the state." Yes, when the ruler, as a father, a son, and a brother, is a model, then the people imitate him. This is what is meant by saying, "The government of his kingdom depends on his regulation of the family."

What is meant by "The making the whole empire peaceful and happy depends on the government of his State," is this: When the sovereign behaves to his aged[③], as the aged should be behaved to, the people become filial; when the sovereign behaves to his elders, as elders should be behaved to, the people learn brotherly submission; when the sovereign treats compassionately the young and helpless, the people do the same. Thus the ruler has a principle with which, as with a measuring square, may regulate his conduct. What a man dislikes in his superiors, let him not display in the treatment of his inferiors; what he dislikes in his inferiors, let him not display in the service of his superiors; what he hates in those who are before him, let him not therewith precede those who are behind him; what he hates in those who are behind him, let him not therewith follow those who are before him; what he hates to receive on the right, let him not bestow on the left; what he hates to receive on the left, let him not bestow on the right: this is what is called "The principle, with which, as with a measuring square, to regulate one's conduct. " In *The Book of Poetry*, it is said, "How much to be rejoiced[34] in are these princes, the parents of the people!" When a prince loves what the people love, and hates what the people hate, then is he what is called the parent of the people. In *The Book of Poetry*, it is said, "Lofty is that southern hill, with its rugged masses of rocks! Greatly distinguished are you, O grand-teacher Yin[35], the people all look up to you. " Rulers of kingdoms may not neglect to be careful. If they deviate to a mean selfishness they will be a disgrace in the empire. In *The Book of Poetry*, it is said, "Before the sovereigns of the Yin Dynasty had lost the hearts of the people, they could appear before Heaven. Take warning from the house of Yin. The great decree is not easily preserved. This shows that, by gaining the people, the kingdom is gained, and, by losing the people, the kingdom is lost. On this account, the ruler will first take pains about his own virtue. Possessing virtue will give him the people. Possessing the people will give him the territory. Possessing the territory will give him its wealth. Possessing the wealth, he will have resources for expenditure. Virtue is the root; wealth is the result. If he makes the root his secondary object, and the result his primary, he will only wrangle with[36] his people, and teach them rapine[37]. Hence, the accumulation of wealth is the way to scatter the people; and the letting it be scattered among them is the way to collect the people. And hence, the ruler's words going forth contrary to right will come back to him in the same way, and wealth, gotten by improper ways, will take its departure by the same.

In *the Announcement to Kang*, it is said, "The decree indeed may not always rest on us", that is, goodness obtains the decree, and the want of goodness loses it. In *The Book of Chu*[38], it is said, "The kingdom of Chu does not consider that to be valuable. It values, instead, its good men. " The prince Wen's uncle, Fan[39], said, "Our fugitive[40] does not account that to be precious. What he considers precious, is the affection due to his parent. " In *the Declaration of the Prince of Qin*[41], it is said, "Let me have but one minister, plain and sincere, not pretending to other abilities, but with a simple, upright, mind; and possessed of generosity regarding the talents of others as though he himself possessed them, and, where he finds accomplished and perspicacious[42] men, loving them in his heart more than his mouth expresses, and really showing himself able to bear them and employ them: such a minister will be able to preserve my sons and grandsons, and black-haired people and benefits likewise to the kingdom may well be looked for from him. But if it be his character, when he finds men of ability, to be jealous and hate them; and, when he finds accomplished and perspicacious men, to oppose them and not allow their advancement, showing himself really not able to bear them: such a minister will not be able to protect my sons and grandsons and black-haired people; and may he not also be pronounced dangerous to the State!"

It is only the truly virtuous man, who can send away such a man and banish[43] him, driving him out among the barbarous tribes around, determined not to dwell along with him in the Middle Kingdom[44]. This is in accordance with the saying, "It is only the truly virtuous man who can love or who can hate others." To see men of worth and not be able to raise them to office; to raise them to office, but not to do so quickly: this is disrespect. To see bad men and not be able to remove them; to remove them; but not to do so to a distance: this is weakness. To love those whom men hate, and to hate those whom men love: this is to outrage the natural feeling of men. Calamities cannot fail to come down on him who does so. Thus we see that the sovereign has a great course to pursue. He must show entire self-devotion and sincerity to attain it, and by pride and extravagance he will fail of it. There is a great course also for the production of wealth. Let the producers be many and the consumers few. Let there be activity in the production, and economy in the expenditure. Then the wealth will always be sufficient. The virtuous ruler, by means of his wealth, makes himself more distinguished. The vicious ruler accumulates wealth, at the expense of his life. Never has there been a ease of the sovereign loving benevolence, and the people not loving righteousness. Never has there been a case where the people have loved righteousness, and the affairs of the sovereign have not been carried to completion. And never has there been a case where the wealth in such a State collected in the treasuries and arsenals[45] did not continue in the sovereign's possession. The officer Meng Xian Zi[46] said,

"He who keeps horses and a carriage does not look after fowls and pigs. The family which keeps its stores of ice does not rear cattle or sheep. So the house which possesses hundred chariots[47] should not keep a minister to look out for imposts[48] that he may lay them on the people. Than to have such a minister, it was better for that house to have one who should rob it of its revenues.[49]" This is in accordance with the saying: "In a State, pecuniary[50] gain is not to be considered prosperity, but its prosperity will be found in righteousness." When he who presides over a State or a family makes revenues his chief business, he must be under the influence of some small, mean, man. He may consider this man to be good; but when such a person is employed in the administration of a state or family, calamities from Heaven, and injuries from men, will be fallen it together, and, though a good man may take his place, he will not be able to remedy the evil. This illustrates again the saying, "In a State, gain is not to be considered prosperity, but its prosperity will be found in righteousness."

(Translated by James Legge)

Ⅲ. 难点释义

① *The Great Learning*，译作《大学》，在此既有"博学"的意思，也有相对于小学而言的"大人之学"的意思。古人八岁入学学习基础文化知识和礼节；十五岁读大学，学习伦理、政治和哲学等。

② illustrious，光明正大的，杰出的。

③ unperturbedness，心情平静的，未受扰乱的。

④ repose，安宁，安稳。

⑤ rectify，使……端正，改正。

⑥ *the Announcement to Kang*，《康诰》，《尚书·周书》的篇名，西周时周成王任命康叔治理殷商旧地民众的命令。

⑦ *the Tai Jia*，《太甲》，又作《大甲》，《尚书·商书》的篇名。

⑧ decrees of Heaven，上天赋予的使命。

⑨ *the Canon of the Emperor Yao*，《帝典》，即《尧典》，《尚书·虞书》的篇名之

一，另一篇为《舜典》，是二帝政书。

⑩ *the Bathing-tub of Tang*，《盘铭》。汤，即成汤，商朝的开国君主。盘铭是刻在器皿上的警醒箴言。

⑪ *The Book of Poetry*，《诗经》，原本叫"诗"，共有诗歌305首，因此又称"诗三百"。

⑫ *li*，中国长度单位，大概为590码。

⑬ Master，大师，教师，这里指的是孔子。

⑭ sovereign，君主，统治者。

⑮ Qi，淇水，河流名，古为黄河支流，位于河南北部。

⑯ accomplished prince，文采风流的君子，泛指有修养、有学问、品行好的人。

⑰ chisel and grind，雕刻，琢磨。

⑱ awe-inspiring deportment，令人敬畏的威武仪态。

⑲ litigation，诉讼，起诉。

⑳ devoid of principle，奸诈，不诚实。

㉑ self-deception，自欺。

㉒ superior man，作"君子"解，指品德高尚的人。

㉓ There is no evil to which the mean man, dwelling retired, will not proceed. 本句意思是，品德低下的人在独处的时候，无恶不作。

㉔ disciple Zeng，弟子曾，孔子的学生，也即本篇的作者。

㉕ despise，轻视，鄙视。

㉖ the object of，喜爱或厌恶的对象。

㉗ adage，箴言，谚语。

㉘ therewith，于是。

㉙ fraternal submission，对兄长的尊敬。

㉚ loving example，家庭中的仁爱。

㉛ Never has there been a man, who, not having reference to his own character and wishes in dealing with others was able effectually to instruct them. 本句意思是，不采取这种推己及人的方式，而想让别人按自己的意思去做，那是不可能的。

㉜ foliage，树叶。

㉝ behave to his aged，尊敬老人。

㉞ rejoice，使快乐。

㉟ O grand-teacher Yin，这里指的是殷朝，即商朝（约前 17 世纪—前 11 世纪）因最后首都定于殷，又称殷商。这里疑有误译。原文"殷之未丧师，克配上帝"是指殷商在未丧失民心之时，尚能与上天旨意相符。

㊱ wrangle with，与……争斗，争论。

㊲ rapine，掠夺。

㊳ *The Book of Chu*，《楚书》，楚昭王时的史书。

㊴ the prince Wen's uncle, Fan，舅犯，晋文公的舅舅，狐偃，字子犯。狐偃在骊姬之乱时劝晋献公的女儿重耳流亡外国。

㊵ fugitive，流亡的人。

㊶ *Declaration of the Prince of Qin*，《秦誓》，《尚书·周书》中的经典章节。秦誓，秦穆公誓众之辞的简称。

㊷ perspicacious，有洞察力的，敏锐的。

㊸ banish，流放，驱逐。

㊹ the Middle Kingdom，引处主要指当时的中原。

㊺ arsenal，府库的财产。

㊻ Meng Xian Zi，孟献子，姬姓，孟氏（亦称仲氏），名蔑，谥献，史称孟献子，是孟氏家族振兴的重要贡献者，春秋中期鲁国的外交家、政治家。

㊼ chariot，兵车，战车。

㊽ impost，课税，这里指聚敛的财富。

㊾ Than to have such a minister, it was better for that house to have one who should rob it of its revenues. 此句意思是，与其有聚敛财富的家臣，还不如有偷盗东西的家臣。

㊿ pecuniary，利益，财产。

Ⅳ. 问题思考

1. What are the main ideas of *the Great Learning*? Using your own words to sum up.

2. What does Confucius suggest by referring to King Wen in *Commentary of the Philosopher Zeng*?

3. What is the root of *the Great Learning*? Why does the author say "the superior man must be watchful over himself when he is alone"? Find some examples to support your understanding of the idea.

4. Do you agree with the saying "Riches adorn a house, and virtue adorns the person"? Why or why not? What is Confucius, attitude toward the cultivation of the person?

5. What can make a virtue ruler in a State? Do you think that it has some significances nowadays? If it is, in what respects? If it is not, why do you think in that way?

V. 经典导读

《大学》是南宋朱熹选自《礼记》中的第42篇,再重新编排而成。分为"经"和"传"两个部分。"经"一章,是孔子的原话,由孔子的学生曾子记录;"传"十章,是曾子对"经"的理解和阐述,由曾子的学生记录。后世儒家学者一般认定整篇作者为曾子。《大学》与《中庸》、《论语》、《孟子》被朱熹并列为"四书",是儒家传世经典。朱熹认为,《大学》是孔子及其门生留下的遗书,是儒学"入德之门",所以将它列在"四书"之首。

《大学》通过"三纲八目"完整地阐述了一个人从格物致知开始,修身正心,仁爱齐家,

古代的私塾学堂

直至治国平天下,超凡入圣的过程,是儒门修心、修身的方法论。此外,有学者也认为,《大学》全篇虽引用《诗经》、《尚书》作立论,但其思想脉络却来自《易经》与《易传》,是纳易学入儒学、用易学思想充实儒家思想并使之融为一体的典范。

《大学》即"大人之学"(朱熹解)。其主要内容是"三纲八目"。什么是"三

纲"？"三纲"就是大学之道，是儒家学说的主旨。开篇的第一段话介绍了这一精华："《大学》之道，在明明德，在亲民，在止于至善。知止而后有定，定而后能静，静而后能安，安而后能虑，虑而后能得。物有本末，事有终始，知所先后，则近道矣。"《大学》的最高目标在于弘扬光明正大的品德，在于弃旧图新，在于使人达到最完善的境界，使人确立坚定的志向，心静泰然，周详思考，有所收获。

"三纲"首先强调的是"明德"，德乃人之本，德是人的一切心性和品德。儒学认为人的心性是至善且至灵的，要德智皆善。第二，亲民，即新民。人是革新和实现至善的主体，人要不断去旧习，求进步，成为新民。如商汤所说，"日日新，又日新"；如《诗经》提倡"虽旧帮，其命维新"，要始终自我更新，为至善至美而不懈努力。"止于至善"则是"三纲"的最高境界。商汤、殷周等各代君王莫不如是。君主是圣贤的楷模，至善至美的德行得到弘扬，人民自然敬仰学习，共同创出安乐生活。"三纲"思想对现代建设和谐社会、管治国家也有着指导意义。

《大学》"八目"，也就是八个条目，其实就是八个关键词，它们相互之间有着因果关系："格物（investigating）、致知（completing knowledge）、诚意（sincere thoughts）、正心（rectifying hearts）、修身（cultivating persons）、齐家（regulating the family）、治国（govering the state）、平天下（tranquilizing the state）"。"欲明明德于天下者，先治其国；欲治其国者，先齐其家；欲齐其家者，先修其身；欲修其身者，先正其心；欲正其心者，先诚其意；欲诚其意者，先致其知，致知在格物。物格而后知至，知至而后意诚，意诚一心正，心正而后身修，身修而后家齐，家齐而后国治，国治而后天下平。"前四目——格物、致知、诚意、正心是一个人的内修，达到充实自身、夯实根基的要求："格物"与"致知"教导人从观察、研究万物去探求并获取知识，知识促使人树立真诚信念，端正心思，不持偏见傲惰，从而培养高尚品性，修正自己；后四目——修身、齐家、治国、平天下是外修的方法，以服务社会为目的。修养自身，孝顺父母，恭敬兄长，家人和睦相亲，齐家治国自成。民众效法，社会和谐。

《大学》一书常常被认为具有由"内圣"而"外王"的重要意义。"内圣"，即自己内心的修行已经圆满，内在成为有学识、有智慧、品德过人的圣人。内心圆满了，然后将所学所得向外扩展延伸，应用到管理家庭、治理国家方面，使天下太平，成为社会上的王者,所以叫"外王"。"内圣外王"之学是儒家治国理论,治国首重人格修养,至善的人格修养是齐家治国的根本。

《大学》之道对中国的知识界、教育界影响深远。"新民"(或"亲民")一词在中国近代史上被多次使用,例如戊戌变法领袖之一梁启超创办的《新民丛刊》和他创作的"新民说"。而中国不少大学校训,如香港大学的"明德格物"、东南大学的"止于至善"、南开大学的"允公允能,日新月异"、厦门大学的"自强不息,止于至善"、台湾成功大学的"穷理致知"等,也无不体现中国高校继承《大学》之道,通过研究求取知识、图新求上的办学精神。

《大学》中"君子必慎其独"、"德润身、心广体胖"和"生财有道"等,无不是现代人修身养性、持正心、走正路的心灵指导。"修身、齐家、治国、平天下"也成为古今仁人志士追求和奋斗的目标。

VI. 译本链接

1. Charles Muller,*The Great Learning*,New York:Routledge,1990.

2. James Legge,*The Sacred Books of the East*,London:Oxford University Press,1861.

3. Joshua Marshman,*The Great Learning*,London:Penguin,1814.

4. 林语堂译:《大学》,纽约:哥伦比亚大学出版社 1938 年版。

5. 辜鸿铭译:《大学》,London:John Murray,1908.

6. 何祚康:《大学·中庸》(汉英对照),北京:华语教学出版社 1996 年版。

Unit Three
The Doctrine of the Mean（《中庸》）

I. 背景简介

Zi Si（483 B. C. – 402 B. C.）, whose family name is Kong, given name is Ji, styled Zi Si. He was Kongli's son and Confucius' grandson. It was said that he was a teacher of Duke Lumiao. He died at the age of eighty-two. He was a renowned philosopher and great thinker in the early Warring States Period.

Zi Si was not Confucius' disciple[①] because he was only 4 years old when Confucius passed away. He took Zeng Shen, a famous disciple of Confucius, as his teacher. He inherited the Confucian spirit and teaching. He elaborated and developed the teaching in the book entitled *The Doctrine*[②] *of the Mean* whose

Zi Si（483 **B. C.** – 402 **B. C.**）

impact was said to surpass *the Great Learning*, the book written by Zi Si's teacher Zeng Zi. *The Doctrine of the Mean* was one of the five classics, and was a required textbook in ancient schools and a must-read as well for imperial competitive examination.

Zi Si was regarded as a great master because he served as a link between Confucius and Mencius. He passed on his thought to his disciple Mencius who later developed his own

theory on the basis of Zi Si's teaching. His thought and Mencius's theory constitute the Simeng (Zi Si – Mencius) School which became an important part of Confucian School.

Zi Si held a special place in Confucian School and was reversed at ancient times. He was conferred different titles in Song Dynasty and Yuan Dynasty. In Ming Dynasty he was ultimately conferred a title "Shusheng".

Zi Si's thought primarily demonstrates the usefulness of a golden way to gain perfect virtue. It focuses on the "way" that is prescribed by a heavenly mandate not only to the ruler but to everyone. To follow these heavenly instructions by learning and teaching will automatically result in a Confucian virtue. Because Heaven has laid down what is the way to perfect virtue, it is not that difficult to follow the steps of the holy rulers of old if one only knows what the right way is.

Ⅱ. 文本选读

[Chapter 1]

Human nature is endowed by Heaven. The right way of behavior is to follow one's nature and all nature should be cultivated in the right way of behavior.

The right way of behavior can not be divorced from[③] the man; if behavior can be divorced, it is not the right way. Even when a gentleman lives alone, he should be prudent[④] and afraid to do wrong, because though no one knows what he has done, he himself will know it all.

When joy, anger, sorrow and happiness are not revealed, they are *zhong*, in the mean. When they are revealed, they are *he*, in harmony. *Zhong* is the base of everything and *he* is the right way to reveal everything. If *zhong* and *he* are achieved, the world would run smoothly.

[Chapter 2]

Confucius said, "Whatever a gentleman does, he should do according to the doctrine of the Mean; only a petty person would do otherwise. A gentleman conforms to the principle of *zhong yong* because he adheres to the mean, going neither too far nor not far enough; a petty person is reckless because he can never be impartial or unbiased. "

[Chapter 8]

Confucius said, "Yan Hui⑤ (Confucius' disciple) chooses to take the Mean course. Once he has learnt something good he keeps it in his mind and never let go of it. "

[Chapter 9]

Confucius said, "It is possible to rule the state well, to decline high posts and handsome salaries, and it is even possible for a man to tramp on sharp knives to move forward, but it is almost impossible for a man to adhere to the Mean forever. "

[Chapter 10]

Zi Lu⑥ (Confucius's disciple) asked the meaning of strong will. Confucius said, "What kind of strong will do you want to learn, the southern one, or the northern one, or the one of self-cultivation? The southern one means to educate people in the spirit of tolerance and forbearance⑦ and not to seek revenge on others even if a man has been ill treated. Gentlemen cherish this kind of strong will. The northern one means to take up all kinds of arms and not to hesitate to fight to the end, even at the cost of his life. Those who are physically strong favor this kind of strong will. Hence, gentlemen are tolerant, do not follow the fashion, adhere to the Mean, do not change their attitude if the state is in order, and do not compromise their personal integrity if the state is in chaos. This is what we call strong will. "

[Chapter 14]

A gentleman should always be satisfied with his own position and act accordingly. If he occupies a high position, he should behave like a high official. If he is poor and in a low position, he should act as a poor and subordinate official. If he lives in a barbarous area⑧, he should do as a barbarian does. If he is in adversity⑨, he should take action appropriate to such circumstances. Whatever his position, he should be contented and cheerful. If he is a superior, he should not treat his subordinates high-handedly⑩. If he occupies a low position, he should not flatter his superior. If he behaves himself and does not blame others, no one will complain about him. He should blame neither God nor others, but accept his fate calmly. A petty person runs risks to make profits. Confucius said, "To gentlemen, to behave well is like shooting an arrow. If he misses the target, he himself is to blame."

[Chapter 20]

Duke Ai of Lu⑪ asked Confucius the way to administer the state. Confucius said, "The orders issued by King Wen⑫ and King Wu⑬ written on bamboo strips⑭ were effective only when there were wise and virtuous⑮ officials. If there were no wise and virtuous officials, the order would not have been effective. The right way to treat people is to govern the state well; the right way to treat the earth is to plant trees. Government affairs are like reeds⑯. Thus the key to govern the state well is to employ wise and virtuous officials. The key to employ wise and virtuous officials is the ruler's self-cultivation. To cultivate himself a man must follow the right course and to follow the right course he must begin with kindness and benevolence.

"Being benevolent means to love people. The greatest benevolence is to love one's own parents. Justice means to treat things properly. The greatest justice is to value wise and virtuous persons. To love one's relatives, a man should take their relation to himself into consideration; to value wise and virtuous persons, he should take their rank into consideration. These are the basis of rite⑰. So a gentleman must first cultivate himself. A man begins his self-cultivation by serving his parents well and he can not serve his parents well unless he knows the people, and one can not know the people well unless he knows the way of Heaven⑱."

"The most important relationships in the world are five in number: rulers and subjects; fathers and sons; husbands and wives; brothers; friends. The maintenance and improvement of these relationships depend on three virtues: wisdom, benevolence and courage. The way to practice them is the same. Some know these relationships by nature, others by learning, still others by hard work. Once they know, what they know is the same. Some practice these relationships naturally, others grudgingly. Others still are inspired by profit. Once these are practiced, the results are the same."

Confucius said, "To be eager to learn indicates wisdom because it may eliminate stupidity. To practice what one knows indicates benevolence because it makes one selfless.

To have a sense of shame indicates courage because it clears one of cowardice[19]. A man who knows these points knows how to cultivate himself; a man who knows how to cultivate himself knows how to rule others; a man who knows how to rule others knows how to administer the state.

"There are nine set principles to administer the state: to cultivate one's moral character, to value virtuous persons, to be on intimate terms with relatives, to esteem[20] high officials, to understand and sympathize with all officials, to care about the common people, to attract all kinds of workers, to appease[21] those who are far away, and to think of the dukes. Self-cultivation enables a man to behave correctly. Valuing virtuous persons makes him wise. Being on intimate terms with relatives, a man will no longer hear complaints from his uncles, cousins and brothers. Esteeming high officials allows him to handle affairs properly. Understanding and sympathizing with all officials will make them reward him with better work and more loyalty. Caring about common people will make them encourage one another. Attracting all kinds of workers will enrich the state. Appeasing those who are far away will make them pledge allegiance. Thinking of dukes finds them obeying in fear.

"To cultivate himself, a man should wear clothes properly as if he is fasting[22], and do nothing that does not conform to the rites. To value virtuous persons, a man should drive away slanderers[23], refrain from sensual pleasures[24], despise[25] material goods and respect virtues. To be on intimate terms with his relatives, a man should raise their ranks and salaries, have the same likes and dislikes. To esteem high officials, a man should place many officials of lower grade at their disposal. To understand and sympathize with all officials, a man should trust them and raise their salaries. To encourage the common people, he should make them serve only in slack seasons[26] and reduce their taxes. To motivate all kinds of workers, a man should check up on their work and their salaries should match with their posts and work. To appease those who are far away, a man should see off those who depart and welcome those who arrive, reward the good and take pity on the weak. To bestow[27] grace upon dukes, a man should adopt heirs for those who have no offspring, restore dukedoms which have been destroyed, put down rebellions for them, help them when they are in trouble, make obeisance to Emperor Zhou at five yearly intervals[28] and dispatch[29] a diplomatic mission at three yearly intervals, present as many gifts as possible and accept as few gifts as possible. Though there are nine ways to govern the state, the underlying principle is the same."

"Preparedness ensures success, unpreparedness spells failure. To think before one speaks ensures fluency; to think before one acts ensures all difficulties will be cleared away; to think before one performs duties ensures easy conscience; to think before one practices principles ensures smoothness in the practice."

"Subordinate officials should not be able to rule over the masses if they are not trusted by their superior. To enjoy the trust of his superior, a man has to gain the trust of friends first. To gain the trust of friends, he should obey his parents. To obey his parents, a man should examine himself to see if he is honest and sincere. To do so, he has to distinguish the good from the bad, otherwise he would not be able to be honest and sincere."

"Sincerity is the way of Heaven. To strive to be sincere is the way of man. Some are born sincere. What they do always conforms to the way of Heaven without strenuous[30] efforts to do so. What they strive for always falls into the way of Heaven without conscious thought. Though they act calmly and leisurely, their actions always agree with the way. This is because they are sages! The one who strives to be sincere is the one who chooses and adheres to the good. One must learn extensively, examine carefully, think prudently, distinguish clearly and practice sincerely the good way. He should not stop learning until he has known all, neither should he stop asking until he has exhausted his questions, nor should he stop thinking until he has found all the answers, nor should he stop distinguishing until he has made the differences clear, nor should he stop acting until he has done his sincere best. If others succeed by making one ounce of effort, I will make a hundred times as much effort; if others succeed by making a hundred ounce of effort, I will make ten hundred times as much effort. If only a man follows this principle, he would be clever even though he has been stupid and he would become strong even though he has been weak."

(Translated by He Zuokang)

Ⅲ．难点释义

① disciple，门徒，弟子。

② doctrine，学说，教义。

③ be divorced from，脱离。

④ prudent，谨慎的，明辨的。

⑤ Yan Hui，颜回，曹姓，颜氏，名回，字子渊，春秋时期鲁国人。出身贫寒，不幸早死，享年仅39岁。他14岁即拜孔子为师，此后终生追随，是孔子最得意的弟子。

⑥ Zi Lu，名仲由，字子路，或称季路，鲁国人，是孔子著名的弟子。被列为"孔门十哲"之一，比孔子年少9岁，也是弟子中侍奉孔子最久的人。子路性格爽直，为人勇武，信守承诺，忠于职守，以擅长"政事"著称。

⑦ forbearance，宽容，克制。

⑧ a barbarous area，异邦，未开化的地区，泛指当时少数民族聚居的地区。

⑨ adversity，逆境，不幸。

⑩ high-handedly，目空一切地，专横地。

⑪ Duke Ai of Lu，鲁哀公，姬姓，名将，是鲁国第二十六任君主。

⑫ King Wen，周文王，姬姓，名昌，是周人崇敬的祖先，周王朝的奠基人。周文王擅长易经卜卦。

⑬ King Wu，周武王，姬姓，名发，周文王之子，是西周王朝的开国君主。

⑭ bamboo strip，竹简，战国至魏晋时代的书写材料。竹简通常用竹片制成，是古代最早的书籍形式。此处泛指古代典籍。

⑮ virtuous，有道德的，正直的。

⑯ reed，芦苇。此处喻指为政容易。

⑰ rite，礼仪，习俗，典礼。

⑱ the way of Heaven，自然的法则，道理，天道。

⑲ cowardice，怯懦，胆小。

⑳ esteem，尊敬，尊重。

㉑ appease，安抚，优待。

㉒ fast，斋戒。此处引申为整洁身心。

㉓ slanderer，诽谤者。

㉔ sensual pleasures，声色享受。

㉕ despise，轻视，鄙视。

㉖ in slack seasons，淡季。此处引申为适时地。

㉗ bestow，赐予，赠予。

㉘ make obeisance to Emperor Zhou at five yearly intervals，此句意思是，命令诸侯每隔五年去朝拜周王。

㉙ dispatch，派遣。

㉚ strenuous，费力的，艰苦的。

Ⅳ. 问题思考

1. How does Confucius explain the concept of "*zhong*"?

2. Why does Confucius say "The doctrine of mean is the supreme principle"?

3. According to Confucius, what should people do to practice the doctrine of mean?

4. Of the nine set principles in *The Doctrine of the Mean*, which do you think is the most important to administer the state? Why do you think so?

5. How does Confucius define sincerity? Why does he say "there is no end to being sincere"? Find more examples in the text to support your understanding of the definition.

6. What is the relationship between sincerity and benevolence, and knowledge?

7. In which aspect of the modern society do you think *The Doctrine of the Mean* can be applied to? Please justify your answer.

Ⅴ. 经典导读

《中庸》原是《礼记》中的一篇，被朱熹誉为"孔门心法"。一般认为是孔子的孙子子思所作。现存的《中庸》，则经过秦代儒家学者修改整理。子思前承孔子，后来其思想通过他的门生又传给了孟子。《中庸》和《孟子》的基本观点也大体相近，所以有"思孟学派"的说法。自西汉时代始,各代都有研究、解读《中庸》的著作,其中以南宋朱熹的《中庸章句》影响最大。朱熹把《中庸》与《大学》、《论语》、《孟子》合在一起,并列为"四书",成为儒家学派传世经典,是后世官定的教科书和科举考试的必读书,对宋、元以后的教育产生了极大的影响。

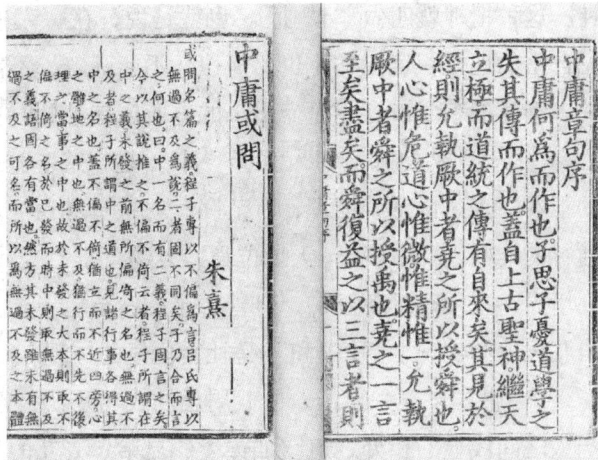

清代木刻版《中庸》内页

据传,《中庸》全书共 45 篇。《中庸》的核心思想是中庸之道。也包括"五达道"、"三达德"、"九经"、诚信和"为学无息"的教育思想。《中庸》凝聚了儒学中的思想精粹,既阐释中庸精神,也提出实践方法,内容丰富,充满哲理。

"中庸之道"的主旨在于修养人性,提高道德修养,教导处世为人之法,倡导修身、齐家、治国的自然之道。"中庸"并非现代人所普遍理解的中立、平庸。"中"是独立、不偏不倚、不高不低、无过与不及,是"合适、合理、适度、适时"。"庸"是平常、恒久的常理。中庸之道的目的是教育人们以唯物主义的思维模式,自觉地进行自我修养、自我监督、自我教育、自我完善,把自己培养成为具有理想人格,至善、至仁、至诚、至道、至德、至圣、合外内之道的理想人物。

《中庸》第一章提出:"天命之谓性,率性之谓道,修道之谓教。"天命即天性,也属于人的本性;"率性之谓道"是说要遵从规律而不是放纵本性;"修道之谓教"是说要学习改善自我。自然所赋予人的是本性,遵循人的本性自然发展就是遵循事物发展的内在规律,学习内省自察,改善内在的品性,教育他人。"道也者,不可须臾离也,可离非道也。是故君子戒慎乎其所不睹,恐惧乎其所不闻。莫见乎远,莫显乎微。故君子慎其独也。"自我教育贯穿于人的一生,人们一刻也离不开自我教育。要将自我教育贯穿于人生的全部过程,就需要有一种强有力的自我约束、自我监督的精神。这种精神就叫做"慎独"。也就是说,在一人独处时,在别人看不到自己、听不见自己的地方,言行举止也要谨慎,不能疏忽,不能懈怠。隐蔽的东西没有不被发现的,细微的东西没有不显露出来的,所以在独处时更要自我约束、自我监督,谨慎小心。《中庸》从情感上切入解释"中"是"喜、怒、哀、乐之未发","中"是天下的根本。表达情感合情理,有节度,就是"和"。"和也者,天下之大道也",即天下通行的准则。"致中和,天地位焉,万物育焉"是实现自我教育,达到不偏不倚的最高境界,也就是具备至仁、至善、至诚、至道、至德、至圣的品德后的效应。中和是自我价值的实现,"致中和"是社会价值的体现。

《中庸》以尧舜禹汤、文武周公的成功秘诀,阐述了中庸的道理及其效用。从人与人之间浅显的相处之道,如夫妻、兄弟、妻儿的和睦相处,说明修习中庸之道要从日常生活做起,先由近处开始、从低处起步,"君子之道,辟如行远,必自迩;辟如登高,必自卑"。以"哀公问政"为例,重申从事政治、从事管理的人提高自身品德修养的关键性和重要性。

"五达道"(君臣也,父子也,夫妇也,兄弟也,朋友之交也)是儒家做人的规范。"三达德"(智、仁、勇)是《中庸》修道的方法论。"好学近乎知,力行近乎仁,知耻近乎勇",即好学不倦就接近于明智、明事理;努力行善就接近于仁义;懂得耻辱就接近于刚勇了。懂得上述三件事就能了解修身;知道修身,就知道如何管理人;知道管理人,就知道如何治理国家。治理国家有"九经":修养自身,尊重贤人,爱护亲族,敬重大臣,体恤群臣,爱护百姓,劝勉各种工匠,优待远方来的客人,安抚诸侯。这些都是《中庸》倡导的"修身、齐家、治天下"的自然法则。《中庸》与曾子的《大学》一脉相承,传递儒家精神。

《中庸》所追求的修养的最高境界是至诚或称至德。内心至诚才明察事理,这叫做自然天性。"唯天下至诚,为能尽其性;能尽其性,则能尽人之性;能尽人之性,则能尽物之性。"内心至诚,能发挥万物本性,进而促进天地生成万物。所以至诚可以与天、地并列。诚是完成自身品德修养的要素,贯穿在万物的始终,没有诚,则没有万物。所以,诚被视为最宝贵的品德。而追求至诚永远没有止境,悠远无穷。通达至诚的途径是"博学之,审问之,慎思之,明辨之,笃行之(learn extensively, examine carefully, think prudently, distrguish clearly, and practise sincerely)"。

　　《中庸》的语言简明精辟，许多表述是至今仍被广为引用的警句名言，例如，"己所不欲，勿施于人"（what you do not like when done to yourself, do not do to others）、"素位而行"、"知耻近乎勇"、"不怨天尤人"、"凡事豫（预）则立，不豫（预）则废"、"非礼勿视、非礼勿听、非礼勿言、非礼勿动"（see no evil, hear no evil, speak no evil, and do no evil at all）等。追求至诚的名句"博学之，审问之，慎思之，明辨之，笃行之"更成为现当代不少高等院校的校训，如中山大学的"博学、审问、慎思、明辨、笃行"、华南理工大学的"博学慎思，明辨笃行"、黑龙江大学的"博学慎思，参天尽物"。"博学笃行"四字更被广泛选用，时刻提醒学子们珍惜学习机会，努力求知、求真、求实，乐于履行义务、勇于承担社会责任。

　　《中庸》对中国传统社会的政治礼制和政治秩序的构建，社会信仰和伦理道德价值观等方面的影响延续至今，对现代管理和人际交往也都有一定的积极意义。

Ⅵ. 译本链接

1. James Legge, *The Sacred Books of the East*, London：Oxford University Press, 1861.

2. 辜鸿铭译：《中庸》, London：John Murray, 1908。

3. 何祚康：《大学·中庸》（汉英对照），北京：华语教学出版社 1996 年版。

Unit Four
The Analects (《论语》)

I. 背景简介

Confucius (551B. C. –479 B. C.), born in the State of Lu which is known today as Qufu in Shandong Province, lived and worked during the Spring and Autumn Period (770B. C. – 476 B. C.). Confucius was a thinker and educator who developed a social and political philosophy that was often considered to be the foundation of subsequent Chinese thought. He was the founder of the Ru School of Chinese thought and the philosophical school of thought that has come to bear his name, Confucianism. He had gained some fame by the time he was 30 but it was not until he was 51 that his official life really assumed great

Confucius (551 **B. C.** –479 **B. C.**)

importance. This eventful career was to last for only four years as he was forced to resign when he found it impossible to agree with the authorities. Such was the opposition to his ideas that he was obliged to leave his country and to travel around the states.

Compared to his frustrated political career, his career as a teacher and philosopher was brilliant and full of achievements. He first promoted the ideas "to educate all despite their social status" and "to teach according to the students' characteristics", and broke with tradition that only the aristocracy had the privilege of education. He also proposed a complete set of principles concerning study. He said, "He who learns but does not think is lost. He who thinks but does not learn is in great danger." The accumulated words of his wisdom have come down to us as *the Analects*, one of the most important of all the Chinese classics. The analects have greatly influenced the moral and philosophical values of China and other countries in Eastern Asia. The text has remained a fundamental course of study for any would-be scholar for over two thousand years.

Confucius' social philosophy largely revolves around the concept of Goodness (*ren*). For Confucius, concern for others is demonstrated through the practice of forms of the Golden Rule: "What you do not wish for yourself, do not do to others." He regards devotion to parents and older siblings as the most basic form of promoting the interests of others before one's own. Central to all ethical teachings found in *the Analects* of Confucius is the notion that the social arena is the extended family. Confucius saw a duty to one's parents and ancestors as instrumental in the cultivating of virtue and as in accordance with ritual. One who behaved morally in all possible parallel structures extending outward from the family probably approximated Confucius' conception of Goodness.

Confucius' political philosophy is also rooted in his belief that a ruler should learn self-discipline, should govern his subjects by his own example, and should treat them with love and concern. He advocated for governance through Goodness and placed a great deal of weight on ruling by what was right. For Confucius, what characterized superior rulership was the possession of "virtue". Such "virtue" would enable the ruler to win a following and to maintain good order in his state without troubling himself and by relying on loyal and effective deputies. A ruler would have to be cognizant of past rituals and traditions but also lead people by example. He should not act out of personal or political gain but instead advocate only for what would be best for his people. It seems apparent that Confucius' warnings about the ill consequences of promulgating law codes were not popular in his time.

Ⅱ. 文本选读

Book Ⅰ

1. 1 The Master[①] said, "To learn and at due times to repeat what one has learnt, is that not after all a pleasure? That friends should come to one from afar, is this not after all delightful? To remain unsoured even though one's merits are unrecognized by others, is that not after all what is expected of a gentleman?"

1. 2 Master You[②] said, "Those who in private life behave well towards their parents and elder brothers, in public life seldom show a disposition to resist the authority of their superiors. And as for such men starting a revolution, no instance of it has ever occurred. It is upon the trunk[③] that a gentleman works. When that is firmly set up, the Way[④] grows. And surely proper behavior towards parents and elder brothers is the trunk of Goodness?"

1. 3 The Master said, "'Clever talk and a pretentious manner' are seldom found in the Good[⑤]."

1. 4 Master Zeng[⑥] said, "Every day I examine myself on these three points: in acting on behalf of others, have I always been loyal to their interests? In intercourse with my friends, have I always been true to my word? Have I failed to repeat the precepts that have been handed down to me?"

1. 5 The Master said, "A country of a thousand war-chariots[⑦] cannot be administered unless the ruler attends strictly to business, punctually observes his promises, is economical in expenditure, shows affection towards his subjects in general, and uses the labor of the peasantry only at the proper times of year."

1. 6 The Master said, "A young man's duty is to behave well to his parents at home and to his elders abroad, to be cautious in giving promises and punctual in keeping them, to have kindly feelings towards everyone, but seek the intimacy of the Good. If, when all that is done, he has any energy to spare, then let him study the polite arts[⑧]."

1. 7 Zi Xia[⑨] said, "A man who treats his betters as betters, wears an air of respect, who into serving father and mother, knows how to put his whole strength, who in the service

of his prince will lay down his life, who in intercourse with friends is true to his word...
Others may say of him that he still lacks education, but I for my part should certainly call
him an educated man. "

1.8 The Master said, "If a gentleman is frivolous[10], he will lose the respect of his
inferiors and lack firm ground upon which to build up his education. First and foremost he
must learn to be faithful to his superiors, to keep promises, to refuse the friendship of all
who are not like him. And if he finds he has made a mistake, then he must not be afraid of
admitting the fact and amending his ways. "

1.9 Master Zeng said, "When proper respect towards the dead is shown at the end and
continued after they are far away the moral force of a people has reached its highest point. "

1.10 Zi Qin[11] said to Zi Gong[12], "When our Master arrives in a fresh country he always
manages to find out something about its policy. Does he do this by asking questions, or do
people tell him of their own accord?" Zi Gong said, "Our Master gets things by being
cordial, frank, courteous, temperate, deferential. That is our Master's way of enquiring—
a very different matter, certainly, from the way in which enquiries are generally made. "

1.11 The Master said, "While a man's father is alive, you can only see his intentions;
it is when his father dies that you discover whether or not he is capable of carrying them out.
If for the whole three years of mourning he manages to carry on the household exactly as in
his father's day, then he is a good son indeed. "

1.12 Master You said, "In the usages of ritual it is harmony that is prized; the Way of
the Former Kings from this got its beauty. Both small matters and great matters depend upon
it. If things go amiss, he who knows the harmony will be able to attune them. But if
harmony itself is not modulated by ritual, things will still go amiss[13]. "

1.13 Master You said, "In your promises cleave to what is right, and you will be able
to fulfill your word. In your obeisance cleave to ritual, and you will keep dishonor at bay.
Marry one who has not betrayed her own kin, and you may safely present her to your
ancestors. "

1.14 The Master said, "A gentleman who never goes in eating till he is sated, who does not demand comfort in his home, who is diligent in business and cautious in speech, who associates with those that possess the Way and thereby corrects his own faults—such a one way indeed be said to have a taste for learning. "

1. 15 Zi Gong said, " 'Poor without cadging, rich without swagger,' what of that?" The Master said, "Not bad. But better still, 'Poor, yet delighting in the Way; rich, yet a student of ritual. '" Zi Gong said, "The saying of the Songs:

As thing cut, as thing field,

As thing chiseled, as thing polished[14]

refers, I suppose, to what you have just said?" The Master said, "Ci[15], now I can really begin to talk to you about the Songs, for when I allude to sayings of the past, you see what bearing they have on what was to come after. "

1. 16 The Master said, " (The good man) Does not grieve that other people do not recognize his merits. His only anxiety is lest he should fail to recognize theirs. "

BOOK II

2. 1 The Master said, "He who rules by moral force (*de*) is like the polestar, which remains in its place while all the lesser stars do homage[16] to it. "

2. 2 The Master said, "If out of the three hundred Songs I had to take one phrase to cover all my teaching. I would say 'Let there be no evil in your thoughts'. "

2. 3 The Master said, "Govern the people by regulations, keep order among them by chastisements[17], and they will flee from you, and lose all self-respect. Govern them by moral force, keep order among them by ritual and they will keep their self-respect and come to you of their own accord. "

2. 4 The Master said, "At fifteen I set my heart upon learning. At thirty, I had planted my feet firm upon the ground. At forty, I no longer suffered from perplexities[18]. At fifty, I knew what the biddings of Heaven were. At sixty, I heard them with docile ear. At seventy, I could follow the dictates of my own heart; for what I desired no longer overstepped the boundaries of right. "

2.5 Meng Yi[19] asked about the treatment of parents. The Master said, "Never disobey!" When Fan Chi[20] was driving his carriage for him, the Master said, "Meng asked me about the treatment of parents and I said, 'Never disobey!'" Fan Chi said, "In what sense did you mean it?" The Master said, "While they are alive, serve them according to ritual. When they die, bury them according to ritual and sacrifice to them according to ritual."

2.6 Meng Wu[21] asked about the treatment of parents. The Master said, "Behave in such a way that your father and mother have no anxiety about you, except concerning your health."

2.7 Zi You[22] asked about the treatment of parents. The Master said, "'Filial sons' nowadays are people who see to it that their parents get enough to eat. But even dogs and horses are cared for to that extent. If there is no feeling of respect, wherein lies the difference?"

2.8 Zi Xia asked about the treatment of parents. The Master said, "It is the demeanor[23] that is difficult. Filial piety does not consist merely in young people undertaking the hard work, when anything has to be done, or serving their elders first with wine and food. It is something much more than that."

2.9 The Master said, "I can talk to Yan Hui[24] a whole day without his ever differing from me. One would think he was stupid. But if I enquire into his private conduct when he is not with me I find that it fully demonstrates what I have taught him. No, Hui is by no means stupid."

2.10 The Master said, "Look closely into his aims, observe the means by which he pursues them, discover what brings him content—and can the man's real worth remain hidden from you, can it remain hidden from you?"

2.11 The Master said, "He who by reanimating the Old can gain knowledge of the New is fit to be a teacher."

2.12 The Master said, "A gentleman is not an implement[25]."

2.13 Zi Gong asked about the true gentleman. The Master said, "He does not preach what he practices till he has practiced what he preaches. "

2. 14 The Master said, "A gentleman can see a question from all sides without bias. The small man[26] is biased and can see a question only from one side. "

2. 15 The Master said, "He who learns but does not think is lost. He who thinks but does not learn is in great danger. "

2. 16 The Master said, "He who sets to work upon a different strand destroys the whole fabric. "

2. 17 The Master said, "You[27], shall I teach you what knowledge is? When you know a thing, to recognize that you know it, and when you do not know a thing, to recognize that you do not know it. That is knowledge. "

2. 18 Zi Zhang[28] was studying the Song Ganlu[29]. The Master said, "Hear much, but maintain silence as regards doubtful points and be cautious in speaking of the rest; then you will seldom get into trouble. See much, but ignore what it is dangerous to have seen, and be cautious in acting upon the rest; then you will seldom want to undo your acts. He who seldom gets into trouble about what he has said and seldom does anything that he afterwards wishes he had not done, will be sure incidentally to get his reward. "

2. 19 Duke Ai[30] asked, "What can I do in order to get the support of the common people?" Master Kong replied, "If you 'raise up the straight and set them on top of the crooked, ' the commoners will support you. But if you raise the crooked and set them on top of the straight, the commoners will not support you. "

2. 20 Ji Kang[31] asked whether there were any form of encouragement by which he could induce the common people to be respectful and loyal. The Master said, "Approach them with dignity, and they will respect you. Show piety towards your parents and kindness towards your children, and they will be loyal to you. Promote those who are worthy; train those who are incompetent; that is the best form of encouragement. "

2. 21 Someone, when talking to Master Kong, said, "How is it that you are not in the public service?" The Master said, "*The Books*[32] says, 'Be filial, only be filial and friendly towards your brothers, and you will be contributing to government. ' There are other sorts of

quite different from what you mean by 'service'."

2. 22 The Master said, "I do not see what use a man can be put to, whose word cannot by trusted. How can a wagon be made to go if it has no yoke-bar or a carriage, if it has no collar-bar?"

2. 23 Zi Zhang asked whether the state of things ten generations hence could be foretold. The Master said, "We know in what ways the Yin modified ritual when they followed upon the Xia. We know in what ways the Zhou modified ritual when they followed upon the Yin. And hence we can foretell what the successors of Zhou will be like, even supposing they do not appear till a hundred generations from now."

2. 24 The Master said, "Just as to sacrifice to ancestors other than one's own is presumption, so to see what is right and not do it is cowardice."

BOOK XVII

17. 1 Yang Huo③ wanted to see Master Kong; but Master Kong would not see him. He sent Master Kong a sucking pig. Master Kong, choosing a time when he knew Yang Huo would not be at home, went to tender acknowledgement; but met him in the road. He spoke to Master Kong, saying, "Come here, I have something to say to you." What he said was "Can one who hides his jewel in his bosom and lets his country continue to go astray be called Good?" "Certainly not." "Can one who longs to take part in affairs, yet time after time misses the opportunity to do so—can such a one be called wise?" "Certainly not." "The days and months go by, the years do not wait upon our bidding." Master Kong said, "All right; I am going to serve."

17. 2 The Master said, "By nature, near together; by practice far apart."

17. 3 The Master said, "It is only the very wisest and the very stupidest who cannot change."

17. 4 When the Master went to the walled town of Wu④, he heard the sound of stringed instruments and singing. Our Master said with a gentle smile, "To kill a chicken one does not use an ox-cleaver." Zi You replied saying, "I remember once hearing you say, 'A

gentleman who has studied the Way will be all the tenderer towards his fellow-men; a commoner who has studied the Way will be all the easier to employ.'" The Master said, "My disciples, what he says is quite true. What I said just now was only meant as a joke."

17. 5 Gongshan Furao^㉟, when he was holding the castle of Mi in revolt (against the Ji Family), sent for the Master, who would have liked to go; but Zi Lu^㊱ did not approve of this and said to the Master, "After having refused in so many cases, why go to Gongshan of all people?" The Master said, "It cannot be for nothing that he has sent for me. If anyone were to use me, I believe I could make a 'Zhou in the East^㊲'."

17. 6 Zi Zhang asked Master Kong about Goodness. Master Kong said, "He who could put the Five into practice everywhere under Heaven would be Good." Zi Zhang begged to hear what these were. The Master said, "Courtesy, breadth, good faith, diligence and clemency. 'He who is courteous is not scorned, he who is broad wins the multitude, he who is of good faith is trusted by the people, he who is diligent succeeds in all he undertakes, he who is clement can get service from the people.'"

17. 7 Bi Xi^㊳ summoned the Master, and he would have liked to go. But Zi Lu said, "I remember your once saying, 'Into the house of one who is in his own person doing what is evil, the gentleman will not enter.' Bi Xi is holding Zhongmou^㊴ in revolt. How can you think of going to him?" The Master said, "It is true that there is such a saying. But is it not also said that there are things 'so hard that no grinding will ever wear them down', that there are things 'so white that no steeping will ever make them black'? Am I indeed to be forever like the bitter gourd that is only fit to hang up, but not to eat?"

17. 8 The Master said, "You, have you ever been told of the Six Sayings about the Six Degenerations?" Zi Lu replied, "No, never." (The Master said,) "Come, then; I will tell you. Love of Goodness without love of learning degenerates into silliness. Love of wisdom without love of learning degenerates into utter lack of principle. Love of keeping promises without love of learning degenerates into villainy^㊵. Love of uprightness without love of learning degenerates into harshness. Love of courage without love of learning degenerates into turbulence. Love of courage without love of learning degenerates into mere recklessness."

17. 9 The Master said, "Little ones, why is it that none of you study the Songs? For the Songs will help you to incite people's emotions, to observe their feelings, to keep company, to express your grievances. They may be used at home in the service of one's father; abroad, in the service of one's prince. Moreover, they will widen your acquaintance with the names of birds, beasts, plants and trees."

17. 10 The Master addressed Boyu[41] saying, "Have you done *the Zhou Nan* and *the Shao Nan*[42] yet? He who has not even done *the Zhou Nan* and *the Shao Nan* is as though he stood with his face pressed against a wall!"

17. 11 The Master said, "Ritual, ritual! Does it mean no more than presents of jade and silk? Music, music! Does it mean no more than bells and drums?"

17. 12 The Master said, "To assume an outward air of fierceness when inwardly trembling is (to take a comparison from low walks of life) as dishonest as to sneak into places where one has no right to be, by boring a hole or climbing through a gap."

17. 13 The Master said, "The 'honest villager'[43] spoils true virtue (*de*)."

17. 14 The Master said, "To tell in the lane what you have heard on the highroad is to throw merit (*de*) away."

17. 15 The Master said, "How could one ever possibly serve one's prince alongside of such low-down creatures? Before they have got office, they think about nothing but how to get it; and when they have got it, all they care about is to avoid losing it. And as soon as they see themselves in the slightest danger of losing it, there is no length to which they will not go."

17. 16 In old days the common people had three faults, part of which they have now lost. In old days the impetuous were merely impatient of small restraints; now they are utterly insubordinate. In old days the proud were stiff and formal; now they are touchy and quarrelsome. In old days simpletons[44] were at any rate straightforward; but now "simple-mindedness" exists only as a device of the impostor.

17. 17 The Master said, "Clever talk and a pretentious manner are seldom found in the Good."

17. 18 The Master said, "I hate to see roan killing red, I hate to see the tunes of Zheng[45] corrupting Court music, I hate to see sharp mouths overturning kingdoms and clans."

17. 19 The Master said, "I would much rather not have to talk." Zi Gong said, "If our Master did not talk, what should we little ones have to hand down about him?" The Master said, "Heaven does not speak; yet the four seasons fun their course thereby, the hundred creatures, each after its kind, are born thereby. Heaven does no speaking!"

17. 20 Ru Bei[46] wanted to see Master Kong. Master Kong excused himself on the ground of ill-health. But when the man who had brought the message was going out through the door he took up his zithern and sang, taking good care that the messenger should hear.

17. 21 Zai Yu[47] asked about the three years' mourning[48], and said he thought a year would be quite long enough: "If gentlemen suspend their practice of the rites for three years, the rites will certainly decay; if for three years they make no music, music will certainly be destroyed. (In a year) The old crops have already vanished, the new crops have come up, the whirling drills have made new fire. Surely a year would be enough?"

The Master said, "Would you then (after a year) feel at ease in eating good rice and wearing silk brocades?" Zai Yu said, "Quite at ease." The Master said, "If you would really feel at ease, then do so. But when a true gentleman is in mourning, if he eats dainties, he does not relish them; if he hears music, it does not please him; if he sits in his ordinary seat, he is not comfortable. That is why he abstains from these things. But if you would really feel at ease, there is no need for you to abstain."

When Zai Yu had gone out, the Master said, "How inhuman Yu is! Only when a child is three years old does it leave its parents' arms. The three years' mourning is the universal mourning everywhere under Heaven. And Yu—was he not the darling of his father and mother for three years?"

17. 22 The Master said, "Those who do nothing all day but cram themselves with food and never use their minds are difficult. Are there not games such as draughts? To play them would surely be better than doing nothing at all."

17. 23 Zi Lu said, "Is courage to be prized by a gentleman?" The Master said, "A gentleman gives the first place to Right. If a gentleman has courage but neglects Right, he becomes turbulent. If a small man has courage but neglects Right, he becomes a thief."

17. 24 Zi Gong said, "Surely even the gentleman must have his hatreds?" The Master said, "He has his hatreds. He hates those who point out what is hateful in others. He hates those who dwell in low estate revile[49] all who are above them. He hates those who love deeds of daring but neglect ritual. He hates those who are active and venturesome, but are violent in temper. I suppose you also have your hatreds?" Zi Gong said, "I hate those who mistake cunning for wisdom. I hate those who mistake insubordination for courage. I hate those who mistake tale-bearing for honesty."

17. 25 The Master said, "Women and people of low birth are very hard to deal with[50]. If you are friendly with them, they get out of hand, and if you keep your distance, they resent it."

17. 26 The Master said, "One who has reached the age of forty and is still disliked will be so till the end."

(Translated by Arthur Waley)

Ⅲ. 难点释义

① the Master，子，中国古代对有地位、有学问的男子的尊称，有时也泛称男子。《论语》中"子曰"的"子"，都是指孔子。

② Master You，有子，孔子的学生，姓有，名若，比孔子小 13 岁，一说小 33 岁，后一说较为可信。在《论语》中记载的孔子学生，一般都称字，只有曾参和有若称"子"。因此，许多人认为《论语》即由曾参和有若所著述。

③ the trunk，本，此处意为"根本"，区分于 the twigs（细枝末节）。

④ the Way，道。在中国古代思想里，道有多种含义。此处的道，指孔子提倡的仁道，即以"仁"为核心的整个道德思想体系及其在实际生活的体现。简单讲，就是治国、做人的基本原则。

⑤ the Good，仁。仁是孔子哲学思想的最高范畴，又是伦理道德准则。还有一种

解释，认为古代的"仁"就是"人"字，为仁之本即做人的根本。

⑥ Master Zeng，曾子，姓曾名参（音 shēn），字子舆，生于公元前505年，孔子的得意门生，以孝出名。据说《孝经》就是他撰写的。

⑦ a country of a thousand war-chariots，千乘之国。乘（音 shèng），意为辆。这里指古代军队的基本单位。每乘拥有四匹马拉的兵车一辆，车上甲士3人，车下步卒72人，后勤人员25人，共计100人。千乘之国，指拥有1 000辆战车的国家，即诸侯国。

⑧ the polite arts，文，古代文献。主要有诗、书、礼、乐等文化知识。

⑨ Zi Xia，子夏。姓卜，名商，字子夏，孔子的学生，比孔子小44岁。

⑩ frivolous，轻率的，孩子气的。

⑪ Zi Qin，子禽。姓陈名亢，字子禽。郑玄所注《论语》说他是孔子的学生，《史记·仲尼弟子列传》却并未载此人，故一说子禽不是孔子的学生。

⑫ Zi Gong，子贡。姓端木名赐，字子贡，卫国人，比孔子小31岁，是孔子的学生。子贡善辩，孔子认为他可以做大国的宰相。据《史记》记载，子贡在卫国做了商人，家有财产千金。

⑬ amiss，出了差错的，有缺陷的。

⑭ as thing cut，as thing field，as thing chiseled，as thing polished，"如切如磋，如琢如磨"，此二句见《诗经·卫风·淇奥》。有两种解释：一说切、磋、琢、磨分别指对骨、象牙、玉、石四种不同材料的加工，否则不能成器；一说加工象牙和骨，切了还要磋，加工玉石，琢了还要磨，有精益求精之意。

⑮ Ci，赐，子贡名，孔子对学生都称其名。

⑯ homage，效忠，顺从。

⑰ chastisement，惩罚。

⑱ perplexity，困惑。此处指掌握知识之后，不被外界事物所迷惑。

⑲ Meng Yi，孟懿子。鲁国的大夫，三家之一，姓仲孙，名何忌，"懿"是谥号。其父临终前要他向孔子学礼。

⑳ Fan Chi，樊迟：姓樊名须，字子迟。孔子的弟子，比孔子小46岁。他曾和冉求一起帮助季康子进行革新。

㉑ Meng Wu，孟武伯：孟懿子的儿子。"武"是他的谥号。

㉒ Zi You，子游，姓言名偃，字子游，吴国人，与子夏、子张齐名，孔子的著名弟子，"孔门十哲"之一。

㉓ demeanor，行为，举止。

㉔ Yan Hui，颜回，字子渊，春秋时期鲁国人。他14岁即拜孔子为师，此后终生师事之。在孔门诸弟子中，孔子对颜回称赞最多，不仅赞其"好学"，而且还以"仁人"相称。

㉕ implement，工具，器具。此句意为"君子不像器具那样（只有某一方面的用途）"。

㉖ the small man，小人，指没有道德修养的人。

㉗ You，由，姓仲名由，字子路。生于公元前542年，孔子的学生，长期追随孔子。

㉘ Zi Zhang，子张，姓颛孙，名师，字子张。出身微贱，且犯过罪行，经孔子教育成为"显士"。孔子死后，独立招收弟子，宣扬儒家学说，是"子张之儒"的创始人。

㉙ Ganlu，干禄，"求福、求禄位、求仕进"之意。南北朝时特指公家所给的俸禄，后来多指求取功名利禄。

㉚ Duke Ai，哀公，姓姬名蒋，哀是其谥号，鲁国国君，公元前494—前468年在位。

㉛ Ji Kang，季康子，姓季孙名肥，康是他的谥号，鲁哀公时任正卿，是当时政治上最有权势的人。

㉜ *The Books*，《书》，指《尚书》。

㉝ Yang Huo，阳货，名虎，字货，春秋时期鲁国人。鲁国大夫季平子的家臣，季平子死后，专权管理鲁国的政事。后来他与公山弗扰共谋杀害季桓子，失败后逃往晋国。是当时炙手可热的人物。

㉞ Wu，武城，鲁国的一个小城，当时子游是武城地方长官。

㉟ Gongshan Furao，公山弗扰，人名，又称公山不狃，字子洩，季氏的家臣。

㊱ Zi Lu，仲由，字子路，又字季路，春秋末鲁国卞人。孔子的得意门生，以政

事见称。性格爽直率真，有勇气有才艺，敢于批评老师。孔子对他评价很高，认为可备大臣之数。

㊲ Zhou in the East，东周，此句意指："将要在东方建立起一个西周式的社会，使文王、武王之道重现于东方。"

㊳ Bi Xi，佛肸（Bì Xī），晋国大夫范氏家臣，中牟城地方官。

㊴ Zhongmou，中牟，地名，在晋国，约在今河北邢台与邯郸之间。

㊵ villainy，恶行，罪恶。

㊶ Boyu，伯鱼，孔子的儿子鲤的字。

㊷ the Zhou Nan，Shao Nan，《周南》、《召南》，《诗经·国风》中的第一、第二两部分篇名。周南和召南都是地名。这是当地的民歌。

㊸ honest villager，乡愿。孔子所说的"乡愿"，是指那些表里不一、言行不一的伪君子，这些人欺世盗名，却可以堂而皇之地自我炫耀。

㊹ simpleton，头脑简单的人，傻子。

㊺ Zheng，郑国。

㊻ Ru Bei，孺悲，鲁国人，鲁哀公曾派他向孔子学礼。

㊼ Zai Yu，宰予，字子我，亦称宰我，孔子著名弟子之一。其人能言善辩，曾从孔子周游列国，游历期间常受孔子派遣，使于齐国、楚国。

㊽ the three years' mourning，三年之丧。古代丧服中最重的一种。臣为君、子为父、妻为夫等要服丧三年。是中国封建社会的基本丧制。

㊾ revile，辱骂，痛斥。

㊿ Women and people of low birth are very hard to deal with，"唯女子与小人为难养也"。孔子轻视妇女的思想由此可见。这是儒家一贯的思想主张，后来则演变为"男尊女卑"、"夫为妻纲"的男权主义。

Ⅳ. 问题思考

1. The teachings in *the Analects* share one central theme：goodness/benevolence. What's Confucius' concept of goodness?

2. Confucius said，"He who learns but does not think is lost. He who thinks but does

not learn is in great danger. " Do you agree with him? Why?

3. According to Confucius, what qualities are "persons of virtue" to have?

4. In a Confucianism society, three main types of relationships were evidently hierarchical: ruler and servant, between brothers, and husband and wife. What's your understanding of this hierarchy?

5. Does Confucianism have any practical value in the commercialized society? Give a brief illustration of your own understanding.

V. 经典导读

《论语》(*The Analects*) 是儒家学派的经典著作之一, 由孔子的弟子及其再传弟子编撰而成。它以语录体和对话文体为主, 记录了孔子及其弟子的言行, 集中体现了孔子的政治主张、伦理思想、道德观念及教育原则等。与《大学》、《中庸》、《孟子》、《诗经》、《尚书》、《礼记》、《易经》、《春秋》并称"四书五经"(Four Books and Five Classics)。通行本的《论语》共20篇。《论语》首创语录之体, 其语言简洁精练, 含义深刻, 其中有许多言论至今仍被世人视为至理。《论语》中所记孔子循循善诱的教诲之言, 或简单应答, 点到即止; 或启发论辩, 侃侃而谈, 富于变化, 娓娓动人。

《论语》中记述孔子的伦理道德观念主要是仁、义、礼。就本质而言, 孔子的仁就是对生命的珍惜、热爱与尊重。大体来看, 主要含三个层次: "爱己"、"孝悌"和"爱人"。孔子的仁有一贯之道: "忠恕"。它贯穿于整个仁学之中。它主要包含正反两方面内

"三人行, 必有吾师"已成为千古名句

容: "忠"包含着"己欲立而立人, 己欲达而达人", 以至"杀身以成仁"(give up

one's life for righteausness）等一系列的道德内容，是一个由己及人，由父母及君王以至整个社会、国家的与人为善、乐于奉献的高贵品德；"恕"要求"己所不欲，勿施于人"，即自己做不到有利于别人的"忠"时，起码要做到不有害于别人。此外，孔子将"义"看作人们必不可少的道德品质。孔子肯定人的本性，重视个人的物质利益（"富与贵是人之所欲也"，"贫与贱是人之所恶也"），但不是片面地追求利，而是将利与义结合起来，先义而后利。主张"见利思义"，"见得思义"。同时，孔子也非常重视礼，认为礼是仁的外在表现，是人的外在规范，"克己复礼为仁"，"不学礼，无以立"。

孔子思想的伦理道德观念具有鲜明的两面性。一方面，它反映了人类社会伦理生活的一般要求，成为其思想中的精华部分。另一方面，由于受到当时时代和阶级的局限，他的部分伦理道德观念成为其思想中的糟粕。孔子的仁爱主义精神，尊重人的价值，主张人与人之间相互爱护、相互关心的人道主义，为人以仁爱为怀的意识，推己及人的道德行为模式等，都具有重要的价值。由此而形成的仁政思想、仁爱情怀、博爱意识、人文主义精神、民本主义思想等也都有重要的意义。相反，孔子的等级主义精神，以及在此基础上发展出来的"三纲五常"（the three cardinal guides and the five constant virtues）、"三从四德"（the three obediences and the four virtues）等封建伦理纲常，强化了人间等级秩序的合理性、正当性，在一定程度上扼杀了人的个性发展，扭曲了人格，不适应社会的发展，应予以摒弃。当然，等级主义精神中的一些具体认识，如上对下关怀、下对上的尊重，长对幼的爱护、幼对长的敬重，亲对子的关爱、子对亲的敬爱等，也有一定的合理因素。

在政治主张上，孔子把以"仁"为核心的伦理道德思想也贯彻其中，他提出"仁政"的学说。他希望统治者"节用以爱人，使民以时"，反对对人民过分剥削、压榨，提出富民、惠民的主张。他又希望统治者"为政以德"，反对一味使用严刑峻法，主张要先用严格的道德标准要求自己、以身作则，通过道德感化搞好政治。孔子主张对老百姓"齐之以礼"，将礼的实施范围扩大到庶民身上，这是对周礼的原则性的修正。这些政治原则，在当时均有较大的进步意义。

与其从政经历相比较，孔子一生在教育领域取得的成就要大得多。春秋以前，学在官府，文化知识被贵族垄断。孔子首创私人讲学，面向社会广泛招收学生，通过传授文化知识来培养从政人才，对随后的历史产生了巨大影响。据说孔子有弟子三千，其中精通六艺者72人。在教育对象方面，孔子主张"有教无类"（In teaching, there should be no distinction of classes），指出人的本性是可以教育的。在教学方法方面，他提出"因材施教"（To teach students in accordance with their optitude），重视启发式教育，注意培养学生的学习自觉性和独立思考能力。孔子的教育目的在于培养"士"，其标准是"君子"。孔子要求培养的君子有两个条件：一要注意自己的道德修养，即要有"德"；二要使老百姓都得到安乐，即要有"才"。要求君子德才兼备，以德为主，尤其注意区别贵贱之礼与泛爱众之仁和推己及人的恕道。在"才"方面，要求君子应有治国安民之术，要有从政的才智，能治"千乘之国"，能长"千室之邑"，能"使于四方，不辱君命"。孔子谆谆告诫弟子："不患无位，患所以立。不患莫己知，求为可知也。"表明孔子办学的目的，就是培养从政的人才。"学而优则仕"（Officialdom is the natural outlet for good）虽然出自子夏之口，却确实代表了孔子的教育思想，也可以说是孔子的教育目的。其对于世袭世禄制度来说是一大进步，但是后来也产生过副作用，即将做官作为求学的唯一目的，作为夺取高官厚禄的敲门砖，"万般皆下品，唯有读书高"（To be a scholar is to be the top of society）就是其流毒弊端。

20世纪的很长一段时间中，《论语》都被作为封建文化的象征，被列为批判否定的对象，而后虽有新儒学的研究与萌生，但是在中国民主革命的大背景下，儒家文化在中国并未形成新的气候，以《论语》为首的儒家文化甚至被批判得一无是处。然而，任何一个社会都不能不对其民族精神及传统文化进行重新反思。特别是民族文化的精粹，更值得人们重新认识，重新探索。客观地看，《论语》有其糟粕或消极之处，但它所反映出来的两千多年前的社会人生精论，富有哲理的名句箴言，却是中华民族文明程度的历史展示。即使在经济、文化飞速发展的今天，《论语》中的许多思想仍相当具有借鉴意义和时代价值。

Ⅵ. 译本链接

1. ［英］James Legge，《中国经典》，伦敦：企鹅图书公司1875年版。
2. Ku—Hungming：*The Discourses and Sayings of Confucius：A New Special Trans-*

lation, Illustrated with Quotations from Goethe and Other Writers, Shanghai: Keely and Walsh co. , 1998.

3. ［英］Arthur Waley,《论语》, 伦敦: 企鹅图书公司 1938 年版。

4. 刘殿爵:《论语》, 伦敦: 企鹅图书公司 1979 年版。

5. 赖波、夏玉和:《论语》, 北京: 华语教学出版社 1994 年版。

6. 王福林:《论语详注及英译》, 北京: 世界图书出版公司 1997 年版。

Unit Five
Mencius (《孟子》)

I. 背景简介

Mencius (about 372 B. C. – 289 B. C.), whose given name was Ke and styled Zi Yu, was a native of Zou in Warring States (now to south-eastern Zoucheng, Shandong Province). He was a great philosopher in the Warring States Period. He travelled around the States of Qi, Song, Wei, Teng and other places, disseminating his political propositions in order to give full play to his political ambition. Later on, because he fell out with the ruler, he withdrew from the public service and started to teach disciples, and wrote books to set up his own theory. The book of *Mencius* is the fruit of his thoughts.

Mencius mainly carries on Confucian thought of benevolence and applies it to the political field. He

Mencius (**about** 372 **B. C.** – 289 **B. C.**)

also puts forward the thought of benevolent governance, which can be seen in the resumed "nine squares" system and private ownership of the land cultivator. He opposes unduly exploitation of the people by the ruler, advocates for relieving punishment and taxes, and for support of the aged and education of the young. He also brings forward the proposal that

"people are the most important force, the State is less important, and the monarch is the least important." He persuades the ruler to ensure people's safety and security, which in his opinion should be regarded as the key to the safety and danger of the State and monarch. His thought of opposing tyrant and despotic rule is of positive social significance.

The theory of benevolent governance is based on the conception of primary kindness. Mencius thinks that human beings are kind by nature, and he regards this inborn kindness as a natural disposition, which can be acquired without thinking and learning. People have morals through continuous self-retrospection and through efforts to seek for their own natural kindness. A Mencius's typical moral personality is one that "neither riches nor honors can corrupt him, neither poverty nor adversity can make him swerve from principles, neither threats nor force can make him give up." Similarly, Mencius identifies his own happiness and worries with the peoples' and regards it as his own duty to ensure the whole world safety and happiness, claiming to be happy when the whole world is happy, to be worried when the whole world is worried. This strong sense of social responsibility has become a cultural tradition of the Chinese nation.

Mencius believed that from the heart come goodness, duty, courtesy, propriety, and wisdom. Anyone lacking these is a slave. Practicing the good is like archery: when one fails to hit the mark, one must correct oneself. If others do not respond to your love, look into your own humanity. If others fail to respond to your governing, consider your own wisdom. If others do not return your courtesy, look into your own respect. In other words, whenever you fail to achieve your purpose look into yourself. Mencius' interpretation of Confucianism has generally been considered the orthodox version by subsequent Chinese philosophers, in which his emphasis on virtue is still important today.

Ⅱ. 文本选读
Book 3　Gong Sun Chou（Ⅰ）

[…]

3.3 Mencius said, "One who uses force under the guise of benevolence will become the leader of the princes, but he must first be the ruler of a large State before he can do so. One who practices benevolence through the virtuous rule will become the unifier of the world, and to do so, his state need not be a large one. King Tang[①] began to be such a ruler with a territory of only seventy li square, and King Wen[②] with one of a hundred. People submit to force not because they do so willingly, but because they are not strong enough. People who submit to the virtuous rule do so sincerely just like the seventy disciples in their submission to Confucius. *The Book of Poetry*[③] says of King Wen:

'East, west, north, south—

In any place really,

People submit sincerely.'

This serves as an illustration of what I have said."

3.4 Mencius said, "Benevolence brings glory, whereas cruelty brings disgrace. Now people who hate disgrace but are cruel are like those who hate dampness but live in a low-lying area. If a prince hates disgrace, nothing will be better for him than to esteem virtuous men and respect the intelligentsia so that virtuous men hold office in the government, and capable men fill various posts. Taking advantage of the time of peace, the ruler can straighten things out in the field of administration and justice. Under such circumstances even states larger than his will surely stand in awe of him. *The Book of Poetry* says:

'When there's no cloud and no rain,

With bark of the mulberry tree,

I mend the window and door.

There now, you people below,

Who dares to bully me?'

Confucius said, 'The author of this poem probably knew the principle of government. If a ruler can run a state well, who will dare to bully him?'"

"But now the rulers take advantage of the time of peace to abandon themselves to pleasure, indolence[④] and loafing[⑤], they are in fact inviting disaster."

"Fortune good or bad is what one oneself has it coming. *The Book of Poetry* says:

'Obey forever Heaven's mandate[⑥],

And seek much blessing for yourself. '

And *the Taijia*⑦ says, ' When trouble befalls you from Heaven, there is still hope of avoidance; when you ask for trouble, there is no hope of escape. ' This is an illustration of what I have said. "

3.5 Mencius said, "If a ruler honors the virtuous and employs the capable so that outstanding people fill responsible positions, then the intellectuals of the world will be pleased to serve at his court. If goods are stored in the marketplace but not taxed, and if goods are purchased by the state according to law when unsalable, then all the traders in the world will be pleased to have stocks in his marketplace. If there is only inspection but no duty at his frontier passes, then all the travelers in the world will be pleased to travel on his roads. If tillers only have to help in the public fields, but pay no taxes on their private land, then all the tillers will be pleased to till the land in his territory. If he abolishes the additional levy⑧ in place of corse and land tax, then all the people in the world will be pleased to come and want to be his subjects. If he can really take these five measures, the people of his neighboring states will look up to him as a parent, and since the appearance of the human race nobody has succeeded in instigating⑨ children against their parents. Thus he will have no adversary in the world, and such a ruler is called a Heaven-ordained official⑩. Never has such a ruler failed to become a unifier of the world. "

3.6 Mencius said, "All men have a sense of compassion. As the ancient kings had such a sense, they had the compassionate system of government. Running such a government with such a sense, one would find it as easy to rule the world as to roll something on the palm of one's hand. The reason why I say all men have a sense of compassion is that, even today, if one chances to see a little child about to fall into a well, one will be shocked, and move to compass on, neither because he wants to make friends with the child's parents, nor because he wants to earn praise from his neighbors and friends, nor because he hates to hear the cry of the child. From this we can see that whoever has no sense of compassion is not human; whoever has no sense of shame is not human; whoever has no sense of modesty is not human; and whoever has no sense of right and wrong is not human. The sense of compassion is the beginning of benevolence; the sense of shame the beginning of righteousness; the sense of modesty the beginning of decorum[11]; the sense of right and wrong the beginning of wisdom. Man possesses these four beginnings just as he possesses four limbs. Anyone possessing these four and saying that he can not do what is required of him is abasing himself. If he says that his ruler can not do what is required of him, he is abasing his ruler. Let a man know how to develop fully all these beginnings he possesses, and it may be compared to the starting of a fire or the gushing[12] out of a spring. If these are fully developed, he can protect the whole world; if not, he will not be able even to serve his parents. "

3.7 Mencius said, "Is the arrow-maker less benevolent than the armor-maker? The former is afraid lest he should fail to hurt people, while the latter is afraid lest he should fail to keep them safe. The same is the case with doctor and coffin-maker[13]. Therefore, great care should be taken to choose one's occupation. "

"Confucius said, 'The fine neighborhood is where benevolence prevails. One can not be considered wise if one does not choose such a neighborhood to live in. ' Benevolence is the greatest honor conferred by Heaven and the secure abode[14] of man. If you do not practice it when there is nothing in the way, it is a sign of lack of wisdom. He who is neither benevolent nor wise, and lacks decorum and righteousness is a menial. A menial ashamed of his menial work is like a maker of bows ashamed of making bows, or an arrow-maker ashamed of making arrows. If a man is ashamed of his doings, his best course of action is to practice benevolence. The practice of benevolence is like archery. An archer first assumes a correct stance[15] and then shoots. If he misses the target, he does not complain against those who do better. He simply seeks the cause of failure in himself. "

3.8 Mencius said, "Zi Lu was pleased when he was told that he had made a mistake. Emperor Yu[16] would bow low before a man who had made a fine proposition. The Great Shun[17] was even more wonderful. He was too ready to fall into line with others, giving up his own incorrect opinions for their correct propositions, and pleased to learn from others the way to do good. From the time that he was successively a farmer, a potter, and a fisherman to the time that he became emperor, there was nothing good in others that he did not draw on. To learn from others the way to do good is to help others do good by doing good along with them. Therefore, there is nothing more important for a gentleman than doing good along with others. "

3.9 Mencius said, "Bo Yi[18] would not serve a ruler he did not approve, nor would he make friends with a man he disliked. He would not take his place at the court of a wicked ruler, nor would he speak with such a man. To do either of these would have been to him the same as to sit in mud and pitch wearing a court robe and court cap. His hatred for evil was intensified to such an extent that if he were standing with a fellow villager who had his cap on askew[19], he would walk away scornfully as if afraid to be sullied. Accordingly, even though a feudal prince summoned him in the finest language, he would decline the invitation. He did so because he thought it beneath him to go to the feudal prince. "

"On the contrary, Hui of Liuxia[20] was not ashamed of a foul ruler, nor did he disdain a low position. Holding office, he did not conceal his considerable ability, but made it a point to do things according to his principles. If overlooked, he would not complain; if reduced to poverty, he would not be sad. That is why he said, 'You are you, and I am I. How could you sully me even if you stood naked beside me?' Therefore it was a complete contentment that he could associate with them without losing his self-possession. He would stay if pressed. The reason was that he thought it was beneath him not to stay. "

Mencius added, "Bo Yi was too strait-laced[21], and Hui of Liuxia was lacking in self-respect. A gentleman will not go to either of the extremes. "

Book 11 Gaozi (Part A)

[…]

11.2 Gao Zi said, "Human nature is like a whirlpool[22]. Given an outlet in the east, the water flows out in the east. Given an outlet in the west, the water flows out in the west. Just as water is not naturally inclined to flow east or west, so human nature is not originally good or bad. " "It certainly is true," said Mencius, "that water flows east or west without showing any preference to either. But does water flow downwards or upwards without showing any preference? Human nature is always good, just as water always flow downwards. No human nature but is good, no water but flows downwards. In fact, water can rise above one's forehead when whipped, it can ascend a mountain when forced to flow backwards. But is it in the nature of water to behave so? No. Circumstances force its way. That man can be made to do wrong shows that his nature can be changed exactly like the flow of water. "

[...]

11. 4 Gao Zi said, "Eating and sex are human nature. Benevolence is internal, not external; while righteousness is external, not internal. "

Mencius asked, "What do you mean by benevolence being internal and righteousness being external?"

"I respect an elderly man because his elderliness is worth my respect, not because there is elderliness in my nature, just as I recognize a white thing as white because it is white. That is why I call this external. "

"Indeed there is not much to choose between the whiteness of a white horse and the whiteness of a white man; but I wonder is the compassion for an old horse no different from the respect for an elderly human being? And in whom does righteousness lie, in the elderly man or in the person who respects the elderly man?"

"I love my younger brother, but I do not love the younger brother of a man from Qin. To love or not to love, it is up to me. So I say love is internal. I respect an elderly person from Chu as well as I respect an elderly person of my family. My respect depends on the elderliness of others. That is why I call it external. "

Mencius said, "My liking for the roast meat of Qin is no different from my liking for the roast meat of my own cooking. So is the case with other things. Can we say the liking for roast meat is also an external thing?"

11. 5 Meng Jizi[23] asked Gong Duzi[24], "Why do you say righteousness is internal?"

"It makes me respect one worthy of my respect. So I say righteousness is internal. "

"When a villager is a year older than your elder brother, then whom do you show more respect to?"

"To my elder brother."

"When they are at table together, whose cup do you fill with wine first, the villager's or your elder brother's?"

"The villager's."

"You respect your brother in your heart, but you show your respect first to the villager. It follows that righteousness is external, not internal."

Gong Duzi was stumped for an answer, and took the matter up to Mencius.

Mencius said, "If you ask him whether a man is to respect his uncle or his younger brother, his answer will be, 'My uncle.' If you ask him which person a man is to respect more, when his younger brother is the person chosen by the family to accept their sacrificial offerings on behalf of their ancestors, his answer will be, 'The younger brother.' If you ask him why at first he said the uncle should be respected in preference to the younger brother, he will say his younger brother is in a position entitled to respect. So you can say, 'It is just because the villager is in a position entitled to respect that you should first fill his wine cup. Everyday respect goes to the elder brother; occasional respect goes to the villager.'" On hearing this, Meng Jizi said, "Since the same respect is due to both one's uncle and one's younger brother, righteousness must be external, not internal."

Gong Duzi said, "In winter we drink water hot, in summer we drink water cool, can we say that drinking and eating is also external?"

[…]

11.6 Gong Duzi said, "Gao Zi once said to me, 'Human nature is neither good nor bad.' Some say, 'Human nature can be either good or bad. That is why during the reign of King Wen and King Wu㉕, the people were good-hearted; during the reign of King You㉖ and King Li㉗, the people were cruel-hearted.' Some say, 'There are men whose nature is good and there are men whose nature is evil. That is why Emperor Yao㉘ had such an evil subject as Xiang㉙, and the Blind Old Man㉚ had such a good son as Shun. Such an evil man as King Zhou had such good uncles as Qi, Viscount of Wei㉛, and Prince Bigan㉜.' Now you say human nature is good. Does it mean the sayings of all the others are wrong?"

Mencius said, "Man is in his essence capable of becoming good. That is why I say human nature is good. That man should become evil is not a question of his essence. Compassion is a feeling shared by everyone, so is shame, so is respect, so is the sense of right and wrong. Compassion means benevolence, shame means righteousness, respect means decorum, and the sense of right and wrong means wisdom. Benevolence, righteousness, decorum, and wisdom are not conferred on me by others, they are in my essence. Only I have never sought to discover them in me. Hence the saying: 'Seek, and you find it; let go, and you lose it.' One may fall short of another by two or five times, even countless times, simply because he has not given full play to his native endowment, *The Book of Poetry* says:

'The human beings made by Heaven,

They have all things and they see why.

People cling to the general rules,

And so they like the virtues high.'

Confucius commented, 'The author of this poem was reasonable. Where there are things, there are rules. In accordance with these general rules, people like high virtues.'"

11. 7 Mencius said, "During a year of bumper[33] harvests, young people are prone to laziness; during a year of crop failures, young people are prone to ferocity. Not that they are evil in nature, but that circumstances make them go evil ways. Take the barley. The seed is sown and covered in the same place and at the same planting time. The barley will all grow luxuriantly, and it will ripen by the summer solstice. In case there is any discrepancy[34] in the yield, it is because the soil varies in fertility, the fall of rain and dew is irregular, and the farming methods are not the same quality. Thus things of the same kind are all similar. Why should we have doubts when it comes to man? The sage and I are the same kind. That is why Long Zi[35] said, 'When someone makes a straw sandal without first seeing the foot, I know he certainly will not make a straw basket.' All sandals are similar because all feet are similar. All palates have similar tastes; Yi Ya[36] was the first to have an exquisite taste for

delicious food. If taste for food should vary from man to man as dogs and horses are different from me in species, then how come all palates have tastes similar to Yi Ya's? In taste all the world follow Yi Ya, which shows all palates are similar. It is the same with ears. In music, all the world follow Shi Kuang[37], which shows men have similar ears for music. It is the same with eyes. In beauty, all the world look to Zi Du[38] for a perfect model, and whoever does not appreciate his beauty is as good as blind, which shows that men have similar eyes for beauty. Hence it is said, 'All palates have the same preference in taste; all ears in sound; all eyes in beauty. Are hearts an exception to this general rule? What is common to all hearts is reason and righteousness. The sage is the first to have these common elements that exist in all our hearts. Thus reason and righteousness appeal to my heart in the same way as animal meats appeal to my palate. "

11. 8 Mencius said, "The trees on the Ox Mountain[39] were once luxuriant, but as they are on the outskirts of a great capital, they are often subject to axe fellings, can we wonder at the loss of their beauty? Of course, during the respites[40] from axe strokes in the daytime, and at night, nourished by rain and dew, they stand there not without fresh shoots sprouting and growing, but again cattle and sheep come to pasture on them, stripping them of tender shoots and rendering them bald and barren. The sight of their baldness and barrenness makes people think the mountain has never had good trees. Is it in the nature of the mountain? Is it in the nature of man to be entirely barren of benevolence and righteousness? He has lost these virtues because he is like the trees under the strokes of the axe every day. How can he flourish in these virtues? In the daytime and at night, he will breathe out some benevolence and righteousness, at dawn his virtues will be nourished by the fresh air he breathes in and his likes and dislikes somewhat resemble those of other people, but his behavior on the morrow[41] nips his virtues in the bud. This happening again and again of course destroys the night air of goodness stored in him; when the night air of goodness is destroyed, he is just like a wild beast. When people see he is just like a beast, they will think he is a creature without ever having a trace of inborn virtues. Is it his true nature? So, getting nourishment, there is nothing that will not grow; losing nourishment, there is nothing that will not perish.

Confucius said, 'Grasp, and it exists; let go, and it perishes; it is not known when it comes and when it goes, or whence it comes and where it goes.' Perhaps these words of his refer to the human heart?"

11. 9 Mencius said, "Do not wonder at the king's inadequate wisdom. Even though there is a plant that is the aptest to grow, if it is placed in sunshine only one day, and then is exposed to the frost ten days, it sure can not remain alive. I have seen less and less of the king, I have retired to my home, leaving the king in the cold to the utmost degree; even if there are some budding of good virtues in his heart, what help have I given him? Take for example playing games of go, which requires only petty skills; yet if we are not devoted to learning it, we can never play it well. Yi Qiu[42] is a master hand at playing go. Suppose he gives lessons to two learners. One of them follows Yi Qiu's instruction attentively. The other learner seems to be listening, but his mind's eye sees a swan flying towards him, his hands itching[43] to take up bow and arrow to shoot it; so even if the two study together, the latter must lag behind. Is this due to the fact that he is less intelligent than the other learner? Of course not. "

11. 10 Mencius said, "Fish is what I desire, and bear's paw is also what I desire; if I can not have both, I will give up fish and take bear's paw. Life is what I desire, and righteousness is also what I desire; If I can not have both, I will give up life for righteousness. Life is what I desire, but there is something even more desirable than life; so I would not drag out an ignoble[44] existence. Death is what I abhor, but there is something even more abhorrent than death, so I would not eschew[45] disaster. If there is nothing more desirable than life, then why will a man not resort to every means to keep alive? If nothing is more abhorrent than death, then why will a man not do everything to eschew disaster? But some people will prefer certain things to life, some people will not do certain things to eschew disaster; that is to say, I desire something even more than life, and I abhor something even more than death. It is not only the man of virtue that has such a feeling in his heart, but everyone has it. Only it is the man of virtue that can retain this feeling. Here is a basket of steamed rice or a bowl of soup, getting it, you live; losing it, you die. Even so,

if it is given in blustering arrogance, a wayfarer[⑩] will not accept it; if it is first trodden on and then given, not even a beggar will deign to accept it. But if the offer is ten thousand bushels of grain, then there are people who have accepted it in disregard of decorum and righteousness. What good will ten thousand bushels of grain do me? Is it the grandeur of palaces, the service of wife and concubine, or the gratitude of poor acquaintances and relations? I once rejected an offer that could keep death away from me, yet now I accept one which promises only the grandeur of palaces; I once rejected an offer that could keep death away from me, yet now I accept one which promises only the service of wife and concubine; I once rejected an offer that could keep death away from me, yet now I accept one that promises only the gratitude of poor acquaintances and relations. Will such things not come to an end? They really mean the loss of the heart proper."

1l. 11 Mencius said, "Benevolence is man's heart; righteousness is man's way. Alas! That man should not go on the way of righteousness nor seek to recover the benevolence of the heart! When chickens or dogs are missing, man will look for them; but when the benevolent heart is missing, man will not try to seek it back. The pursuit of learning is just to recover this missing benevolent heart. This, and nothing more."

(Translated by Zhao Zhentao)

Ⅲ. 难点释义

① King Tang，商汤（？—约前 1588），子姓，名履，庙号太祖，为商太祖，河南商丘人。商朝的创建者，今人多称商汤，又称武汤、天乙、成汤、成唐。

② King Wen，文王，姬姓，名昌，周王朝的缔造者。《毛诗序》："文王受命做周也。"郑玄笺注："受天命而王天下，制立周邦。"

③ *The Book of Poetry*，《诗经》，下面的诗句均出自《大雅·文王》。

④ indolence，懒散，懒惰；好逸恶劳。

⑤ loafing，游荡；游手好闲；虚度光阴。

⑥ mandate，授权；委托管理。

⑦ *the Taijia*，《太甲》，《尚书》中的一篇。

⑧ levy，征兵；征税。

⑨ instigating，唆使；煽动。

⑩ Heaven-ordained official，天吏，顺从上天旨意的执政者。这里的"吏"不是指小官吏。

⑪ decorum，礼仪；礼节。

⑫ gushing，涌出；迸出。

⑬ coffin-maker，木工。

⑭ abode，住所，住处。

⑮ stance，立场；姿态；位置。

⑯ Emperor Yu，大禹，是传说中与尧、舜齐名的贤圣帝王。他最卓著的功绩，就是治理滔天洪水，又划定中国国土为九州。

⑰ The Great Shun，舜（生卒年不详），传说中的父系氏族社会后期部落联盟首领，中国历史传说中的古帝王（五帝）之一。传称号有虞氏，姓姚，名重华，字都君，谥曰"舜"。

⑱ Bo Yi，伯夷，为商末孤竹国（今河北卢龙西）孤竹君之长子，姓墨胎氏，名允。一开始，孤竹君想以次子叔齐作为继承人，等到他父亲死后，叔齐让位给伯夷。伯夷认为这样会违背父命，于是逃走，而叔齐亦不肯继承家业，亦逃往他处。

⑲ askew，不正的；歪的。

⑳ Hui of Liuxia，柳下惠（前720—前621），展氏，名获，字禽，一字季，春秋时期鲁国柳下邑（今山东新泰柳里）人，鲁孝公的儿子公子展的后裔。"坐怀不乱"的典故正是出于他。

㉑ strait-laced，极拘谨的；固守道德观念的。

㉒ whirlpool，漩涡；湍急的水。

㉓ Meng Jizi，孟季子，其人不详。翟灏《四书考异》以为原文本无"孟"字，季子即是"季任为任处守"之季任。

㉔ Gong Duzi，公都子，孟子的学生。

㉕ King Wu，周武王姬发在位3年，西周王朝开国君主，周文王次子。因其兄伯邑考被商纣王所杀，故得以继位。他继承父亲遗志，于公元前11世纪消灭商朝，夺

取全国政权，建立了西周王朝，表现出卓越的军事、政治才能，成为中国历史上的一代明君。死后谥号"武"，史称周武王。

㉖ King You，周幽王，（前795—前771），姓姬，名宫涅（shēng）。周宣王之子，西周第十二代君王。《史记》形容他"性暴戾，少思维，耽声色"。

㉗ King Li，周厉王，姬胡（？—前828）即周厉王，周夷王之子。在位期间，任用荣夷公实行"专利"，即以国家名义垄断山林川泽，不准国人（指工商业者）依山泽而谋生，借以剥削人民，违背了周人共同享有山林川泽以利民生的典章制度。

㉘ Emperor Yao，尧（前2377—前2259），姓伊祁，名放勋，史称唐尧。20岁时，其兄帝挚为形势所迫让位与他，尧成为中国原始社会末期的部落联盟长。90岁禅让与舜。

㉙ Xiang，象，舜的异母弟。性傲狠，相传他在父亲瞽瞍（gǔ sǒu）示意下，多次谋杀舜，未遂。后被舜流放。

㉚ Blind Old Man，指瞽瞍，古代皇帝虞舜之父。

㉛ Qi，Viscount of Wei，宋微子，子姓，名启，世称微子、微子启（"微"是国号，"子"是尊称），宋国（今河南商丘）开国元祖，第一代国君。

㉜ Prince Bigan，比干，子姓，名干，沬邑人（今卫辉市北）。为殷商贵族商王太丁之子。一生忠君爱国，倡导"民本清议，士志于道"。从政40多年，主张减轻赋税徭役，鼓励发展农牧业生产，提倡冶炼铸造，富国强兵。

㉝ bumper，丰盛的；丰富的。

㉞ discrepancy，不符；矛盾；差异。

㉟ Long Zi，龙子，古代的贤人。

㊱ Yi Ya，易牙，春秋时齐国最擅长烹调的人，齐桓公的宠臣。

㊲ Shi Kuang，师旷，字子野，山西洪洞人，春秋时著名乐师。他生而无目，故自称盲臣、瞑臣。尤精音乐，善弹琴，辨音力极强。

㊳ Zi Du，子都，春秋时代美男子。

㊴ Ox Mountain，牛山，齐国首都临淄郊外的山。

㊵ respite，缓解；暂缓。

㊶ morrow，次日，重大事件后紧接着的日子。

㊷ Yi Qiu，弈秋，春秋时期鲁国的下棋圣手。

㊸ itching，渴望。

㊹ ignoble，不光彩的；卑鄙的。

㊺ eschew，避免；远避。

㊻ wayfarer，旅人，过路人。

Ⅳ. 问题思考

1. Why does Mencius talk more about the imperturbation of the mind and courage?

2. What's Mencius' attitude towards the concept of "Benevolence"? How does he explain such a concept?

3. Mencius said that："a man who commands our liking is what is called a good man. He whose goodness is part of himself is what is called real man. He whose goodness has been filled up is what is called beautiful man. He whose completed goodness is brightly displayed is what is called a great man. When this great man exercises a transforming influence，he is what is called a sage. When the sage is beyond our knowledge，he is what is called a spirit-man." Do you agree with his definition of "good man"，"great man"，"beautiful man"，"a sage"，"a spirit-man"? Why or why not? Try to find more examples in real life to support your statement.

4. How does Mencius carry on Confucian thought of benevolence and applies it to the political field? Why has his interpretation of Confucianism generally been considered the orthodox version by subsequent Chinese philosophers?

5. Why does Mencius pay much attention to such four persons as Emperor Yu, The Great Shun，Bo Yi，Hui of Liuxia? What does he want to tell us by emphasis on these four persons?

Ⅴ. 经典导读

根据司马迁在《史记·孟荀列传》中所说，孟子周游列国，因所述"唐虞三代之德"与"所如者不合"，不被采纳，于是"退而与万章之徒序《诗》、《书》，述仲尼之意，作《孟子》七篇"，就是我们今天所见到的《梁惠王》、《公孙丑》、《滕文公》、《离娄》、《万章》、《告子》、《尽心》。七篇各分上下，篇内分若干章，篇章之间没有必然联系。

《孟子》一书是儒家重要经典之一，是由孟子本人和他的弟子万章、公孙丑等撰写的。此书以叙事和对话的方式记载了孟子一生的政治活动、学术活动以及在政治、哲学、伦理道德、教育等各方面的主要观点。

此书的主要内容大致可以概述为以下几个方面：

第一，宣传"仁政爱民"的思想。游说各诸侯国君，如齐宣王、梁惠王、滕文公、鲁平公等，宣传自己"仁义"的主张。孟子十分重视民心向背，通过大量历史事例反复阐述这是关乎得天下与失天下的关键。强调"民为贵，社稷次之，君为轻"；主张保民、养民，行仁政。提倡王道，反对霸道；提倡仁政，反对暴政。揭露和批判各国诸侯的贪婪残暴，关注人民的生存状态。

第二，主张"性善说"。孟子认为，人人生而具有善的萌芽。"恻隐之心，人皆有之；羞恶之心，人皆有之；恭敬之心，人皆有之；是非之心，人皆有之。恻隐之心，仁也；羞恶之心，义也；恭敬之心，礼也；是非之心，智也。仁义礼智非由外铄我也，我固有之也。"人性有善端，而此善性，需要认真存养才能发挥功能，才能成为君子圣贤。自暴自弃的人，乃不知存养。至于存养之道，则要养其大者，不能以小害大，因贱害贵。

第三，在品德修养方面，孟子提倡善养浩然之气，并主张"杀身成仁，舍生取义。"对伟人和大丈夫提出了很高的要求，何为大丈夫？孟子认为，大丈夫之人必须是"天将降大任于斯人也，必先苦其心志，劳其筋骨，饿其体肤，空乏其身，行拂乱其所为，所以动心忍性，曾益其所不能"，"居天下之广居，立天下之正位，行天下之大道；得志与民由之；不得志，独行其道。富贵不能淫，贫贱不能移，威武不能屈"。

第四，崇尚"孝悌忠信"，提倡"五伦"规范。"孝悌忠信"是《孟子》伦理道德的基本要求；是家庭的伦理规范，善事父母为孝，敬顺兄长为悌。孟子把道德规范概括为四种，即仁（benevolence）、义（righteousness）、礼（properiety）、智（wisdom）。他认为"仁、义、礼、智"是人们与生俱来的东西，不是从客观存在着的外部世界所取得的。同时他把人伦关系概括为五种，即"父子有亲，君臣有义，夫妇有别，长幼有序，朋友有信"。孟子认为，仁、义、礼、智四者之中，仁、义最为重要。仁、义的基础是孝、悌，而孝、悌是处理父子和兄弟血缘关系的基本道德规范。他强调，如果每个社会成员都用仁、义来处理人与人之间的各种关系，封建秩序的稳定和天下的统一就有了可靠保证。

第五，树立"仁者爱人"的好风气。孟子强调"仁之实，事亲是也"，"仁者爱人"，"亲亲而仁民，仁民而爱物"。"仁者爱人"就是一种爱护他人、关心他人、体谅他人、帮助他人的同情心，是对他人发自内心的一种尊重和关切。全社会都要做到"老吾老，以及人之老；幼吾幼，以及人之幼"。怎样才算是仁呢？根据《孟子》一书可以概括为：首先要亲民；其次要用贤良，"尊贤使能，俊杰在位"，"贤者在位，能者在职；明其政刑"；最后是要尊重人权。

《告子章句上》集中讨论人性问题，是孟子"性善论"思想较为完整的体现。文中重点谈论了仁义道德与个人修养的问题，并论证了恻隐、羞恶、恭敬、是非"四心"以及它们与仁、义、礼、智之间的内在联系，对精神与物质、感性与理性、人性与动物性等问题也有所涉及。

《孟子》是儒家经典之一，书中所蕴含的政治、伦理、哲学、教育等思想学说，不仅对中国两千年来的封建社会产生了巨大的影响，而且对中华民族的性格塑造和道德情操的培养也起着至关重要的作用。哲学家朱熹称《孟子》为"出处大概，高不可及"，并称"六经"为"千斛之舟"。《孟子》一书与"五经"并列。明清以降，朱熹版的《孟子》更是被当作开科取士的必读之书。

农夫揠苗助长

　　《孟子》里的许多文章因铺陈排比而气势逼人，善设机巧而引人入彀，欲擒先纵而后发制人，长于譬喻而说理生动；文章巧于辩论，语言流畅，富有文采和感染力，对于后世的散文也有较大的影响。《孟子》在语言（包括书面语和口语）方面对后世的影响也是不可忽视的。时至今日，汉语中的许多成语典故都源于《孟子》，例如"五十步笑百步"（the one who ran fifty paces laughs at the one who ran a hundred）、"缘木求鱼"、"揠苗助长"、"出尔反尔"、"上有好者，下必甚焉"、"尽信书，不如无书"（one would rather be short of books than believe all that the books say），"人之患，在好为人师"等，至今还经常出现于文章和口语中，其中的许多典故都成为千古名句。

Ⅵ. 译本链接

1. James Legge，*The Sacred Book of the East*，London：Oxford University Press，1861.

2. E. Fabes：《孟子学说类编》，New York：Harper Collins，1882 年版。

3. L. A. Lyall：《孟子》，纽约：蓝登书屋 1932 年版。

4. D. C. Lau：《孟子》，伦敦：企鹅图书公司 1970 年版。

5. 赵甄陶等译：《孟子》，长沙：湖南人民出版社 1999 年版。

Unit Six
The Book of Changes (《易经》)

Ⅰ. 背景简介

The Book of Changes, also known as *the Yi Jing* (*pinyin*), *Classic of Changes* or *Zhou Yi*, is one of the oldest of the Chinese classic texts. Originating from divination practice by the people living between the late Yin dynasty (about 17th century B. C. – 11th century B. C.) and early Zhou dynasty, the text of this book was completed at the early period of the Western Zhou Dynasty (about 1046B. C. – 771 B. C.). Rather than being the work of one legendary or historical figure, several great people are believed to have contributed to the completion of the book. Among them are Fu Xi (伏羲), Shen Nong (神农), Yu, King Wen of Zhou (周文王), the Duke Zhou (周公) and Confucius.

The Eight Hexagrams

Though controversial among ancient scholars concerning the implication of the two-character title of the book itself, a textual analysis and study of the development of changeology (易学) indicate that the meaning of Zhou (周) should be the Zhou Dynasty, distinguishing itself from the Yin Dynasty; and the basic meaning of Yi (易) should refer to alternation of the sun and the moon, and also of *yin* and *yang*.

The Book of Changes is made up of two parts: the text and the appendices. The text

consists of hexagrams（卦象）, hexagram names（卦名）, hexagram judgments（卦辞）, linear titles（爻题）and linear judgments（爻辞）. The basic components for a hexagram are a yang line（阳爻）and a yin line（阴爻）. Three lines form a trigram and altogether there are eight trigrams as the cardinals. They respectively symbolize heaven, earth, thunder, wind, water, fire, mountain and lake. Trigrams are doubled as hexagrams, and eight hexagrams multiplied by eight hexagrams are sixty-four hexagrams. One hexagram can be divided into two trigrams as the lower and the upper or the inner and the outer trigrams. Each hexagram has a name, for instance, the Qian hexagram（乾卦）, the Kun hexagram（坤卦）, the Zhun hexagram（屯卦）and so on. The sixty-four hexagrams symbolize sixty-four different contexts or processes and can be used as metaphors for and analogies to different situations and changing processes. Each hexagram is attached with some hexagram judgment. The six lines of each hexagram are named from bottom to top as the bottom line, the second line, the third line, the fourth line, the fifth line and the top line. The yang line is called nine for an odd number in divination calculation and the yin line six for an even number. Thus the titles for each line of a hexagram are, for instance, nine at the bottom line, nine at the second line, six at the third line, or six at the top line. Each linear title is followed by a linear judgment. For the Qian and Kun hexagrams, each has an extra line and their titles are "all changeable nines" and "all changeable sixes" respectively.

The obscurity of the meanings and uncertain cohesion and coherence of the text of the hexagram and linear judgments in *The Book of Changes* caused difficulty in understanding the book.

The Book of Changes was created out of two reasons. According to the first part of *the Survey*, the creation of *The Book of Changes* was intended to reveal principles of all objects and their states to accomplish all work and embrace all principles under heaven. The second was for a full expression of thought and in language. Obviously, *The Book of Changes* was an accumulation of wisdom and wishes of our forefathers in life through ages. Based on the historical materials and life experience of the ancient people, the book explored both the historical wisdom in the development of the ancient kingdoms, society and man and the wisdom of living for the present and future by means of integrating natural elements with mathematical deduction and logical thinking. Like a long chain of cultural genes, Chinese thought and culture has inherited considerably from *The Book of Changes* which has influenced countless Chinese philosophers, artists and even business people throughout history over centuries.

As one of the media of traditional Chinese culture, *The Book of Changes* has been widely spread throughout the world. The book was introduced to Europe in the 17th century by the missionaries in China and Thomas Mcclatchie was the first person to translate the book into English in 1880. Changeological studies became even more popular in the West in the second half of the 20th century. In Asia, *the Book of Changes* was mainly spread to Japan, the North Korea and the Republic of Korea and Vietnam. Since the 1970s, translations in different languages and books and academic papers on *The Book of Changes* have increased and studies adopting western methods and integrating western philosophies have greatly enriched changeological studies.

Ⅱ. 文本选读

The Qian Hexagram[1]

The Qian Hexagram (the symbol of heaven) predicts supremacy[2], success, potentiality and perseverance[3].

1. The dragon is lying in wait. The time for action is not ripe.

2. The dragon appears in the fields. It is time for the great man to emerge from obscurity[4].

3. The gentleman strives hard all day long. He is vigilant[5] even at nighttime. By doing so, he will be safe in times of danger.

4. The dragon will either soar to the sky or remain in the deep. There is nothing to blame in either case.

5. The dragon is flying in the sky. It is time for the great man to come to the fore[6].

6. The dragon has soared to the zenith[7]. It will regret sooner or later. None of the dragons claims to be the chief; this is a sign of good omen[8].

The Kun Hexagram⑨

The Kun Hexagram (the symbol of earth) predicates supremacy and success. There is potentiality in perseverance⑩ with the submissiveness⑪ of a mare. When a gentleman goes anywhere, he will go astray⑫ if he takes the lead⑬ and he will have guidance if he follows behind. The potentiality lies in finding friends in the southwest and losing friends in the northeast. Peaceful perseverance is a sign of good omen.

1. When you tread on hoarfrost⑭, solid ice will appear soon.

2. If you are fair and square⑮, you will reap⑯ benefits without exertion⑰.

3. Keep your brilliance concealed⑱; you'd better persevere in doing this. If you have the chance to serve the king, you should claim no credit⑲ but do good service.

4. If you are reticent⑳ like a tied-up sack, you will receive neither blame nor praise.

5. You are dressed in yellow like an official; this is a sign of supreme omen.

6. When the dragon comes to fight in the wilderness, blood runs black and yellow.

7. Potentiality lies in eternal perseverance.

The Xu Hexagram㉑

The Xu Hexagram (the symbol of waiting) predicates sincerity, a bright prospect and success. Perseverance will bring good fortune. It is time to cross a great river.

1. Waiting in the suburbs, you should exercise your patience. You will not receive any blame.

2. Waiting on the beach, you may face some gossip, but will have good fortune in the end.

3. Waiting in the mire㉒, you are threatened by imminent danger㉓.

4. Waiting in jeopardy㉔, you will get out of the trap.

5. Waiting in leisure, you will have good fortune.

6. You have fallen into the trap. When three unexpected guests arrive, you will have good fortune in the end if you show respect to them.

The Bi Hexagram[25]

The Bi Hexagram (the symbol of fellowship[26]) predicates good fortune. Prudence[27] will bring about virtue[28], constancy[29] and integrity[30]. Even when the rebellious princes come to be presented at court, misfortune will fall on those who come late.

1. Establishing fellowship with sincere people will not evoke[31] blame. Sincerity is like a full jug, which will bring unexpected blessing[32].

2. Sincerity from the bottom of your heart will bring about good fortune if you persevere.

3. You are establishing fellowship with ignoble[33] people.

4. Following the wise superior will bring about good fortune if you persevere.

5. Be open and aboveboard[34] toward others, like the king hunting from three sides and leaving one side for the game to escape[35]. Thus, the citizens are all at ease; this is a sign of good omen.

6. You are not capable enough to be a superior; you will have misfortune.

The Qian Hexagram[36]

The Qian Hexagram (the symbol of modesty) predicates success. The gentleman is modest all his life.

1. A truly modest gentleman can overcome all difficulties; he will have good fortune.

2. If you are known for modesty and persevere in it, you will have good fortune.

3. Meritorious[37] but modest, the gentleman is like this all his life; he will have good fortune.

4. You will prosper in every respect if you practice modesty.

5. Modesty wins support from your neighbours. It is time to be on the offensive[38]; you will be ever-victorious.

6. Since you are known for modesty, it is time to take military action[39] in order to pacify[40] your own country.

The Sui Hexagram[41]

The Sui Hexagram (the symbol of following) predicates supreme success. There is potentiality in perseverance. There is nothing to blame.

1. When you follow the change of times, you will have good fortune if you persevere. If you find friends outside your family, you will win merits.

2. If you cling to an inferior man[42], you will lose the company of a superior man.

3. If you cling to a superior man, you will lose the company of an inferior man. Although you may get what you seek after, you'd better stick to yourself.

4. You may benefit from your followers; this is a sign of ill omen. If you are sincerely doing what is right and remain open and aboveboard, what is there to blame?

5. If you are sincere to the good people, you will have good fortune.

6. You give firm allegiance[43] and are loyal to the king. The king entrusts you to attend the sacrificial rites[44] on the West Mountain[45].

The Guan Hexagram[46]

The Guan Hexagram (the symbol of observation) predicates devotion, with which the king washes his hands before making offerings in the sacrificial rites. The people below are observing with the same devotion or piety[47].

1. Observing with the ignorance of a child is blameless for the inferior man, but grievous[48] for the gentleman.

2. Observing stealthily[49] from behind the door is the proper behavior for the woman.

3. Observe your own behavior to decide on your advance or retreat.

4. Observe the situation in the country, and you may serve the king.

5. Observe his own behavior, and the gentleman will not receive any blame.

6. Observe the life of the people, and the gentleman will not receive any blame.

The Yi Hexagram[50]

The Yi Hexagram (the symbol of gain) predicates benefit. It is time to take action. It is time to cross a great river.

1. It is time to take major actions. You will have supreme fortune and will not receive any blame.

2. When you are offered a lot of money, you will not change your mind. Eternal⑤¹ perseverance will bring good fortune. The king is making offerings to the gods; this is a sign of good omen.

3. If you benefit people who are in misfortune, you will not receive any blame. Be sincere and upright⑤²; always show respect to your superior.

4. Be upright, always ask for instructions, and the superior will follow your advice. You will be relied on⑤³ in important matters such as moving the capital.

5. Sincerity in benefiting the people will doubtlessly bring good fortune. People will also be sincere and repay your kindness⑤⁴.

6. Nobody will bring you benefit and somebody may attack you because you are not steadfast⑤⁵; this is a sign of ill omen.

Ⅲ. 难点释义

① Qian Hexagram，乾卦。下卦、上卦皆为乾，象征天。Hexagram，本指数学里的六线形。因《周易》里的 64 卦象皆由六根横线（即阳爻和阴爻）按照不同的规律组合而成，故用 hexagram 一词译出较为妥当。以下同。

② supremacy，最高地位。由于乾卦象征天，体现了至高无上的初始状态。

③ perseverance，坚贞，毅力。

④ obscurity，地位卑微。

⑤ vigilant，警醒的。

⑥ come to the fore，崭露头角。

⑦ zenith，顶点。

⑧ omen，征兆。

⑨ Kun Hexagram，坤卦。下卦上卦皆为坤，象征着大地、母马、母亲等。坤卦以"柔顺利贞"的宁静来赞扬"厚德载物"的君子之美。

⑩ potentiality in perseverance，蕴藏于坚毅中的潜力。

⑪ submissiveness，顺从。

⑫ go astray，误入歧途。

⑬ takes the lead，抢先，带头。

⑭ hoarfrost，霜。

⑮ fair and square，光明正大。

⑯ reap，收获。

⑰ exertion，尽力而为。

⑱ keep your brilliance concealed，不要显露才华。

⑲ claim no credit，不邀功请赏。

⑳ reticent，慎言少语。

㉑ Xu Hexagram，需卦。下乾，象征天，上坎，象征水。按《说卦》，坎为水，乾为天，水在天上，故有下雨之情。需卦象征着等待。

㉒ mire，泥潭。

㉓ imminent danger，即将发生的危险。

㉔ jeopardy，危险。

㉕ Bi Hexagram，比卦。下坤，象征地，上坎，象征水。"比"象征归附顺从，比卦强调人与人之间的和谐关系。

㉖ fellowship，此处意为交情。

㉗ prudence，谨慎。

㉘ virtue，美德。

㉙ constancy，恒久。

㉚ integrity，正直。

㉛ evoke，引起。

㉜ unexpected blessing，意外的祝福。

㉝ ignoble，卑鄙的。

㉞ aboveboard，光明正大。

㉟ like the king hunting from three sides and leaving one side for the game to escape，好像君王围猎时，三面围拢，仅张开一面网，任前面的猎物走离。Game，猎物。

㊱ Qian Hexagram，谦卦。下艮，象征山，上坤，象征地。谦卦象征谦虚。

㊲ meritorious，有功劳的。

㊳ on the offensive，准备进攻。

㊴ take military action，采取军事行动。

㊵ pacify，使安定。

㊶ Sui Hexagram，随卦。下震，象征雷，上兑，象征泽。随卦象征随从、顺应。

㊷ cling to an inferior man，依附一个寒微的人。

㊸ firm allegiance，绝对的忠诚。

㊹ sacrificial rites，祭礼。

㊺ West Mountain，西山。在周代时，应指岐山，因在镐京之西，故曰西山。

㊻ Guan Hexagram，观卦。下坤，象征地，上巽，象征风。观卦阐发观察的意义和方法。

㊼ piety，虔诚。

㊽ grievous，本意为事态严重，此处意为"羞耻"。

㊾ stealthily，暗地里。

㊿ Yi Hexagram，益卦。下震，象征雷，上巽，象征风。益卦象征着增益。

51 Eternal，永恒的。

52 upright，正直的。

53 rely on，信赖。

54 kindness，善良。

55 steadfast，坚定不移的。

Ⅳ. 问题思考

1. What is the basic structure of *The Book of Changes*?

2. What is the relationship between hexagram judgment and linear judgment?

3. We cannot deny the possibility that the evolution of sixty-four hexagrams was the result of long development of life and production activities in ancient China. How do you understand the relationship between the hexagrams and their symbolic meanings?

4. Can you feel the influence of *The Book of Changes* in modern life? How should we regard the divination practice by fortune-tellers making use of the principles and methods from *The Book of Changes* in modern times?

5. Inspired by the dialectic principles implied in *The Book of Changes*, people regard it as the embodiment of philosophy of life, believing that human existence and life much always adapt to changes. Please explain with an example.

6. Why was *The Book of Changes* promoted the primary classic in China?

V. 经典导读

《周易》是一部体现深邃的中华民族智慧和灿烂的中华文明的巨著。虽然《周易》成书的起源是殷末周初的人们卜筮时的一套符号系统，但是其内容上涉天文，下盖地理，中及人事，从画符取象到术数推演，从天地之道到经世治国，从帝王将相到平民百姓，弥纶天地，广大精微，包罗万象，超越时空。因此《周易》早已超越了其原始的宗教迷信性质，成为中国古代学术思想的源头活水，启迪和推动了中国古代科技文明发展，正因为如此，它被誉为"群经之首，大道之源"。

《周易》包括两个部分，即《易经》和《易传》。《易经》包括卦画、卦名、爻题和爻辞。古人根据直观朴素的观察，把天地、男女、昼夜、炎凉、上下、胜负等宇宙中变化万端、纷繁复杂的事物分为阴、阳两大类，用"╍╍"表示阴，用"━━"表示阳，象征广泛的相互对立的事物和现象。在此基础上，古人称阴、阳符号为"爻"（yáo），每三爻叠成一卦画，于是出现了"八卦"。八卦有各自的名称和形式，分别是乾（☰）、坤（☷）、震（☳）、巽（☴）、坎（☵）、离（☲）、艮（☶）、兑（☱），它们分别象征天、地、雷、风、水、火、山、泽。八种卦画又可上下重叠、排列组合成六十四个卦画，即六十四卦。六十四卦的每一个六画卦都有一个名称，如屯、需、贲、咸等，而且每个六画卦可拆分为下卦和上卦。六画卦的每一爻，从下往上分别称作初、二、三、四、五、上。阳爻为奇数九，阴爻为偶数六，合称为爻题，如初九、九二、六三和上六。每一爻题后附有爻辞。爻辞以"假象喻义"的表现形式，阐释卦画和爻形所蕴含的事物运动、变化和发展的哲理。六十四卦相承相受，从六十四种角度展示不同的环境条件下的事理特征和变化规律。这就是《周易》的

"经文"，即《易经》部分。

《易传》是解释《易经》大义的说明性文字，共七种十篇，附于经文之后，如同经文的羽翼，因此又称为"十翼"，它们分别是《文言》、《彖》上下、《象》上下、《系辞》上下、《说卦》、《序卦》、《杂卦》。其中，《文言》是专门补充解说乾、坤两卦的。《彖》随上下经分为上下两篇，分释六十四卦卦名和卦辞。《象》亦随上下经分为上下两篇，阐释各卦的卦象和各爻的爻象。《系辞》对《易经》的卦画演变历史，《周易》产生的时间和原因，卦画的原理、形成和含义，《周易》成书的原因和目的，卦爻象与卦爻辞的关系、孔子与《易传》的关系、《周易》的精神实质等各方面内容作了全面的辨析和阐发，是《易传》中内容和哲学思想最丰富的部分。《说卦》专论八卦象例。《序卦》旨在解说《周易》六十四卦的编排次序，揭示各卦相承的意义。《杂卦》则打散《序卦》所揭示的卦序，把六十四卦重新分成三十二组，两两对举，以精要的语言概括卦旨。

本单元遴选《周易》上经《乾》、《坤》、《需》、《比》、《谦》、《随》、《观》凡七篇，下经《益》一篇。考虑到本书的编写意图和读者对象，只辑录各卦的卦爻辞，略去《易传》或"十翼"部分。

乾卦，下卦、上卦皆为乾，象征天。乾卦为六十四卦之首，它最大的特点是六爻皆为阳爻。乾卦以"天"来喻指刚健、正大的美德，以"龙"为喻宣扬"天"之纯阳刚健的精神。乾卦开篇就以"元、亨、

天坛的建筑来自五行学说的灵感

利、贞"四言，高度概括"天"具有至高无上、开创万物并使之亨通吉利、和谐富裕、光大正直的功德。乾的卦辞以龙设喻，描绘龙在不同时间和地点的不同状态。它或潜或隐，时而现身于田，时而翻腾于深水池之中，又冲天而起，升腾翱翔于九霄之上。它运行不止，变化不定，目标高远，充满力量。如此生动的形象可以说是对天道，即世界的普遍法则和宇宙的生命力的最好的喻示，也是对人的自强不息、雄健顽强、奋发向上、一往无前的精神的精彩刻画，又是对人的微妙神奇、变化莫测、出神

入化的智慧的深刻描绘。

坤卦，下卦、上卦皆为坤，象征地。该卦以六根阴爻来象征"含弘广大"的大地。坤卦的卦辞用牝（pìn）马，即柔顺的雌马为隐喻，象征次要的、被动的、顺从的、温和的处下之道。坤卦以纯阴卦象显示了一种极为柔弱的状态，所以卦辞说君子有所往，先迷失方向，然后终究有所归。《周易》并不认为阴阳的地位与强弱是固定不变的，而是认为世界处于阴阳消长的变化之中。坤卦从让人不寒而栗的初爻辞开始，最后一根爻辞却充满了鼓舞人心的战斗气息和不畏牺牲的英勇精神，中间的爻辞又多鼓励人们努力地言语。可见，坤卦中的处下之道不是要人们总是消极地顺从或保持无所作为的谨小慎微，它一方面要人们面对艰难险恶的处境和形势时谨慎小心，明智应对，另一方面则是大力增强人的精神生命力，引导人们在完善自我和增强才干上采取积极进取的态度，并且总是让人们对前途充满希望。

需卦，下乾，象征天，上坎，象征水，水在天上，有下雨之情。《京房易传》曰："需，云上于天，凝于阴而待于阳，故曰需者待也。"在六十四卦中，凡言有"利涉大川"的卦，多有进取之象，需卦就是这样的一个卦。但是进取需要耐心、稳步、有序，而不是轻举妄动。需卦中六爻，初言"无咎"，二言"终吉"，三言"慎不败"，四言"顺以德"，五言"贞吉"，上又言"终吉"，皆无凶象，这表明以诚实、耐心、慎重的态度进取，就会吉祥有利。

比卦，下坤，象征地，上坎，象征水。水流于地，亲而附之，附之无间，相融相合。该卦强调人与人之间的和谐关系。比卦从德、人、上下、内外等方面来说明"比"的意义。初六以"比"而"有孚"，强调人欲与人有"比"，必要心怀诚信；六二以"自内"提示，"比"应内附而不应外索；六三以"匪人"来指明所"比"之人应有正直的品德；六四则以外比于贤，来说明"比"应以贤人为友，而不应有内外之分；九五因以中正居尊，故以"显比"来宣扬其亲比于下的仁爱之德；上六则以"无首"来揭示不能终"比"则必终于"凶"。比卦的理想是要实现上下皆亲的"和谐"状态。

谦卦，下艮，象征山，上坤，象征地。本来山高地低，而现在山在地下，表示高大者自居于下位，是谦虚的表现。谦卦的卦名、卦象、卦辞和大多数爻辞，都直接明确地赞扬谦虚，一卦的各组成部分如此高度集中于一个抽象的概念，这在六十四卦中是罕见的。此外，该卦的卦辞和六爻爻辞都言吉利，这在六十四卦中仅此一例。该卦的前三爻都为吉，据有高位的人，如果谦虚谨慎，就能渡过任何艰险。后三爻稍次，但也无不利，小至一举一动，大至出兵征伐，都因虚怀若谷，恪尽职守，遵循准则，而最后得到好的结果。正所谓"谦虚使人进步"，在几千年的华夏文化中，谦虚始终被视为君子所奉行的美德。

随卦，下震，象征雷，上兑，象征泽。上兑为悦，下震为动。这种内动外悦的卦象隐含着"刚来而下柔"的"随从"之举。该卦以"元亨，利贞"来赞美随从于善道的品德。具体到六爻：初九"出门"而"有功"，六二随从"小子"而有"失"，六三失"小"得"大"，九四"有孚"而"无咎"，九五因"孚"而"吉"，上六则"穷"与随道。晏子曰："君子居必择邻，游必有士。"故君子之"随"比"择善而从"。

观卦，下坤，象征地，上巽，象征风。"观"的意思是观察、观看。事物的运行像风一样变化无常，唯有仔细观察，看到事物的本质而不是现象，才能适应事物的发展变化，才能避免行动错误以致损失。观卦辞蕴含的意义在于：当参与和观看祭祀神明、宗祖的盛人场面出现时，应秉持诚信，它强调庄严肃穆的祭祀场面对人心的净化作用。观卦由此与政治统治有关。"观"的方式和内容因人而异。初六因观之以幼稚而"无咎"；六二说明女子之"观"应悄然而观，这是两种不可取的观察方式。六三是观察自己的所作所为，可知"进退"。唯六四因近于君王之侧，而得"观国"之"观"，成为王之座上宾，九五、上九则从上往下观，观下之民风而知其政治得失，所以君王观民之时也是自观。

益卦，下震，象征雷，上巽，象征风。卦下多阴，卦上多阳，阴虚阳实，阳以实授之，阴以虚承之，象征着增益。上三爻以损而得益，下三爻以守正而受益，故益卦"损上益下"。初九以阳德居卑下之位，居中而为受益之爻，故能大有所为。六二以柔中为美，所以能获"十朋之龟"。六三虽不当位，然若在受益之时，有救济之心，也可"无咎"。六四柔怀善志，处益下之始，有尊上而益下之德，所以"有喜"而"无咎"。九五能广施恩惠于天下，所以得"元吉"之喜。上九处上，其位不正，所以不能自损而益下，故被"击"而有"凶"。由此看来，唯损于彼，才能益于此。

Ⅵ. 译本链接

1. ［英］麦格基：《（易经）之译——附注解与附录》，伦敦：企鹅图书公司

1876 年版。

2. ［英］理雅各：《易经》，伦敦：牛津大学出版社 1882 年版。

3. ［德］卫礼贤德译，贝恩斯英译：《易经》，纽约：纽约大学出版社 1950 年版。

4. 傅惠生：《周易汉英对照》，长沙：湖南人民出版社 2008 年版。

5. 汪熔培：《英译易经》，上海：上海外语教育出版社 2007 年版。

6. 卫礼贤英译：《周易全二卷》，长沙：岳麓书社 2013 年版。

Unit Seven
Dao De Jing （《道德经》）

Ⅰ. 背景简介

Lao Zi, or Lao Dan (about 571 B. C. – 471 B. C.) with a birth name of Li Er, was a native of the southern feudal state of Chu in the later Spring and Autumn Period. As an adult, he held a minor government post as a librarian in the imperial archives of the Eastern Zhou Dynasty. Confucius was said to have consulted the royal archives to find information on certain rituals. At some point he relinquished this post. According to legend, Lao Zi got disgusted because of the decline in morality and the dishonesty prevailing in politics in the area where he lived, and decided to go away and live as a hermit. When he reached the entrance to the state of Ch'in, the famous Hangu Pass, he met Yin Xi, the guardian of the pass, who asked him to prove his wisdom by writing a book. When Lao Zi finished the book, he left it to Yin Xi and little was known about him thereafter.

Lao Zi (**about** 571 **B. C.** – 471 **B. C.**)

The only book written by Lao Zi was the famous *Lao Zi or Dao De Jing* on which Taoism was based. The book is a short, poetic text of about 5,000 Chinese characters, divided into

81 chapters, but has been a great source of inspiration for poets, artists, philosophers and theologians all over the world. In the West, the translations of *Lao Zi* are only next to that of *the Bible* in number. The philosophy of Lao Zi presented in *Dao De Jing* is mainly about the universe, human life and politics.

The concept of "Dao" signifies the primordial essence or fundamental nature of the universe. In the foundational text of Taoism, the *Dao De Jing*, Lao Zi explains that Dao is not a 'name' for a 'thing' but the underlying natural order of the universe whose ultimate essence is difficult to circumscribe. Dao is thus "eternally nameless" and to be distinguished from the countless 'named' things which are considered to be its manifestations. As to preservation of life, the main ideas in Lao Zi include: few desires, no addition to one's vitality, and to keep vital *qi*. The political views in the book of *Lao Zi* can be mainly expressed in three sentences: "Kingdoms can only be governed if rules are kept, battles can only be won if rules are broken. But the adherence of all under heaven can only be won be letting-alone."

Ⅱ. 文本选读
Chapter 1
The Way[①] that can be told of is not an Unvarying Way;
The names that can be named are not unvarying names.
It was from the Nameless that Heaven and Earth sprang;
The named is but the mother that rears the ten thousand creatures, each after its kind.
Truly, "Only he that rids himself forever of desire can see the Secret Essences";
He that has never rid himself of desire can see only the Outcomes.
These two things issued from the same mould, but nevertheless are different in name.
This "same mould" we can but call the Mystery,
Or rather the "Darker than any Mystery",
The Doorway whence issued all Secret Essences.

Chapter 2

It is because every one under Heaven recognizes beauty as beauty that the idea of ugliness exists.

And equally if every one recognized virtue as virtue, this would merely create fresh conceptions of wickedness.

For truly, Being and Not-being grow out of one another;

Difficult and easy complete one another.

Long and short test one another;

High and low determine one another.

Pitch and mode give harmony to one another.

Front and back give sequence to one another.

Therefore the Sage relies on actionless activity[2],

Carries on wordless teaching,

But the myriad creatures are worked upon by him; he does not disown them.

He rears them, but does not lay claim to them,

Controls them, but does not lean upon them.

Achieves his aim, but does not call attention to what he does;

And for the very reason that he does not call attention to what he does.

He is not ejected from fruition[3] of what he has done.

Chapter 8

The highest good is like that of water[4]. The goodness of water is that it benefits the ten thousand creatures; yet itself does not scramble, but is content with the places that all men disdain[5]. It is this that makes water so near to the Way.

And if men think the ground the best place for building a house upon,

If among thoughts they value those that are profound,

If in friendship they value gentleness,

In words, truth; in government, good order;

In deeds, effectiveness; in actions, timeliness—

In each case it is because they prefer what does not lead to strife,

And therefore does not go amiss⑥.

Chapter 9

Stretch a bow to the very full,

And you will wish you had stopped in time;

Temper a sword-edge to its very sharpest,

And you will find it soon grows dull.

When bronze and jade fill your hall.

It can no longer be guarded.

Wealth and place breed insolence⑦.

That brings ruin in its train.

When your work is done, then withdraw!⑧

Such is Heaven's Way.

Chapter 13

"Favor and disgrace goad⑨ as it were to madness; high rank hurts keenly as our bodies hurt."

What does it mean to say that favor and disgrace goad as it were to madness? It means that when a ruler's subjects get it they turn distraught, when they lose it they turn distraught. That is what is meant by saying favor and disgrace goad as it were to madness. What does it mean to say that high rank hurts keenly as our bodies hurt? The only reason that we suffer hurt is that we have bodies; if we had no bodies, how could we suffer?⑩

Therefore we may accept the saying: "He who in dealing with the empire regards his high rank as though it were his body is the best person to be entrusted with rule; he who in dealing with the empire loves his subjects as one should love one's body is the best person to whom one can commit the empire."

Chapter 16

Push far enough towards the Void,

Hold fast enough to Quietness[①],

And of the ten thousand things none but can be worked on by you.

I have beheld them, whither they go back.

See, all things howsoever they flourish,

Return to the root from which they grew.

This return to the root is called Quietness;

Quietness is called submission to Fate;

What has submitted to Fate has become part of the always-so.

To know the always-so is to be illumined;

Not to know it, means to go blindly to disaster.

He who knows the always-so has room in him for everything;

He who has room in him for everything is without prejudice.

To be without prejudice is to be kingly;

To be kingly is to be of heaven;

To be of heaven is to be in Tao.

Tao is forever and he that possesses it,

Though his body ceases, is not destroyed.

Chapter 22

"To remain whole, be twisted!"

To become straight, let yourself be bent.

To become full, be hollow.

Be tattered, that you may be renewed.

Those that have little, may get more,

Those that have much, are but perplexed.

Therefore the Sage

Clasps the Primal Unity,

Testing by it everything under heaven.

He does not show himself; therefore he is seen everywhere.

He does not define himself, therefore he is distinct.

He does not boast of what he will do, therefore he succeeds.

He is not proud of his work, and therefore it endures.

He does not contend,

And for that very reason no one under heaven can contend with him[12].

So then we see that the ancient saying "To remain whole, be twisted" was no idle word; for true wholeness can only be achieved by return.

Chapter 25

There was something formless yet complete,

That existed before heaven and earth;

Without sound, without substance,

Dependent on nothing, unchanging,

All pervading, unfailing.

One may think of it as the mother of all things under heaven.

Its true name we do not know;

"Way" is the by-name that we give it.

Were I forced to say to what class of things it belongs,

I should call it Great (ta).

Now ta also means passing on,

And passing on means going far away,

And going far away means returning.

Thus just as Tao has "this greatness" and as earth has it and as heaven has it, so may the ruler also have it.

Thus "within the realm there are four portions of greatness," and one belongs to the king.

The ways of men are conditioned by those of earth.

The ways of earth, by those of heaven.

The ways of heaven, by those of Tao, and the ways of Tao, by the Self-so. [13]

Chapter 42

Tao gave birth to the One [14]; the One gave birth successively to two things [15], three things [16], up to ten thousand. These ten thousand creatures cannot turn their backs to the shade without having the sun on their bellies, and it is on this blending of the breaths that their harmony depends.

(To be orphaned, needy, ill-provided is what men most hate; yet princes and dukes style themselves so. Truly, "things are often increased by seeking to diminish them and diminished by seeking to increase them." The maxims that others use in their teaching I too will use in mine. Show me a man of violence that came to a good end, and I will take him for my teacher.)

(Translated by Arthur Waley)

Ⅲ. 难点释义

① the Way，道。"道"的概念，作为老子的哲学思想体系的核心，其含义博大精深。老子认为"道"不可以用语言来说明，而是深邃奥妙的，并不是轻而易举就能够领会的，需要一个从"无"到"有"的循序渐进过程。

② actionless activity，无为之事。老子提出的"无为"的观点，不是无所作为，随心所欲。他以圣人为例，教导人们要有所作为，但不是强作妄为。

③ fruition，成就，实现。

④ The highest good is like that of water. 上善若水。意思是说，最高境界的善行就像水的品性一样，泽被万物而不争名利。水有滋养万物的德行，它使万物得到它的利益，而不与万物发生矛盾冲突。

⑤ disdain，蔑视，不屑于做。

⑥ amiss, 出差错的, 有缺陷的。

⑦ insolence, 傲慢, 无礼。

⑧ When your work is done, then withdraw! 功遂身退。老子指出, 知进而不知退、善争而不善让会给人带来祸害, 希望人们把握好度, 适可而止。

⑨ goad, 激励, 刺激。

⑩ The only reason that we suffer hurt is that we have bodies; if we had no bodies, how could we suffer? 此句多理解为: "我之所以有大患, 是因为我有身体; 如果我没有身体, 我还会有什么祸患呢?" 然而结合众多前人所注, "身" 理解为 "自己" 或 "人的欲望 (发自身体感觉器官)" 似乎较妥。

⑪ Push far enough towards the Void, hold fast enough to Quietness. 老子特别强调致虚守静的功夫。他倡导人们应当用虚寂沉静的心境, 去面对宇宙万物的运动变化。

⑫ He does not contend, and for that very reason no one under heaven can contend with him. 此句充分体现了老子 "柔弱胜刚强" 的哲学思想。老子所谓 "不争", 不是放弃一切, 而是要以不争反立于不败之地。后世流传的 "难得糊涂"、"吃亏是福" 等思想意识都与之相关。

⑬ The ways of earth, by those of heaven. The ways of heaven, by those of Tao, and the ways of Tao, by the Self-so. "道"、"人"、"天"、"地" 这四个存在, 老子把 "道" 放在第一位。它不会随着变动、运转而消失。"道" 是事物得以产生的最基本、最根源的地方。

⑭ One, "一", 这是老子用以代替 "道" 这一概念的数字表示, 即道是绝对无偶的。

⑮ two things, "二", 指阴气、阳气。"道" 的本身包含着对立的两方面。阴阳二气所含育的统一体即是 "道"。因此, 对立着的双方都包含在 "一" 中。

⑯ three things, "三", 即是由两个对立的方面相互矛盾冲突所产生的第三者, 进而生成万物。"三" 在先秦是多数的意思。

Ⅳ. 问题思考

1. Lao Zi's idea of "non-action" (*wu wei*) has been believed by many to be a passive

escapism from the reality. Do you agree? Why or why not?

2. Do you agree with the idea that "When your work is done, then withdraw"? Give your reasons for it.

3. What's your understanding of "He does not contend, and for that very reason no one under heaven can contend with him"? How can it be applied to the modern life?

4. Is there any conformity between Lao Zi's philosophy of life and his philosophy of governing? If yes, please briefly explain it.

5. In what way and how are Lao Zi's thoughts valuable for you?

V. 经典导读

《道德经》（又称《老子》）大约成书于公元前6世纪，一般认为，它是春秋时期一位叫老聃的隐者所作。《道德经》只有五千多个汉字，共81章，分为道篇和德篇两部分。虽然简短，但它在中国文化发展中的作用却毋庸置疑：以它为基础，中国古代产生了与儒家并列的哲学派别道家；根据它的思想，中国古代产生了以老子为始祖的宗教派别道教，这是华夏民族本土产生的最具影响的宗教。《道德经》的思想直接影响了中国人的民族特性、思维倾向和审美趣味。《道德经》在15世纪左右就开始被介绍到欧洲，它是译本最多的中国古代哲学著作之一。据联合国教科文组织统计，《道德经》在被译成外国文字发行量最多的文化名著中排名第二，仅次于《圣经》。哲学家尼采曾说过："老子思想的集大成——《道德经》，像一个永不枯竭的井泉，满载宝藏，放下了，唾手可得。"

《道德经》是中国哲学史上第一部具有完整哲学体系的著作，涵盖了老子的宇宙观、人生观和社会政治观。

老子认为宇宙万物的本原是"道"。"道冲，而用之或不盈。渊兮，似万物之宗"，"道生一，一生二，二生三，三生万物。"天下万物生于有，而有则生于无。道作为老子哲学的最高范畴，从根本上否定了天作为人格神的至上权威，使无神论的思想

老子在各地传道授业

理论化，是一种历史的进步。"道"的含义虽然很多，但是它有两种最突出的规律：对立转化和返本复初。老子说："反者道之动。"这里所说的"反"有两层含义，一是"相反"的"反"，二是"复返"的"返"。两层意思又互相关联，反映出老子哲学的独特智慧。在阐述相反相成的思想时，老子习惯采用"正言若反"的思路。在老子看来，"天下皆知美之为美，斯恶已；皆知善之为善，斯不善已。故有无相生，难易相成，长短相形，高下相倾，音声相和，前后相随。是以圣人处无为之事，行不言之教。万物作焉而不辞"。老子认为，少则得，多则惑，世界的高下美丑，是人的一种判断。人给世界作判断、分高下，乃至确定世界的意义，其实是对真实世界的误解。即如美丑而言，当天下人知道追求美的时候，就有了美丑的区分，就有了分别的见解。老子并不反对人们追求美，但他认为这种追求美的方式，并不能得到真正的美。真正对美的欣赏，是对美和丑的超越。

在人生观方面，老子从他的自然无为哲学出发，对于人的行为方式，提出了"以柔弱胜刚强"的观点。老子"以柔弱胜刚强"的哲学，立足点在"不争"。老子认为，争强好胜，是衰落的根源；而清静无为，则可以合于自然无为的生命之道。老子说"上善若水"（The hightest good is like that of water）——水具有最高的善。老子以水来作比喻，突出他的"不争"哲学思想与恶意争斗的丛林法则之间的区别所在。老子说："水善万物而不争。"水的最高德行就是"不争"。人往高处走，水往低处流。人情受欲望驱动，好高而恶下，而水却永远地往下流淌。水是生命之源，可以滋润万物，给大地带来生命，没有水也就没有生命。水在最低、最平、最静之处，包容天下一切，映照万物。水选择了一条和利欲熏心的人完全不同的道路。

当然，老子哲学并不是弱者的哲学，他的哲学充满了力量感。老子认为，水在柔弱宁静中，积聚了强大的力量，可以冲破世界上的一切障碍。他说："天下莫柔弱于水，而攻坚强者莫之能胜。"水是柔弱胜刚强的典型。水因为不争，不为利欲所驱动，所以能无往而不胜。老子总结说："我有三宝，持而保之。一曰慈，二曰俭，三曰不敢为天下先。慈故能勇；俭故能广；不敢为天下先，故能成器长。"这便是老子"以柔弱胜刚强"思想的最好注解。

老子社会政治观的核心是"无为而无不为"（Not-doing, nothing is left undone）。"无为"作为老子哲学的重要概念，是对"自然"的保护。"自然"是老子哲学最重要的概念之一，它并非指外在的自然物，而指一种自然而然、顺应世界的态度。老子的无为政治，是基于天道无为而提出的。没有"无为"，也就没有"自然"。老子说："无为而无不为"，意思不是说什么都不做，消极等待事情的成功。而是说，人的一切事业应该在顺应自然的基础上去做，不能强行改变自然的节奏。

老子反对"人为"，并不是否定人的积极创造，而是反对破坏自然节奏的盲目乱为。老子所提倡的创造，是契合自然精神的创造。老子告诫人们，放下左右世界的欲望，顺应自然，这样才是解决人与世界冲突的根本途径。老子的政治观同人生观是紧密联系的，人生观讲求柔弱处上，政治观讲求无为而治，这都是柔性的哲学观。

老子提出了很多治国的观点，例如"圣人无常心，以百姓心为心"，"治大国若烹小鲜"，"鱼不可以脱于渊，国之利器不可以示人"，"我无为，而民自化；我好静，而民自正；我无事，而民自富；我无欲，而民自朴"，"大国下小国，则取小国；大国以下小国，则取大国"等，不一而足。虽然有一些像"以智治国，国之贼；不以智治国，国之福"，"小国寡民"（Lct there be a small country with few people）之类的观点不能令所有人接受，但从总体看来不无道理。桃花源式的国家，并不能存在于今日，但从老子政治观中所提炼出来的治国方法，依然可以借鉴。

老子哲学在中国思想史上有着重要的地位，后代不少哲学家都在不同程度上受到它的影响。自汉以后注释《道德经》者不下千家，这在中国古籍中是罕见的。老子不但创立了我国三大宗教之一的道教，而且他的思想可以说影响了后来整个中国哲学史的发展，直到今天，《道德经》还在参与塑造中华民族的思想。

Ⅵ. 译本链接

1. ［英］亚瑟·韦利：《道及其威力》，伦敦：企鹅图书公司 1934 年版。

2. Stephen Mitchell：*Tao Te Ching*，New York：Harper Collins，1988.

3. 辜正坤：《老子英译》，北京：北京大学出版社 1995 年版。

4. 林语堂：《老子的智慧》，纽约：蓝登书屋 1948 年版。

5. 陈荣捷：《老子之道》，纽约：鲍波斯·麦瑞尔股份有限公司 1963 年版。

6. 刘殿爵：《道德经》，伦敦：企鹅图书公司 1963 版。

7. 林振述：《老子〈道德经〉及王弼注译本》，Paud J. Lin：*A Translation of Lao*

Tzu's Tao Te Ching and Wang Pi's Commentary. Ann Arbor：Center for Chinese Studies，University of Michigan，1977.

8. ［美］韩禄伯：《老子〈道德经〉——最新发现马王堆帛书新译》，New York：Ballantine Books，1989.（Henricks, R. G.：*Lao-Tzu Te-Tao Ching—A New Translation Based on the Recenthy Discovered Ma-wany-tui Texts*，New York：Ballantine Books，1989.）

9. 陈乃扬：《英译老子》，上海：上海外语教育出版社 2012 年版。

Unit Eight
Zhuang Zi (《庄子》)

I. 背景简介

Zhuang Zi (about 396 B. C. – 286 B. C.),
whose given name was Zhou, was born in Meng,
the State of Song in Warring States Period (now to
north-eastern Shangqiu, Henan province). He was
a great philosopher of the Warring States Period,
and an important representative of Taoism.

Zhuang Zi, which is generally regarded as the
work written by Zhuang Zi, reflects his main
thoughts with Taoism as the core. The basic attribute
of Taoism is "inaction and invisibility". The basic
spirit of Taoism is keeping natural, which, in
Taoism, is considered as an ideal state. Zhuang Zi

Zhuang Zi (**about** 396 B. C – 286 B. C)

thinks that it is the final target for people to return to the original nature and a natural state.
Zhuang Zi advocates a natural outlook on life, showing a pursuit of spiritual freedom and
personal independence. He criticizes the bondage imposed on the human nature by rites and
music, benevolence and justice. From the book we can find his typical personality of
aloofness from the world and arrogant reserve, which sets a striking contrast with genial,
cultured and elegant Confucian character, honest, sincere and thrifty.

The basis of Zhuang Zi's theory is relativism. He blurs out the differences between concrete matters, exaggerates their similarities, and claims that "everything is all the same in the world". He gains a complete emancipation in spirit through aloofness from the mortal life and through indifference to the differences between right and wrong, matter and self-gene, life and death. In Zhuang Zi's thought there is a fundamental element of dialectics. He thinks matter can be divided limitlessly, and contradiction can be inverted. Once he says, "It is possible to turn the rotten into the real and ethereal, and vice versa. So it is said one stroke can run through the world."

Ⅱ. 文本选读

Chapter 1 **Wandering in Absolute Freedom**

In the northern Sea there is a kind of fish by the name of *kun*, whose size covers thousands of *li*. The fish metamorphoses[①] into a kind of bird by the name of *peng*, whose back covers thousands of *li*. When it rises in flight, its wings are like clouds that hang from the sky. When the wind blows over the sea, the *peng* moves to the South Sea, the Celestial Pond.

According to *Qi Xie*, a collection of mysterious stories, "On its journey to the South Sea, the *peng* flaps sprays for 3,000 *li* and soars to a height of 90,000 *li* at the windy time of June." The air, the dusts and the microbes float in the sky at the breath of the wind. Does the sky display the blueness as its true color? Or does it reach an unattainable distance? When the *peng* looks from above, it must have observed a similar sight.

If a mass of water is not deep enough, it will not be able to float large ships. When you pour a cup of water into a hole on the floor, a straw can sail on it as a boat, but a cup will get stuck in it for the water is too shallow and the vessel is too large. If the wind is not strong enough, it will not be able to bear large wings. Therefore, the *peng* must have a strong wind under it as its support so as to soar to a height of 90,000 *li*. Only then can it brave the blue sky and clear all obstacles on its southward journey.

A cicada and a turtle-dove derided the *peng*, saying, "We fly upward until we alight on an elm or a sandal tree. Sometimes when we cannot make it, we just fall back to the ground. What's the sense of soaring to a height of 90,000 *li* on your journey to the south?" If you are going to the green suburbs, you only have to bring three meals and you will come back with a full stomach. If you are going 100 *li* away, you have to bring enough grain to last you three months. How could these two little creatures know about all this?

Little learning does not come up to great learning; the short-lived does not come up to the long-lived. How do we know that this is the case? The fungi that sprout in the morning and die before evening do not know the alternation of night and day; cicadas do not know the alternation of spring and autumn. Those are cases of the short-lived. In the south of the state of Chu there is a miraculous tortoise, for whom each spring or autumn lasts 500 years; in the remote ages there was a huge toon three, for which each spring or autumn lasted 8,000 years. Those are cases of the long-lived. But today, Pengzu, who lived over 700 years, is uniquely acknowledged for his longevity. It is not lamentable that he is an object of envy to all!

Tang, the first king of the Shang Dynasty, asked his minister Ji a similar question.

Tang asked Ji, "Are there limits up and down, east and west, north and south?"

Ji answered, "There are limits beyond limits. In the remote and barren north, there is a dark sea, the Celestial Pond, where lives a kind of fish by the name of *kun*, whose size covers thousands of *li*. There also lives a kind of bird by the name of *peng*, whose back is like a lofty mountain and whose wings are like clouds that hang from the sky. Soaring like a whirlwind to a height of 90,000 *li*, the *peng* flies above the heavy clouds and against the blue sky on its southward journey toward the South Sea. A quail in the marsh laughed at the *peng*, saying, 'where does he think he's going? I hop and skip and fly up, but I never fly up more than a dozen meters before I come down and hover above the reeds. That's the highest I ever fly! And where does he think he's going?'"

Such is the difference between the small and the great.

For those who are intelligent enough to take a minor office, well-behaved enough to impress a district, virtuous enough to please a lord and to win the confidence of a state, their complacency is like that of the cicada, the turtle-dove or the quail. Song Rongzi[②] is a philosopher who mocks at them, for he himself does not feel flattered when the whole world praises him and does not feel discouraged when the whole world blames him. He can differentiate the internal from the external; he can distinguish between honor and disgrace. But that is all he can do. Although he is not entangled in worldly affairs, he still has something unattained.

Then there is Lie Zi③, who can travel by riding the wind in a free and easy manner, returning to earth in fifteen days. He is never entangled in worldly fortunes, but although he does not have to walk, he is still dependent on something.

However, suppose someone rides on the true course of heaven and earth and harnesses the changes of the six vital elements④ of yin, yang, wind, rain, darkness and brightness to travel in the infinite. What is there for him to be dependent on?

Therefore, as the saying goes, "The perfect man cares for no self; the holy man cares for no merit; the sage cares for no name."

King Yao wished to abdicate his throne to Xu You⑤, saying, "If you do not put out the torch fire when the sun or the moon is shining, isn't it hard to see the torch light? If you continue to water the fields when timely rains are falling, isn't it a waste of labor? If you take the throne, the world will be in good order. Yet I am now still vainly occupying the place, and I consider myself inadequate. Please allow me to hand over the empire to you."

Xu You answered, "Since you took over the throne, the empire has been in good order. If I were to take your place, would I be seeking after name? Since name is but the shadow of reality, do you want me to be the shadow? The wren that builds a nest in the deep forest occupies only a single branch; the mole that drinks from the river takes only a bellyful. Go back, my lord, and forget about it. I have no need for the empire. Even if the cook is not attending to his duties, the priest at the offering ceremony will not come to the kitchen to do it for him."

Jianwu sought for advice from Lian Shu, "I heard Jie Yu⑥ telling high tales, impressive but fantastic, never coming to the point. I was confounded by his words—boundless as the Milky Way and quite unreasonable."

Lian Shu asked, "What did he say?"

"He said, 'There is a holy man living on the faraway Mount Guye. With his skin as white as ice and snow, he is as amiable as a virgin. He does not eat the grains, but sucks the wind, drinks the dew, rides on the cloud, harnesses the flying dragon and roams beyond the four seas. By concentrating his spiritual power, he protects the creatures from the plague and ensures a bumper harvest.' I think his tale is ridiculous and simply do not believe it."

Lian Shu said, "Indeed! We cannot share the beautiful patterns and colors with a blind man; we cannot share the music of bells and drums with a deaf man. There is not only physical blindness and deafness, but also mental ones. These words apply to you exactly. This holy man with all his integrity can merge everything under heaven into one. When the people expect him to rule over the world, how can he busy himself in doing anything about it? Nothing can harm this holy man. He will neither be drowned in a great flood that rises to the sky nor feel the heat in a drought that melts the metal and the rocks and scorches the earth and the hills. When from his dust and chaff alone you can mould wise kings like Yao and Shun, how can he be willing to bother himself with worldly affairs?"

"A man from the state of Song carried some ceremonial caps to the state of Yue for sale. But the men in Yue used to cut off their hair and tattoo their bodies, so the caps were useless to them."

"King Yao brought order to the people in the empire and reigned successfully over the land within the four seas. After his return from his visit to the Holy Four[7] on Mount Guye north of the Fen River, he lost his interest in his rule over the land."

Hui Zi[8] said to Zhuang Zi, "The marquis of Wei gave me some seeds to grow huge gourds. I planted them and they bore gourds big enough to hold five bushels of grain. As containers, they were not strong enough to hold the water or the soup; as ladles when they were cut in two, they were too large to be used anywhere. They were large enough, but I broke them up because they were useless."

Zhuang Zi said, "You are certainly not well versed in using big things. There was a man in the state of Song who was an expert in making an ointment for chapped hands. For generations, the family had been working on bleaching silk floss as its occupation. A traveler heard about the ointment and offered a hundred pieces of gold for the recipe. The Song man gathered the family members together and said, 'We have been working on bleaching silk floss for generations and have earned no more than a few pieces of gold. Now that we can make a hundred pieces of gold within one morning by selling the recipe, I propose we sell it to him.' The traveler got the recipe and offered it to the Duke of Wu, who was at war with the state of Yue. The Duke of Wu made him commander of his fleet, which fought a naval battle that winter with the men of Yue, and put them to rout. The traveler was awarded a piece of occupied land. By the same recipe for chapped hands, one man gained a piece of land while others never went beyond bleaching the silk floss—it is because they used it in different ways. Now that you have gourds big enough to hold five bushels, why don't you tie them around your waist as buoys when you go floating over the river or the lake instead of worrying that they are too large to be used anywhere? It seems to me that your mind is not open enough yet."

Hui Zi said to Zhuang Zi, "I have a big tree people call Tree of the Heaven. Its trunk is so gnarled and knotty that a carpenter can hardly measure it with his inky line; its branches are so twisted that squares and compasses can hardly be applied to them. It stands by the road, but no carpenter would give it a glance. Now your words are like my tree—so big and useless that no one would care to listen to you."

Zhuang Zi said, "Haven't you ever seen a wild cat or a weasel? It crouches on the ground and lies I wait for its prey. Right and left it pounces, up and down it leaps until it happens to be caught by the snare and dies in the trap. Then there is the yak, as big as the clouds hanging from the sky. Big as it is, it cannot catch rats or mice. Now you have a big tree, but are worried about its uselessness. Why don't you plant it in the land of nothingness, a wilderness where nothing grows and no one comes? There you may roam idly around it and sleep carefreely beneath it. No one will apply an axe to it or do any harm to it. Useless as it is, how can it ever come to harm?"

(Translated by Wang Rongpei)

Chapter 17 **Autumn Floods**（Excerpted）

At the time of autumn floods when hundreds of streams poured into the Yellow River, the torrents were so violent that it was impossible to distinguish an ox from a horse from the other side of the river. Then the River God was overwhelmed with joy, feeling that all the beauty under the heaven belonged to him alone. Down the river he travelled east until he reached the North Sea. Looking eastward at the boundless expanse of water, he changed his countenance[9] and sighed to the Sea God, saying, "As the popular saying goes, 'There are men who have heard a lot about Tao but still think that no one can surpass them.' I am one of such men. Upon hearing people belittle Confucius' learning and humiliate Bo Yi's[10] righteousness, I simply could not believe a word they said. Now that I have seen your boundless expanse, I realize that I would have been in danger if I had not come to you. I would always be sneered at by those who are well-versed in Tao."

The Sea God said, "You cannot discuss the sea with a frog at the bottom of a well because it is confined to its dwelling place; you cannot discuss ice with a summer moth because it is limited to one season; you cannot discuss Tao with a bookworm because he is restrained to the book knowledge. Now that you have left the riverside and seen the vast sea, you are aware of your insignificance. Thus it is possible now to discuss Tao with you. Of all the waters under the heaven, nothing is greater than the sea. It receives the endless flow of ten thousand rivers but it is never full. It is leaking endlessly but it is never empty. It does not change with spring or autumn; it does not know flood or drought. It holds so much more water than the Yangtze River and the Yellow River that it is absolutely beyond measure. Yet I am never conceited about the amount. I assume my shape form the heaven and the earth, and accumulate my vigor from *yin* and *yang*. I stay here between the heaven and the earth, just like a small stone or a small tree on a huge mountain. How can I over-estimate myself when I know that I am so insignificant! Don't the four seas between the heaven and the earth resemble small holes in a large swamp? Don't the central states within the four seas resemble grains of millet in a large granary? There are hundreds and thousands of things in the world; humanity is but one of them. Human beings live in regions where grains grow and where boats and carts come and go; an individual man is but one of them. Compared with the hundreds and thousands of things, isn't an individual man but a tiny down[①] on a horse? The succession of the five kings, the strife between the three emperors, the worries of the humane gentleman, and the efforts of the capable officials—all is no more than this. Bo Yi gained fame by refusing to accept the throne; Confucius displayed his learning by lecturing all around. Isn't this self-lauding very much the same as what you did not long ago about your water?"

The River God said, "In that case, can I take the heaven and the earth as something great and the tiny down as something small?"

The Sea God said, "No, you can't. There is no limit for the size of things, no stand-still for time, no set rules for gains and losses, and no fixed point for beginning and ending. Therefore, with a sharp observation for everything far and near, men of great intelligence neither regards the small as insignificant nor regards the large as important, for they know that there is no limit for the size of things. With a profound knowledge of things past and present, they neither worry about the remote past nor attempt to seize the immediate present, for they know that there is no stand-still for time. With a keen insight into gains and losses, they neither rejoice over gains nor grieve over losses, for they know that there are no set rules for gains and losses. With a clear understanding of the smooth passage of life and death, they neither take life as a pleasure nor take death as a disaster; for they know that there is no fixed point for beginning and ending. If you make a calculation, you will find that what man knows is much less than what he does not know and that the time when man is alive is much shorter than the time when he is dead. If you try to pursue unlimited knowledge with your limited life, you will only be puzzled and will achieve nothing. From this point of view, how can you take the tiny down as something small and take the heaven and the earth as something great?"

The River God said, "The worldly men are all of the opinion that the tiniest thing has no from and the largest thing has no boundary. Is that true?"

The Sea God said, "From the viewpoint of the small, you cannot get a comprehensive picture of the large; from the viewpoint of large, you cannot discern the distinctive features of the small. The tiny is the smallest of the small; the huge is the largest of the large. The large and the small have their respective advantages, depending on the circumstances. The small and the large are confined to things with forms while formless things are indivisible and boundless things are inexhaustible. What can be verbalized is something large; what can be mentally visualized is something small; what can be neither verbalized nor mentally visualized has nothing to do with smallness or largeness. "

"Therefore, the truly great man neither harms others nor brags about his humaneness or graces. He neither seeks after profit nor despises the profit-seekers. He neither grabs from wealth and property nor prides himself from declining them. He neither relies on others nor lauds over his self-reliance nor belittles avarice. He neither complies with the vulgar world nor aims at eccentricity. He neither acts differently from others nor scorns the flatterers. He neither takes position and stipend as stimuli nor takes penalty and humiliation as disgrace. He knows that right and wrong cannot be distinguished and that small and great cannot be defined. "

The Sea God said, "From the viewpoint of Tao, there is nothing noble or mean; from the viewpoint of things, an individual often thinks highly of himself and thinks lowly of others; from the viewpoint of worldly learning, the distinction lies outside things themselves. From the viewpoint of distinctions, if we say that something is large because it is relatively large, then everything can be said to be large. If we say that something is small because it is relatively small, then everything can be said to be small. Once you know why the heaven and the earth are like grains of millet and why a tiny down is like a hill, you will understand the distinctions between large and small. From the viewpoint of functions, if we say that something is useful because it is useful in one respect, then everything can be said to be useful. If we say that something is useless in another respect, then everything can be said to be useless. Once you know that east and west are opposite and mutually indispensable, you will understand the functions and usages of things. From the viewpoint of preference, if we say that something is right because it is right in one sense, then everything can be said to be right. If we say that something is wrong because it is wrong in another sense, then everything can be said to be wrong. Once you know that both King Yao and King Jie[12] justified himself and condemned the other, you will understand the preferences of things."

"In the past, when King Yao abdicated his throne to Shun and the latter became the king; when Prince Kuai[13] in the state of Yan abdicated his throne to Zi Zhi[14], the latter was killed. Tang and Wu seized the throne by resorting to military forces while Baigong Sheng[15] failed in a like attempt. From the seizure and abduction of power, and from the deeds of King Yao and the deeds of King Jie, it can be seen that the noble or the mean is but a matter of timing: there are no fixed rules for it. A battering-ram can be used to knock down a city-wall but cannot be used to fill a hole, for the uses of the implements are different. A good steed can gallop a thousand *li* a day but cannot equal a cat or weasels in catching the mice, for the skills of the animals are different. An owl can catch fleas and see the tip of a down at night but cannot see a hill with its eyes wide open at daytime, for the inborn natures of the birds are different. People often say, 'Why don't you adopt the right and discard the wrong? Why don't you adopt order and discard disorder?' People say this because they do not know the law of heaven and earth or nature of things in the world. This is like saying 'Adopt the heaven and discard the earth; adopt *yin* and discard *yang*', which is clearly impossible. If one keeps on blabbing about this incessantly, he is either stupid or absurd. The Three Emperors and Five Kings abdicated their thrones in different forms; the three dynasties of Xia, Shang and Zhou succeeded in different ways. Those who are ill-timed and run counter to the people's will are called usurpers; those who are well-timed and conform to the people's will are called men of humaneness and righteousness. Keep your mouth shut, River God! How can you know the distinction between the noble and the mean, between the large and the small?"

The River God said, "In that case, what am I to do and what am I not to do? What am I to do at all when I accept or reject something, when I adopt or discard something?"

The Sea God said, "From the viewpoint of Tao, nothing can be called noble or mean because the noble and the mean succeed each other endlessly. Don't stick to one point of view, or you will be away from Tao. Nothing can be called too little or too much because the little and the much transform into each other. Don't adhere to one way of behavior, or you will run counter to Tao. Be as solemn as the ruler of a state who is fair and just, and be as dispassionate as the deity of the consecration who is disinterested and unbiased. Be as broad-minded as the water which is all-pervasive and boundless. If your mind is all-embracing, whom are you to show special favor to? This is called impartiality. Since all things are equal, where lies the long and the short of anything? While Tao is infinite, all other things have their life and death, impermanent in their perfection. Now better, now worse, they never remain in the same state. Past years cannot be restored; flowing time cannot be stopped. They grow and decay; they wax and wane — there is a beginning for every ending. That is how we describe he general tendency of Tao and the universal truth of things. The life of things elapses as swiftly as a galloping horse, changing in every movement and shifting at any time. What is to be done? What is not to be done? You only have to wait and see, for everything will follow its natural course of development."

The River God said, "In that case, what is to be valued about Tao?"

The Sea God said, "Those who are well verse in Tao will be acquainted with the universal truth of things; those who are acquainted with the universal truth of things will adapt themselves to the situation; those who adapt themselves to the situation will not get themselves harmed by things. Those who are endowed with perfect virtue will not be burnt by fire, or drowned by water, or hurt by heat or cold, or injured by birds and beats of prey. This does not mean that they are immune to the injuries, but that they are aware of the fortune and misfortune. Not disturbed by whatever comes to them, they are prudent in making their decisions, thus avoiding injuries. Therefore, it is said, 'The inborn human nature resides within and the enforced human behaviors reside without while perfect virtue lies in the inborn nature.' Once you understand the inborn nature and the enforced behaviors, you will adapt yourself to the situation and make the right decision. By so doing, you will be able to restore your inborn nature and be said to have reached perfection."

[...]

(Translated by Wang Rongpei)

Ⅲ. 难点释义

① metamorphose，变形，变质。

② Song Rongzi，宋荣子，又名宋钘，战国时期的思想家。

③ Lie Zi，列子，名寇，又名御寇，相传是战国前期的道家人。其学道于黄帝老子，主张清静无为。后汉班固《艺文志》"道家"有《列子》八卷，已佚。

④ the six vital elements，六气。指自然气候变化的六种现象，即阴、阳、风、雨、晦、明。

⑤ Xu You，许由，上古时代高尚清节之士。相传尧帝要把君位让给他，他推辞不受，逃于箕山下，农耕而食；尧帝又让他做九州长官，他到颍水边洗耳，表示不愿听到这些世俗浊言。

⑥ Jie Yu，接舆，春秋楚国的著名隐士，姓陆，名通，字接舆。平时"躬耕以食"，因对当时社会不满，剪去头发，佯狂不仕，所以也被人们称为"楚狂接舆"。

⑦ the Holy Four，四子。旧注指王倪、齧（niè）缺、被衣、许由四人，实为虚构人物。

⑧ Hui Zi，惠子，战国中期著名政治家、辩客和哲学家。惠子是合纵抗秦主张最主要的组织者和支持者。

⑨ countenance，表情；面孔。

⑩ Bo Yi，伯夷，商末孤竹国孤竹君的长子，姓墨胎氏，名允。相传孤竹君欲以次子叔齐为继承人，孤竹君死后，叔齐让位于伯夷，伯夷不受，而叔齐也不肯登位，先后都逃到周国。

⑪ down，绒毛；汗毛。

⑫ King Jie，桀，又名夏桀，是夏朝第16代君主发之子，在位52年（前1818—前1766），生卒年不详。其人文武双全，赤手可以把铁钩拉直，荒淫无度，暴虐无道。商汤起兵伐桀，桀被放逐而饿死。

⑬ Prince Kuai，燕王哙，战国时期的燕国国君。

⑭ Zi Zhi，子之。战国时期燕国人，燕王哙于前320年即位后，任用子之为燕相，子之为相邦时，办事果断，善于监督考核臣属，得到燕王的赏识和重用。

⑮ Baigong Sheng，白公胜。春秋末期楚国大夫，其父为郑人所杀，欲伐郑报仇而未能，后自缢而死。

Ⅳ. 问题思考

1. What is the highlights of Zhuang Zi's "Absolute Freedom"? And how do you interpret such a freedom?

2. "The perfect man cares for no self; the holy man cares for no merit; the sage cares for no name." In what way should we balance oneself, merit, and name in modern society?

3. What is your comment on Hui Zi's saying "Now your words are like my tree, so big and useless that no one would care to listen to you"?

4. Zhuang Zi said the world "does not need governing; in fact it should not be governed", and, "Good order results spontaneously when things are let alone." To what extent do you agree with this saying? Please illustrate your idea with more examples.

5. Despite sharing some foundational ideas, the two Daoist works *Lao Zi* (*Dao De Jing*) and *Zhuang Zi* discuss the Way very differently. Please briefly summarize the differences.

Ⅴ. 经典导读

庄子（约前369—前286），名周，战国时期著名思想家、哲学家、文学家。是道家学派的代表人物，老子思想的继承和发展者。后世将他与老子并称为"老庄"。当代学者流沙河曾对庄子的为人作了四点概括，"一曰立场，站在环中。二曰方法，信奉无为。三曰理想，追慕泽稚。四曰修养，紧守心斋"。

《秋水》篇与秋水秋色

《庄子》一书亦称《南华经》，共三十三篇。现在通行的《庄子》是郭象注本，包括《内篇》七，《外篇》十五，《杂篇》十一。一般认为，《内篇》为庄子自作，《外篇》和《杂篇》则基本是其弟子和后学所作。有一些篇目则被认为肯定不是庄子学派的思想，如《盗跖》、《说剑》等。《内篇》最集中表现庄子哲学的是《齐物论》、《逍遥游》、《大宗师》等。

《庄子》的核心思想大致可以概括为以下三个方面：

第一，继承和发展老子的"道"，泯灭一切是非标准的相对主义。庄子把老子的道解释为精神的本体，化育万物的本根。人们修养得道，将自己视为自然一物，忘怀自我，淡情寡欲，不计得失，不虑生死，达到天人合一。将老子辩证法的相对性加以夸大，发展为相对主义，认为事物的大小、寿夭、善恶、美丑都是相对而言，进而不谴是非，否定评判是非的一切客观标准。从《秋水》"河伯观海"的寓言中，我们可以读到这些。

第二，主张无为治国，反对礼法治国。庄子与老子一样，主张无为治国，任其自然，认为"绝圣弃知而天下大治"，君主要"无容私"，"汝游心于淡，合气与漠，顺物自然而无容私焉，而天下治矣。"庄子心中的"至德之世"，主要体现为"不尚贤，不使能，上如标枝，民如野鹿。端正而不知以为义，相爱而不知以为仁，实而不知以为忠，当而不知以为信，蠢动而相使，不以为赐。是故行而无迹，事而无传"。庄子反对儒家的以礼法治国和法家的以法律治国。庄子认为，儒家的仁义、礼法违背人性，使百姓"失其朴"。庄子反对儒家和法家的治国方法的核心，是以知治国。庄子认为，知是"争之器"，而且知往往会被大盗所利用，所谓"盗亦有道"，便是如此。

第三，一切顺应自然，无待无为的宿命论。庄子追求绝对的精神自由，逍遥无为，即不受时间和空间的任何限制，超越物质世界的束缚，做到无名、无功、无己、无待、无为。他在《养生主》中的名言充分表明了这种宿命论："吾生也有涯，而知也无涯。以有涯随无涯，殆矣。已而为知者，殆而已矣。为善无近名，为恶无近刑，缘督以为经，可以保身，可以全生，可以养亲，可以尽年"，"依乎天理，批大郤，导大窾，因其自然。"庄子推崇"道法自然"，一生以做官为名缰利锁。司马迁《史记·庄子传》写到庄子这么一件事：楚威王听说庄子很贤良，派人带上厚礼，想聘其为相。庄子笑着对使者说："你快走吧，别玷污我。我宁可在泥涂中玩玩游戏，自得其乐，也不会被什么官职名位绑着，落得个不自在。庄子我一辈子不做官，笑傲于江湖。”

《逍遥游》是《庄子》的代表篇目之一，充满奇特的想象和浪漫的色彩，寓说理于寓言之中，生动的比喻寓言深刻，浅显易懂。前半篇以鲲鹏为主，反复引譬设喻，层层否定，推论世间万物无论大小寿夭，凡是受到时间、空间的限制和物质世界的束缚，就不可能达到逍遥的境界。后半篇以辩论的形式，反复引譬设喻，层层递进，分别阐述圣人无名、神人无功、至人无己。指出如想真正达到自由自在的境界，就必须"无己"、"无功"、"无名"。做到无为才能达到逍遥。第三部分论述什么是真正的有用和无用，说明不能为物所滞，要把无用当作有用，进一步表达了庄子本人反对积极投身社会，志在不受任何拘束，追求悠然自得的生活旨趣，喻指功名利禄是人生的束缚，只有彻底摆脱功名利禄的束缚，才能获得充分的自由。

《秋水》是《庄子》的又一重要长篇，用篇首的两个字作为篇名，主要讨论人应怎样去认识外物。全篇由两大部分组成。前一部分写北海海神跟河神的谈话，一问一答，一气呵成，构成本篇的主体。后一部分写了六个寓言故事，每个寓言故事自成一体，各不关联，跟前一部分海神与河神的对话也没有任何结构上的关联，对全篇主题的表达可谓毫无帮助，似有游离之嫌。

庄子的文章气势磅礴，纵横恣肆。文章的结构没有固定模式，《内篇》以题概篇，《外篇》和《杂篇》取篇首关键词为篇名，但并非后人所加。结构上分总自然，意到笔随，得心应手，千姿百态，想象奇特，寓意深远。庄子文章的寓言将自然万物赋予灵性，历史人物加以虚构，寓言的主题具有多义性，寓言形象的客观含义往往超越作家的主观动机，构成形象大于思想的特征。庄子文章的风格嬉笑怒骂，无拘无束；他的文笔变化多端，具有浓厚的浪漫主义色彩和幽默讽刺的意味，对后世的文学语言具有深远的影响。

一般说来，孔子思想的核心是仁，老子思想的核心是清静无为，但人们对庄子思想的评价则显得褒贬不一。历代对《庄子》的解读都会烙上时代印记，根据当时的背景和人们的需求对庄子寓言的主题有所折中或曲解。因此，阅读《庄子》时必须疏理庄学三义：本义、释义和取义。按照《中国大百科全书》的说法，庄子在天道观上是唯心主义、泛神论；在人道观上是相对主义、宿命论；在认识论上是相对主义、不可知论；在"天人"之辩和"名实"之辩方面是相对主义。对庄子哲学思想的评价，褒贬不一。有人认为庄子的思想反映了没落奴隶主贵族的意识，是主观唯心主义和相对主义；也有人认为，庄子的思想代表了自由农民的意识，具有唯物主义的倾向；还有人认为，庄子在人生论上有宿命论的因素。虽然如此，但古往今来，庄子还是受到了极高的评价。明末清初的文学家金圣叹，就把《庄子》列为"六才子书"之首。（金圣叹说的"六才子"是庄周、屈原、司马迁、杜甫、施耐庵、王实甫。）鲁迅在其《汉文学史纲要》中对庄子的散文也给予了高度的评价——"汪洋阖，仪态万方，晚周诸子之作，莫能先也。"郭沫若认为，"庄子在中国文化史上是一个特异的存在，他不仅是一位出类的思想家，而且是一位拔萃的文学家，""秦汉以来的一部中国文学史，差不多大半是在他的影响之下发展。"

Ⅵ. 译本链接

1. James Legge, *The Sacred Books of the East*, London: Oxford University Press, 1891.

2. Burton Watson, *Chuang Tzu: Basic Writings*, New York: Columbia University Press, 1964.

3. Angus Charles Graham, *Chuang-tzu: The Seven Inner Chapters and Other Writings from the Book Chuang-tzu*, London: George Allen & Unvoin, 1982.

4. 冯友兰英译：《庄子》，北京：外文出版社 1989 年版。

5. 汪榕培英译：《庄子》，长沙：湖南人民出版社 1997 年版。

Unit Nine
Wenxin Diaolong （《文心雕龙》）

Ⅰ. 背景简介

Liu Xie（about 465 – 520）, alias Yanhe, was a native of Ju County, now in Shandong Province. He was probably born and then grew up in Jingkou, the present Zhenjiang City in Jiangsu Province. He was an accomplished Confucian and Buddhist scholar; he did not enjoy any social or literary distinction in his lifetime. According to "The Life of Liu Xie" in *The History of the Liang Dynasty*, he came from a poor family, his father died when he was still young, and he never married. At the age of 23 or 24, he started living in the Dinglin Temple under the

Liu Xie（**about** 465 – 520）

distinguished Buddhist monk Seng You. As a result, Liu became well versed in Buddhist sutras. Liu Xie probably wrote *Wenxin Diaolong* in the same period, spending a total of five to six years on the book and completing it in about A. D. 501.

It is useful to note that the systematic structure of *Wenxin Diaolong* seems to resemble that of a Buddhist sutra more than a typical text of Chinese literary criticism. Liu Xie proves to be illusive, because he declares in the last chapter that the organization of the book into 50 chapters is modeled on the cosmological system embodied in *The Book of Changes*. Besides, he also explicitly considers himself a Confucian disciple, as shown by his remarks in the postscript:

At the age of seven, I dreamed of colorful clouds like brocade, and I climbed up to pick them. After 30, I dreamed of following Confucius southward, holding red-lacquered vessels of rites in hand. I woke up in the morning in jubilance. Hard as it was to behold the Saint, he descended in the dream of an obscure fellow like me!

(Chapter 50, *My Intentions, or Postscript*)

Actually, *Wenxin Diaolong* did not gain immediate recognition. Liu Xie tried to bring it to the attention of Shen Yue, the literary doyen of his time. The story goes that because Shen was hard to approach, Liu Xie pretended to be a peddler and waited outside Shen's house. When Shen Yue appeared, Liu stepped in front of Shen's carriage and presented the book. Shen was said to judge it highly.

After staying for about ten years in Dinglin Temple, Liu Xie left for an official career in A. D. 503, consecutively taking up several minor positions in the court. For some time, he was attendant to Xiao Tong the Crown Prince (501 – 531), a patron of literature. This association could have given the Prince inspiration when he compiled *the Literary Anthology*, one of the most influential literary anthologies in Chinese history. In A. D. 520, Liu Xie took Buddhist vows in Dinglin Temple and died one year later.

A possible paraphrase of the book title would be "the expression of feeling and thought in embellished language". "Dragon-Carving" (雕龙) and "the Literary Mind" (文心) combines the bipartite constitution of writing—language and the mind. "Dragon carving" refers to the use of language and linguistic embellishments. "Literary mind" refers to what is manifest in literary composition. The character *xin*, here translated as mind, is a polysemant referring to both mind and heart. Therefore, the literary mind represents the feeling and thinking person.

Wenxin Diaolong was a convergence and culmination of early statements on literature; which explored many other important issues of literature and literary criticism. Its 50 chapters fall neatly into two parts. The first part, consisting of the first 25 chapters, begins by providing a general statement of Liu Xie's philosophy of literature and critical framework. Then Chapters 6 through 25 cover studies of various literary genres. The second part consists of the remaining 25 chapters, including the postscript. It covers such critical issues as literary imagination, style, rhetoric, literary history, literary appreciation, and the integrity of the author's character.

Running up to 37,000 characters in 50 chapters, Liu Xie's magnum corpus *Wenxin Diaolong* was the single longest treatise in Chinese literary criticism up to its time. Over the centuries, but especially since the Qing Dynasty, *Wenxin Diaolong* has been regarded as a classic of literary criticism. Today, as the numerous studies and modern Chinese translations can attest, *Wenxin Diaolong* "reigns supreme in the field of traditional literary scholarship" —so much so that studies of this literary text have achieved a quasi-disciplinary status with its own name: Dragonology.

Wenxin Diaolong is more than a work of literary criticism. It is also a classic text of Chinese culture. In it Liu Xie develops a philosophy of literature that embodies the literary spirit of Chinese culture.

Ⅱ. 文本选读
Chapter 26   Shensi, or Imagination

26.1 An ancient said, "my physical form is on the sea; my heart lingers in the court." This is "shensi"[①], or imagination, at work. A writer's imagination travels far. When he is absorbed in silent thought[②], his mind ranges across a thousand years; without opening his eyes, his vision penetrates a distance of ten thousand *li*. He produces pearl-like sounds in recitation and conjures up whirling winds and rolling clouds[③] before his eyes. Is this not due to the magical power of imagination! The mystery of imagination lies in the merging of the spirit with the physical world[④]. Vital energy holds the key to the spirit, which resides in the heart. Words and speech control the hub of the physical world, which greets the ears and the eyes. When the hub works smoothly, no forms of the world can be hidden. When the key is clogged, the spirit wants to flee.

26. 2 Therefore, mental void and emotional tranquility[5] are essential for cultivating literary thought. Dredge the heart, purify the spirit. Use diligence to accumulate knowledge, judgment to enrich talent, experience to achieve thorough understanding, taste to select language. Then with a heart of thorough understanding, one can start writing in accordance with the rules of prosody[6]; with a mind of unique perception, one can wield the writing-brush to capture the images in one's vision. This is the foremost art of writing and a main feature of composition.

26. 3 When imagination is bestirred, ten thousand avenues compete to open up. The shapeless is given shape[7]; the unformed begins to take form. If at this moment the writer ascends a mountain, his feeling will permeate the mountain. If he surveys the sea, his emotion will overflow the sea. Thus the capacity of his talent will sweep along with winds and clouds. Holding up his brush, he feels too overwhelmed by his vital energy to concentrate on the choice of words. When he finishes writing, he finds himself only half expressed. Why? Because ideas, being intangible, rush in like a miracle; words, being concrete, cannot be easily made ingenious. Ideas come from the mind; the choice of words is guided by ideas. Ideas and words can be so closely knit as to be in perfect harmony[8]; they can fit so badly as to fall totally apart. Sometimes a thought is close to the heart, but the writer's mind will wander to the end of the world in search of it. Sometimes an idea is right at hand, yet he cannot step over to get it, as if blocked by mountains and rivers. Therefore instead of racking his brains, a writer should nourish his heart and cultivate his art. To master the rules of writing and produce fine works, there is need to labor the mind.

26. 4 The talents of men are divided into the slow and the quick. Literary writings vary in length and weight. Sima Xiangru[9] spoiled a brush in his mouth while thinking. Yang Xiong[10] had nightmares after finishing a composition. Huan Tan[11] was taken ill because of painful thinking. Wang Chong[12] exhausted his vitality in rumination. Zhang Heng[13] spent a decade on his rhyme-prose about the capitals. Zuo Si[14] expended twelve years on his rhyme-prose about the capitals. These are grand compositions, but the products of slow thinking.

Some shorter pieces are completed with wondrous speed. The Prince of Huainan[15] wrote a work of rhyme-prose in one morning; Mei Gao[16] penned one right in front of the emperor. Cao Zhi[17] wrote as easily as if reciting a piece from memory; Wang Can[18] as quickly as if he had been prepared in advance. Ruan Yu[19] dispatched a letter on horseback; Mi Heng[20] drafted a report to the throne over a meal. Although they are short pieces, they showed the authors' nimble mind.

26.5 A quick-witted scholar has a clear grasp of the rules of composition. His mind works so fast that he can write without deliberation. A deliberate person tends to work his mind along winding paths. He weighs over all possibilities and uncertainties before starting to write. The quick writer achieves instant success; the careful writer makes accomplishments with longer delay. Quick or slow, they must rely on both learning and experience. I have never heard of anybody accomplishing anything who, lacking learning, works slowly, or having no talent, writes quickly.

Hence the two worries in writing—A slow mind languishes[21] in penury[22] of ideas; a verbose man jumbles. Experience and learning are food for overcoming poor ideas; a sense of unity is medicine for disorder. Experience, learning and a sense of unity together can assist the working of the mind.

26.6 Human feelings are subtle and complex; literary styles are diverse and changeable. Ingenious meaning may be extracted from coarse words; fresh ideas may come out of commonplace discussions. This is like weaving hemp into cloth[23] although the hemp is worthless in itself, the shuttle and the loom can turn it into valuable fabric. As for the subtleties of thought and intricacies of meaning between the lines, words cannot capture them fully and a writer's brush knows when to halt. The subtleties can only be illuminated by the most insightful; the laws of change can only be grasped by the most versatile. If Yi Yin cannot explain his art of cooking, if Wheelwright Bian cannot talk about his art of using the axe, there is some mystery indeed!

26.7 Summary: the spirit enters the world by way of images, thus the multitudes of feeling and emotion are born in literary writing. The world is comprehended through appearances; the mind responds with reason. Write according to the rules of prosody, and learn to use comparison and metaphor. Remember the rules of writing, diligence leads to success.

Chapter 31　Feeling and Art

31.1 The writings of the sages are called "wen zhang"[24], the bright and colorful. Is this not because they are works of art? Water by nature is fluid, plants solid. If one forms ripples and the other bears flowers, it shows how art depends on substance. However, without their colorful patterns, tigers and leopards would not be much different from dogs and sheep. Without the red varnish, armor made from rhinoceros-hide would lose its glamour. Thus substance must be complemented by art. In describing human spirit or physical forms, in organizing thoughts into words and committing words in writing, excellence comes from art.

31.2 There are three kinds of art: the art of patterns related to the five colors[25], the art of music related to the five tones[26], and the art of feeling related to the five natures. When the five colors are blended, pretty patterns come forth. When the five sound scales are harmonized, music is produced. When the five emotions[27] are stirred, works of literature appear. This is the way of Divine Reason.

31.3 *The Book of Filial Piety*[28] stipulates that words of mourning forego ornament. From this we can infer that the daily speech of a virtuous man is not necessarily unadorned. Lao Zi abhorred dishonesty, so he said, "Fine sounding words are untrue." But his book of five thousand characters is full of subtle beauty. He did not ignore art after all. When Zhuang Zi talked about using ingenious language to depict the physical forms of the world, he referred to ornament. When Han Feizi[29] mentioned strengthening an argument with linguistic art, he referred to embellishment. To use embellished language in argument and ornament in description represents the ultimate change in writing.

31.4 A careful study of *The Book of Filial Piety* and *Lao Zi* shows that ornateness or plainness of style is determined by the writer's temperament. A scrutiny of the words of Zhuang Zi and Han Feizi proves that excessiveness and extravagance result from the imbalance of matter and ornament. If one can trace back to the source to distinguish the clear stream from the turbid, if one can tell the deviant path from the right course, then he will be able to manipulate the art of ornament. Powder and paint can add to female beauty, but real charm comes from natural looks. Language can be adorned with art, but real force and beauty spring from the heart. Therefore, as feeling and thought are the warp of language, so words are the woof of thought and feeling. Only when the warp is set straight does the woof take shape; only when feeling and thought are well arrayed does language become smooth. This is an essential rule of writing.

31.5 In *The Book of Poetry* art is used to express genuine feeling. Later works of rhyme-prose counterfeit feeling for art. How do we know this? The airs and odes in *The Book of Poetry* were written as expressions of feeling and grievances. As their authors had feeling and grievances to convey to their ruler, so poetry became an outlet. However, writers of rhyme prose had no grievances or frustrations in their heart. They feigned feeling in order to win fame and theirs are works of counterfeit feeling. Writings that express genuine feeling are succinct and truthful; works of mere artistry are flowery and extravagant. Later writers, imitating the excessive rather than the truthful abandoned *The Book of Poetry* and turned instead to modern works of rhyme-prose. Consequently works of genuine feeling have become more and rarer while writings of mere artistry are flourishing.

31.6 Some people cherish worldly ambitions yet sing of secluded lives. Some are busy with worldly affairs yet write about unworldly joy. There is no authentic feeling in their works and their words are contrary to their thought. Peach and plum trees do not talk, but paths are trodden out to them by the fruit-gatherers. Orchids grown by men have no fragrance, because men are not inclined to grow orchids by temperament. If even trivial things like trees and flowers depend on feeling to nourish their fruits, how much more so does literature, whose central purpose it is to express feeling! If language belies feeling, what worth will the work have?

31.7 Therefore, language and ornaments are used to express ideas. If ornaments become excessive or the language is eccentric, ideas will only be obscured. That is why a cassia bait[30] and a line made of kingfishers' feathers[31] will only cause one to miss the catch. This agrees with the saying "Meaning is lost in embellishments". That is why a man once wore a coarse linen coat over brocade in order to avoid gaudiness. The image of the hexagram "grace"[32] in *The Book of Changes* traces its source to plain white: It values the natural color. A writer should arrange ideas in the right place and choose the right emotional tone; he should start writing only after his feeling and ideas are well sorted out; he should not allow form to overweigh substance or excessive ornament to overwhelm his heart; he should exalt the natural colors[33] of red and blue and reject the secondary colors of pink and purple. Only then can he be considered to have integrated ornament and substance and accomplished himself as a writer.

31.8 Summary: It is true indeed that words are perpetuated by art. When feeling rises from the heart, language becomes fertile and rich. The brocade made in Wu fades easily[34], the mallow-flower withers soon. Excessive ornament and destitute feeling, do not appeal to the taste.

(Translated by Yang Guobin)

Ⅲ. 难点释义

① Shensi，神思，是《文心雕龙》里的重要概念。相当于西方文艺理论体系中的"imagination"一词，即"想象"的意思。这是一种精神活动，与现代文论所说的形象思维相似。

② silent thought，虚静。这是刘勰从先秦道家和荀子那里引入文学创作并加以改造的理论，包含两层意思：一是虚才能全面接纳各种事物并很好地认识事物形象的各方面；二是虚才能在文学创作过程中排除干扰，专心一意，更好地驰骋想象，释放感情。

③ conjures up whirling winds and rolling clouds，意思是指呈现风云变幻的景象。

④ the merging of the spirit with the physical world，这里强调的是精神和外物一起活动，亦即思维或想象会受到外物的影响。

⑤ mental void and emotional tranquility，虚心和宁静。刘勰强调，文思的酝酿重在虚静，必须清除内心杂念，做到精神纯净。

⑥ the rules of prosody，声律规则。

⑦ shapeless is given shape，在没有定型的文思中构思形象。强调作家要有丰富的想象力。

⑧ Ideas and words can be so closely knit as to be in perfect harmony，本句强调文章的内容、作者的思想感情和文章的言辞三者必须结合紧密。只有这样，写出来的文章才能贴切而天衣无缝。

⑨ Sima Xiangru，司马相如，西汉著名辞赋家。相传他的文思很不敏捷，常常是笔浸在墨汁中，毛笔都被浸泡腐烂了，他也写不出好文章来。

⑩ Yang Xiong，扬雄，西汉官吏兼学者。西汉蜀郡成都（今四川成都郫县）人。少好学，口吃，博览群书，长于辞赋，为汉赋"四大家"之一。

⑪ Huan Tan，桓谭，东汉政治家、哲学家。他在《新论·祛蔽篇》中说，自己年少时羡慕扬雄文章写得好，因苦思太甚而发病卧床。

⑫ Wang Chong，王充，东汉哲学家，会稽上虞（今浙江绍兴）人。其代表作《论衡》是中国历史上一部不朽的无神论著作。

⑬ Zhang Heng，张衡，东汉著名天文学家、文学家、思想家，南阳西鄂（今河南省南阳市石桥镇）人。虽然他发明了地动仪、浑天仪、指南车，把中国古代自然科学和哲学推向了一个新的高度，但据《后汉书·张衡传》说，张衡学习班固的《两都赋》作《二京赋》（《西京赋》、《东京赋》），总共花了十年时间。

⑭ Zuo Si，左思，西晋著名文人。《晋书》上说，左思《三都赋》的构思写作花了十余年时间。

⑮ The Prince of Huainan，淮南王刘安。他接受汉文帝的诏令，文思泉涌，仅用一个早晨的时间就写完了《离骚赋》。

⑯ Mei Gao，枚皋，西汉辞赋家枚乘之子。17 岁时上书梁共王，被召为郎，长期当武帝文学侍从。皋以文思敏捷著称。

⑰ Cao Zhi，曹植，三国时期的魏国诗人，文学家。沛国谯（今安徽省亳州市）人，字子建，是曹操与武宣卞皇后所生第三子。曹植才华横溢，曾以《七步诗》闻名天下。据记载，曹植拿着木片写文章，好像把背诵过的文章抄写下来一样。

⑱ Wang Can，王粲，山阳高平人，三国时曹魏名臣，著名文学家。他举笔便成，

好似预先写好了文章。

⑲ Ruan Yu，阮瑀，陈留尉氏（今属河南开封市）人，东汉文学家，建安七子之一，阮瑀的儿子阮籍位列"竹林七贤"之一，文章写得很出色。

⑳ Mi Heng，祢衡，东汉末年名士，文学家。与孔融等人亲善。后因出言不逊触怒曹操，被遣送至荆州。他的天赋极高，目所一见，辄诵于口，耳所暂闻，不忘于心，"博闻强记之能，亦无人能及"。

㉑ languish，憔悴。

㉒ penury，贫穷的。

㉓ weaving hemp into cloth，这里以织造原料麻的质量虽差，但经过加工，依然可以成为上乘之作，来比喻运用想象进行文学的创作构思。

㉔ "wen zhang"，这里的文章指纹彩显明，不是文章作品的意思。绘画与刺绣上交错的彩色，即纹彩。

㉕ the five colors，五色，即红、黄、蓝、白、黑。

㉖ the five tones，五音，即宫、商、角、徵、羽。用于写作则为语言文辞的声律。

㉗ the five emotions，五性，即喜、怒、哀、乐、怨。

㉘ *The Book of Filial Piety*，《孝经》。传说是孔子自作，但南宋时已有人怀疑是出于后人附会。清代纪昀在《四库全书总目》中指出，该书是孔子"七十子之徒之遗言"，一般认为，此书成书于先秦。

㉙ Han Feizi，韩非子，战国时期韩国人。与李斯同学于荀子，喜好刑名法术之学，是法家学派的代表人物。

㉚ a cassia bait，肉桂。

㉛ kingfishers' feathers，翡翠鸟的羽毛做成的纶线钓丝。

㉜ the hexagram "grace"，贲象穷白：《周易·贲卦》中的"贲"是文饰的意思，可是它的象却归于白色。穷，探究到底。白，指本色，因为丝的本色是白的。

㉝ the natural colors，正色。古代以青、赤、黄、白、黑为正色。正色代表雅正的好文采。

㉞ The brocade made in Wu fades easily，吴地（现江浙一带）美丽鲜艳的锦绣容易变色。

Ⅳ. 问题思考

1. Modern scholars have debated heatedly about Liu Xie's conception of literature. The debate was triggered by an argument that proposes that "Liu's principal, theoretical orientation corresponds with remarkable fidelity to the definition of expressive theories generally which M. H. Abrams distilled from his researches in European critics". This argument gets a rebuttal from James Liu, who views Liu Xie's conception of literature as primarily metaphysical, with strains of pragmatic, expressive, aesthetic, and technical concepts subordinating to it. Stephen Owen also argues in his book *Traditional Chinese Poetry and Poetics* that Liu Xie's conception of literature is neither mimetic nor expressive; Owen believes that Liu Xie's conception of literature is free of such deficiencies, because it views literature as a natural stage of a universal process of manifestation. Make a brief comment on such an argument according to your own understanding.

2. "Le style c'est l'homme meme." It seems that long before Comte de Buffon (1707 – 1788) made his famous statement, and Liu Xie had developed a stylistic theory based on a similar idea. The basic elements of Liu Xie's stylistic theory are outlined in Chapter 27 on imagination, where Liu's emphasis on the purification of the mind and the dredging of the heart finks literary creation to self-cultivation. Make a comparison study of Comte de Buffon and Liu Xie in terms of stylistic theory.

3. According to Liu Xie, style is seen here as the sum-total of an individual—his talent, vitality, learning, and cultivation. Differences in these respects yield different styles. Do you agree or disagree with his idea? Why or why not?

4. Liu Xie emphasizes tranquility, the cleansing of the heart and the purification of the spirit as preparations for the workings of shensi, while 19th century English romantic poets Coleridge believes that imagination needs a time of patient preparation. Make a brief analysis of similarities and differences of the concept of "imagination" in the eyes of Samuel Taylor Coleridge and Liu Xie.

5. What is the implication of the title of Liu Xie's treatise "Dragon-Carving and the Literary Mind" (*Wenxin Diaolong*)?

V. 经典导读

《文心雕龙》是南北朝时著名文学理论家刘勰（约465—520）创作的中国第一部系统的文艺理论巨著。分为上、下两编，每编25篇，包括"总论"、"文体论"、"创作论"、"批评论"、"总序"等五部分，共10卷50篇，分别对文体文风、创作过程、作家风格、文质关系、写作技巧、文辞声律、批评方法等问题作了探讨。

本单元的两篇选文，其主要内容概述如下：

《神思》主要讨论如何运用神思来进行文学创作构思。全篇分三部分：其一，阐述艺术构思的特点和作用。为了更好地构思，作家需要积极地积累知识，辩明事理，运用好生活经验和提高情致修养。其二，通过列举过去的作家，阐述了艺术构思的不同类型。强调在构思中要抓住重点，这样才能取得创作成功。其三，提出艺术加工的必要性以及艺术构思的复杂性。

《情采》是《文心雕龙》50篇中至关重要的一篇。主要论述文学艺术的内容和形式之间的辩证关系。全篇可分三个部分：首先，论述内容和形式的关系：形式只有依附一定的内容才有意义，内容也

现代插图本《文心雕龙》的封面

只有通过一定的形式才能更好地表达。其次，从"为情而造文"（Art is used to express genuine feeling）与"为文而造情"（Prose counterfeit feeling for art）的角度总结了两种不同的文学创作道路。最后，驾驭文采的原则和方法，首先确立内容，然后造文施采，使内容和形式密切结合，写成文质兼备的理想作品。

总体上来看，《文心雕龙》继承并发挥了儒家的文学思想，把原道、徵圣、宗经作为理论核心，贯穿全书的始终。刘勰认为儒家经典是一切文体的本源，如赋、颂、赞等都源于《诗经》。他从儒家经典的风格特色出发，提出关于文学批评的根本原

则："故文能宗经，体有六义，一则情深而不诡，二则风清而不杂，三则事信而不诞，四则义直而不回，五则体约而不芜，六则文丽而不淫。"全书的主要内容概括如下：

第一，对形象思维的进一步探索。刘勰把"神思"视为一种自由的想象活动，对之作了生动的描绘，说："文之思也，其神远矣，故寂然凝虑，思接千载；悄焉动容，视通万里。吟咏之间，吐纳珠玉之声；眉睫之前，卷舒风云之色。"在他看来，"神思"虽受理的支配，但不像抽象的逻辑思维那样受着概念的规定，而是与物、象、言相结合，始终在感性形象中运动，并伴随着主体情感的体验和自由抒发。"夫神思方远。万涂竞萌，规矩虚位，刻镂无形；登山则情满于山，观海则意溢于海，我才之多少，将与风云而并驱矣。"

第二，对文学史观的反思。《文心雕龙》的文学史观认为，文学的发展变化，终归要受到时代及社会政治生活的影响。所谓"时运交移，质文代变……歌谣文理，与世推移"、"文变染乎世情，兴废系乎时序"。刘勰很重视义学本身的发展规律。他提出了所谓的"通变"主张，即文学创作上继承和革新的关系。他要求作家要大胆创新，只有不断创新，文学创作才能不断发展。与此同时，它又强调任何"变"或创新都离不开"通"，即继承。文学创作只有通晓各种"故实"，只有将"通"与"变"，"因"与"革"很好地结合和统一起来，才有可能"骋无穷之路，饮不竭之源"，获得长足的、健康的发展。

第三，关于文学批评方法论的探讨。在《知音》篇里，刘勰批评了"贵古贱今"、"崇己抑人"、"信伪迷真"、"各执一隅之解"的不良风尚，要求批评家"无私于轻重，不偏于憎爱"。与此同时，他还提出了"六观"的批评方法：一观位体，看其内容与风格是否一致；二观置辞，看其文辞在表达情理上是否确切；三观通变，看其有否继承与变化；四观奇正，看其布局是否严谨妥当；五观事义，看其用典是否贴切；六观宫商，看其音韵声律是否完美。这在当时是最为全面和公允的品评标准。不仅如此，《文心雕龙》还提出了批评的态度问题、批评家的主观修养问题等。由于文学创作从内容到形式都是丰富多样的，因此，刘勰非常强调批评应该全面，而不应"各执一隅之解，欲拟万端之变"，否则就会出现"所谓'东向而望，不见西墙'"的现象。刘勰认为，任何批评中的真知灼见，只能是建立在广博的学识和阅历基础之上。"圆照之象，务先博观。""操千曲而后晓声，观千剑而后识器。"

第四，强调情感在文学创作全过程中的作用。要求文学创作要"志思蓄愤，而吟咏情性"，主张"为情而造文"；反对"为文而造情"。创作构思为"情变所孕"，结构是"按部整伍，以待情会"，剪裁要求"设情以位体"，甚至作品的体裁、风格，也无不由强烈而真挚的感情起着重要的作用。他的这一认识相当深刻，非常符合文学创作的特点和规律。

第五，对于风格和风骨的比较研究。刘勰继承曹丕关于风格的意见，作了进一步的发挥，认为形成作家风格的原因，有先天的才情、气质的不同；也有后天的学养和习染的殊异。他将各种不同的文章分为四组八体，每一组各有正反两体——"雅与奇反，奥与显殊，繁与约舛；壮与轻乖"；但它们又互相联系——"八体虽殊，会通合数，得其环中，则辐辏相成"。作者在这八体中参差演化，就会形成自己独特的风格。刘勰关于风格的研究，对后来的《诗式》、《二十四诗品》等，都曾产生直接的影响。在风格论的基础上，刘勰特别标举"风骨"的理论。"风"是要求文学作品要有较强的思想艺术感染力，"骨"则是要求表现上的刚健清新。

第六，对各种文章体裁和源流的总结和阐述，也是《文心雕龙》的重要内容。《文心雕龙》从第5篇《辨骚》起，到第25篇《书记》止，就成为中国现存的南朝时代关于文章体制和源流的唯一重要著作，也是关于这一问题的重要历史文献。其中不乏细致、中肯以至精辟的见解。

毋庸置疑，《文心雕龙》是一部"体大思精"、"深得文理"的文章写作理论巨著。正如范文澜先生所说的那样，"系统地、全面地、深入地讨论文学，《文心雕龙》实是唯一的一部大著作。"鲁迅在《论诗题记》中也有评价："东则有刘彦和《文心》，西则有亚里士多德《诗学》，解析神质，包举洪纤，开源发流，为世楷模。"《文心雕龙》反对了当时文风的"浮诡"和"讹滥"，纠正了过往文论的狭隘偏颇，它在文学批评史上的突出贡献是不言而喻的。

VI. 译本链接

1. Shi Wenzhoug, *The Literary Mind and the Carving of Dragons*, New York: Columbia University Press, 1959.

2. Huang Zhaojie, etc. *The Book of Literary Design*, Hong Kong: The University of Hong Kong Press, 1999.

3. Yang, Xianyi and Gladys Yang, Carving a Dragon at the Core of Literature, *Chinese Literature*. Vol. 1~2, 1962.

4. Ernest Richard Hughes, *The Literary Mind and Its Carving of Dragons*, London: Oxford University Press: 1951.

5. H. Mair, *Buddhism in the Literary Mind and Ornate Rhetoric*, San Francisco: Stanford University Press, 2001.

6. 杨国斌英译,《文心雕龙》, 北京: 外语教学与研究出版社 2003 年版。

Unit Ten
Records on the Warring States Period
(《战国策》)

Ⅰ. 背景简介

Records on the Warring States Period (*Zhan Guo Ce*) is a renowned ancient Chinese historical work and compilation of sporadic materials on the Warring States Period compiled between 3rd and 1st century B. C. It is an important literature in the research of Warring States Period as it accounts the strategies and political views of the School of Negotiation and reveals the historical and social characteristics of the period. It was thought to be composed by Liu Xiang (about 77 B. C. –6 B. C.), a Confucian scholar of the Western Han Dynasty. The author of *Records on the Warring States Period* is unknown. The edition extant today was

the antiquated edition of Record on *the Warring States Period* in 1910

compiled by Liu Xiang under the title "Records on the Warring States Period". Significant contents of *Records on the Warring States Period* were lost in subsequent centuries. Zeng Gong of the Northern Song Dynasty reclaimed some lost chapters from private collectors, proofread and edited the modern version. It is compiled according to 12 states as The East

Zhou, West Zhou, Qin, Chu, Qi, Zhao, Wei I, Han, Yan, Song, Wei II and Zhongshan in 33 books.

Records on the Warring States Period is also the history of individual kingdoms, documenting the events of Western and Eastern Zhou dynasties and their subject kingdoms, including Qin, Qi, Chu, and Zhao. The content is made up of mostly the proposals and activities of counselors. *Records on the Warring States Period* is accomplished in narration and uses many metaphors. The characterization in this book is very accomplished.

Sophisticated intellectual contents of *Records on the Warring States Period* mainly reveal the intellectual inclination of the followers of the School of Diplomacy and illustrate the intellectual wealth and multicultural aspects of the period. *Records on the Warring States Period* displays the social aspects and scholastic habitat of the Warring States Period. Major events and historical information of the period are represented in objective and vivid descriptions. Detailed records of speeches and deeds by followers of the School of Diplomacy reveal the mental makeup and intellectual expertise of the characters. Acts of righteousness, bravery and determination by numerous characters are also recorded.

The literary achievement of *Records on the Warring States Period* is also outstanding—it signifies a new era in the development of ancient Chinese literature. Among other aspects, character description, language usage and metaphorical stories demonstrate rich and clear literary quality. Nevertheless, its intellectual aspects have also been disputed, mainly due to its stress on fame and profit and its conflicts with Confucian ideology. The book appears to overemphasize the historical contributions from the School of Diplomacy, devaluing the book's historical importance.

Ⅱ. 文本选读
Su Qin[1] Started Suggesting Qin to Unite with the Six States

When Su Qin started persuading King Hui[2] of the state of Qin to take his advice to unite Qin with the Six States, he said, "Regarding Your Majesty's state, there are fertile places such as Ba, Shu, Hanzhong and so on in the west. In the north, there are furs produced in the Hu area and swift horses produced in the Dai area. There are dangerous places such as Mount Wu and Qianzhong in the south, and natural forts like Mount Xiao and the pass of Hangu Valley in the east. Moreover, the land of your state is very fertile, and the people are rich. You have ten thousand chariots and one million tough soldiers. You own one thousand *li* of fecund[3] land and your state has lots of assets. The geographic condition is very good. So your state is the so-called Depot of Heaven and is the most powerful country in the world. Relying on Your Majesty's wisdom and capability, the large number of scholars and the masses, the use of chariots and horses, and the spreading of the art of war among the officers and men, surely you can annex[4] other sovereigns' territory, unify the whole world, become a Di and rule the world. Please pay a little attention to my words, Your Majesty, and allow me to explain to you the benefit of my advice."

The king of Qin said, "As far as I know, if a bird's feathers are not well developed, it cannot fly high in the sky; if the law is not complete, it should not be used to punish criminals; if one is not virtuous enough, he cannot employ the people; if one's policies and moral education are not successful, he should not trouble his high-ranking court officials. Now you have travelled one thousand *li* here to my court to give me instructions. Let's discuss that later."

Su Qin said, "I did doubt that Your Majesty might take my advice. Previously, Shen Nong attacked Bu Sui[5]. The Yellow Emperor launched military operations in Zhuolu to attack Chi You[6] and held him captive. Yao attacked Huan Dou[7]. Shun attacked San Miao[8]. Yu attacked Gong Gong[9]. Tang attacked the Xia Dynasty. King Wen attacked the state of Chong. King Wu attacked Zhou, the last king of the Shang Dynasty. Duke Huan of Qi[10] established one of the most powerful states through military actions. By this token, how can military forces be put into disuse? In ancient times, numerous diplomats travelled all over the world and their carriages almost bumped into each other on the road. They made agreements after discussions and negotiations. Thus the world was unified. At present, propositions of Lianheng (referring to Qin's tactics of uniting with other states to consolidate its own power and unify the world) and Hezong[11] (referring to Qin's tactics of allying the six eastern states to counteract Qin) prevail. Armor and weapons are taken out and used again. Scholars and eloquent people try to extend their well prepared arguments. Sovereigns of all the states are confused. Various problems are provoked and cannot be settled correctly. If the law and all the related regulations are complete, the people will simply comply with them falsely. There are numerous documents, but the people still don't feel satisfied. Sovereigns and officials blame each other for the problems, and the common people don't have any means to support themselves. The more rational and warranted the arguments seem to be, the more frequently military actions occur. The more skillful the persuaders are, and the more luxurious their clothes are, the less hope there is for a ceasefire. The more sophisticated and deliberate the viewpoints are, the more disordered the world is. Even though the persuaders try their best to persuade the sovereigns, their ideas are still not accepted. Even though the sovereigns try to extend righteousness and advocate honesty, people all over the world don't feel close to them. As a result, culture and education go into disuse and military operations are undertaken. Suicide warriors are trained at great cost. Armor is made and weapons are sharpened. Soldiers are sent to the battlefront to win every possible victory. Even wise sovereigns of ancient times such as the Five Di-ancestors[12], the Three King-ancestors[13] and the Five Lord-protectors[14] wanted to obtain great benefit and enlarge their territory without effort. But in fact, they could not do that. So they had to resort to military action to gain what they wanted. Great achievements can only be made either by troops fighting each other fiercely or by soldiers fighting to death in a close battle. Thus, if the troops win every war outside the state, righteousness will be extended inside, and if the state establishes a high prestige, the people will be obedient. Nowadays, if you want to unify the whole world, outdo those states yield to your authority, take firm control over the world, govern the people successfully and put other sovereigns at your service, you can do nothing but take military action! Contemporary sovereigns often overlook this crucial fact. Moral education makes them muddle-headed[15]. Their states are in disorder. They are confused by some sophisticated debates and arguments. No wonder none of them is able to unify the world."

Su Qin wore ten letters to persuade the king of Qin, but all his efforts resulted in failure. His black marten coat was worn, his one hundred *jin* of gold was used up, he ran out of money, and finally he had to leave Qin and return home. He wrote leg wrappings and a pair of straw sandals, carrying his books on his back and shouldering his luggage. He looked exhausted and his face was tanned by the sun. He also appeared ashamed. When he arrived home, his wife was weaving and didn't stop to welcome him. His sister-in-law didn't cook anything for him to eat. And his parents didn't talk to him. Su Qin groaned, "My wife does not regard me as her husband. My sister-in-law does not regard me as her brother-in-law. My parents do not regard me as their son. This is my own fault." Then he studied very hard every night. He opened scores of book cases and found *Yin Fu* written by Duke Tai[16]. He read it very carefully and studied its keystone carefully. Every time he felt too tired and sleepy, he would stab his thigh with a wimble[17]. As a result, blood flowed to his feet. He said, "If one persuades the sovereign of a state, he will surely be presented with gold, jade and fine silk fabric and be appointed to a position as powerful as the highest-ranking court official or the prime minister." One year later, he mastered the main ideas of the book very well. He said, "These ideas are the right ones for advising contemporary sovereigns!"

Then he went through the Yan-Wu-Ji Gate and met and advised the king of the state of Zhao in a luxurious hall. The king of Zhao was very satisfied with his ideas, conferred upon him the title of "Lord of Wu'an" and appointed him to be prime minister of Zhao. Su Qin was presented with one hundred chariots, one thousand *chun* of fine silk fabric, one hundred pairs of white jade and ten thousand *yi* of gold. Then he started to travel across the world with these things to persuade the sovereigns of the Six States to unite with each other and counteract the powerful state of Qin together. During the time when Su Qin was prime minister of Zhao, every state cut its ties with Qin.

At that time, everything was decided by Su Qin even though the world was big, the people were numerous, sovereigns and marquises were powerful, and advisors were experienced and astute[18]. Without using one *dou* of provender, bothering one soldier or officer, breaking one bowstring or wasting one arrow, Su Qin made all the sovereigns be friendly to each other like brothers. If a person is wise and capable, he will win over people all over the world. If a wise and capable person is appointed to the right position, people all resorting to military forces, you should resort to policy. Instead of taking action outside your own territory, you should make the right decisions at the court. When Su Qin's power reached its summit, he owned ten thousand *jin* of gold, administrated numerous carriages and horses, and travelled with splendor. The states located east of the mountain range yielded to his authority like grass bending to the wind. As a result, Zhao became the most powerful state of that time. As for Su Qin, he used to be a poor scholar living in a shanty. Now he travelled across the world by carriage to persuade sovereigns of all other states at their courts. No one dared to argue with him and his power was matchless.

When he was on the way to persuade the king of Chu, he passed by Luoyang. When his parents heard this, they cleaned the house and the street, arranged a concert and a banquet to greet him. And they also walked thirty *li* to the suburbs to welcome him. His wife dared not look at him directly in the eye, and paid much attention to listening to every word he said. His sister-in-law crawled out like a snake to pay her respect. She bowed four times before him and knelt down to beg him to forgive her former inhospitality. Su Qin asked, "My sister-in-law, why were you so arrogant before but so humble now?" His sister-in-law replied, "Because now you are powerful and rich." Su Qin said, "Oh! When I was poor, my parents would not regard me as their son. But if I am rich and powerful, even my relatives will be afraid of me. How can one simply overlook power and wealth when he is alive?"

Zou Ji[19] Was More Than Eight *Chi* Tall

Zou Ji was more than eight *chi* tall. He was very handsome and glowed with health. One morning, he got dressed and looked at himself in the mirror. He asked his wife, "Who do you think is more handsome, Mr. Xu living in the northern part of the capital or I?" His wife said, "You are very handsome. Mr. Xu cannot match you!" Mr. Xu who lived in the northern part of the capital was the most handsome man in the state of Qi. Zou Ji was not so confident about his own looks, so he asked his concubine the same question: "Who do you think is more handsome, Mr. Xu or I?" The concubine replied, "How can Mr. Xu match you!" The next day, a guest came to visit Zou Ji. They sit down and talked. Zou Ji asked him, "Who do you think is more handsome, Mr. Xu or I?" The guest said, "Mr. Xu is not as handsome as you!"

Mr. Xu himself came the next day. Zou Ji observed him thoroughly and thought that he himself was not as handsome as Mr. Xu. He then looked in the mirror and found that he was much less handsome than Mr. Xu. He thought it over and over from morning till night and said, "My wife considered me more handsome than Mr. Xu because of her favoritism towards me. My concubine considered me more handsome, because she was afraid of me and therefore wanted to please me. My guest considered me more handsome, because he was going to ask me for help."

Then Zou Ji went to the court to see King Wei of Qi[20] and said, "I know for sure that I am not as handsome as Mr. Xu. However, my wife loves me, my concubine is afraid of me and my guest is going to ask me for help, so they all said that I am more handsome than Mr. Xu. Now Qi has one thousand *li* of land and owns one hundred and twenty cities and towns. All the women and beloved ones in the palace love you. All the court officials are afraid of you. And all the people living within our borders on all four sides are going to seek for your help. From this point of view, you must have been cheated very badly, Your Majesty." King Wei said, "You are right." Then he issued an order as follows: "Among all the high-ranking court officials, officers and ordinary people, those who can point out my errors frankly will be rewarded with top awards. Those who write to me to remonstrate[21] with me will be rewarded with medium awards. Those who can openly discuss my mistakes will be rewarded with third-class awards."

After this order was issued, all the high-ranking court officials and officers vied[22] with each other to remonstrate with the king. The front of the court was as crowded as the market. A few months later, someone would come to argue with the king. When the states of Yan, Zhao, Han and Wei heard this story, they all went to say congratulations and show their respect to the king of Qi. This is regarded as defeating the enemy states without stepping out of the court hall.

A Man from Qi Named Feng Xuan[23]

Once in the state of Qi, there was a man named Feng Xuan. He was too poor to support his family. So he asked someone to tell Lord Mengchang[24] that he wanted to become one of the lord's hangers-on[25] to make a living. Lord Mengchang asked Feng Xuan, "What's your hobby?" Feng Xuan replied, "I have no hobby." Lord Mengchang asked, "What talent do you have?" Feng Xuan said, "I have no talent at all." "I see. You can stay here." Lord Mengchang smiled and accepted him. The people around Lord Mengchang thought that the lord looked down upon Feng Xuan, so they only gave him simple food.

After some time, Feng Xuan leaned on a post, played his sword and sang, "My long sword, let's go. I am not served with fish." Other people there told Lord Mengchang about it. Lord Mengchang said, "Serve him with fish. Give him the same food as that of other hangers-on." After some time, Feng Xuan played his sword again and sang, "My long sword, let's go. When I go out, I don't have a carriage." All the people there laughed at him and they told the lord about it. Lord Mengchang said, "Prepare a carriage for him. Treat him the way we treat those who have carriages." Then Feng Xuan took his sword to visit his friend in his carriage and told him, "Look, Lord Mengchang has accepted me as one of his hangers-on." Some time later, he played his sword and sang again, "My long sword, let's go. I don't feel settled here." All the other people then disliked him and considered him too greedy to be satisfied. Lord Mengchang asked Feng, "Do you have a family, Mr. Feng?" He replied, "I have a mother who is very old." Lord Mengchang then sent some people to support his mother with enough food, cover all her expenses and make sure that she was short of nothing. Feng Xuan didn't sing again.

After that, Lord Mengchang put up a notice looking for an accountant. And he asked his hangers-on, "Who is familiar with accounting and able to collect money from my debtors in Xue for me?" Feng Xuan wrote his name on the notification and said, "I can do that."

Lord Mengchang wondered about this and asked, "Who is this man?" The people around him said, "That's the one who used to sing 'let's go, my long sword'." Lord Mengchang smiled and said, "As expected, he is talented. I am sorry that I have not visited him." He then invited Feng to his home and apologized to him, "I am very tired of everyday trifles and often disturbed by some problems. Moreover, I am not born wise and am also very busy with government affairs. Thus I have offended you (referring to having not visited him in person). Yet you are not angry with me and still want to ask the debtors in Xue to settle their debts to me?" Feng Xuan said, "Yes, I want to do that for you." Then he prepared his carriage, took his luggage and all the bills and said good-bye to the lord. He asked, "After I collect the debts, shall I buy anything for you before I come back?" Lord Mengchang said, "You can buy something I don't have at home."

Feng Xuan drove to Xue and asked the officers in charge of Xue to summon all the debtors owing money to the lord to come to him to check their bills. After all the bills were checked, Feng Xuan stood up and issued a false order to exempt all the debts on behalf of the lord. Subsequently, he burnt all the bills. All the people there jubilantly[26] and loudly expressed their thanks to the lord.

Then Feng Xuan drove directly back to Qi and went to see the lord in the morning. Lord Mengchang wondered why he came back so quickly, so he got dressed to meet him and asked, "Have you collected all the debts? Why did you come back so quickly?" Feng Xuan said, "Yes, I have finished the task." "What did you buy for me then?" asked the lord. Feng Xuan replied, "You told me to buy something you don't have at home. I think your buildings are full of treasures, all the stalls are crowded with dogs and horses, and you also have many beautiful women. So I believe that the thing you don't have here is righteousness. So I bought righteousness for you without asking for your permission." Lord Mengchang said, "How could you buy righteousness?" Feng Xuan replied, "Now you own Xue. However, you don't treat the people there as if they were your own children. On the contrary, you take advantage of them to make huge profits for yourself. I issued a false order in your name to exempt all their debts. Then I burnt all the bills, and the people celebrated and applauded you. That's how I bought righteousness for you. " Lord Mengchang was not happy with him and said, "Hold your tongue!"

After a year, the king of Qi told Lord Mengchang, "I dare not employ the high-ranking court officials of our deceased king at my court. " Lord Mengchang then resigned and went back to his fief[27] Xue. When he was still one hundred *li* from Xue, all the people, young and old, came to welcome him on the road. Lord Mengchang turned around and told Feng Xuan, "Now I witness first hand the righteousness you bought for me. " Feng Xuan said, "A sly hare digs three dens for itself[28]. Then it can merely survive. Now you only have one 'den', so you are still not safe. Please allow me to dig more 'dens' for you. " Lord Mengchang then gave him fifty carriages, five hundred *jin* of gold and sent him to travel to the west to consult with the king of Wei. Feng Xuan told the king, "Qi has dismissed its high-ranking court official—Lord Mengchang—from office and thus provided him the chance to serve other states. The sovereign who employs him first will enrich his state and strengthen his military forces. " Hence, Wei's king emptied out the highest position (referring to an opening for prime minister), appointed the former prime minister to be Commander-in-Chief and sent emissaries with one thousand *jin* of gold and one hundred chariots to invite Lord Mengchang to work for him. Feng Xuan drove back to the lord first and warned him, "One thousand *jin* of gold is a very generous gift. One hundred chariots show the importance of this diplomatic mission. The king of Qi should have heard it. " The emissaries of Wei came three times, but Lord Mengchang flatly refused them. When the king of Qi heard that, both he and his court officials were terrified. Then the king sent the Grand Tutor[29] with one thousand *jin* of gold, two well-decorated carriages, a sword and a letter to apologize to the lord. The letter said, "I am a person of no good. I have suffered from disasters caused by the deceased sovereigns at the ancestral temple and been cheated by devilish and toady court officials. As a result, I offended you. I know that I am not worthy to ask you to work for me again. But would you please come back to govern the people for the sake of our deceased sovereigns?" Feng Xuan cautioned Lord Mengchang, "Please ask for the utensils used in rituals to worship our deceased sovereigns and build an ancestral temple in Xue. " After the ancestral temple was finished, Feng Xuan returned to report to Lord Mengchang and said, "Now all the three 'dens' are already. You can rest easy and enjoy yourself."

Lord Mengchang served as prime minister for dozens of years and was not involved in any problems because of Feng Xuan's schemes.

Ⅲ. 难点释义

① Su Qin, 苏秦（前337—前284），字季子，东周战国时期著名的纵横家。提倡合纵（联合其他国家）对付秦国。相传他是鬼谷子的徒弟。

② King Hui, 秦惠王（前356—前311），战国时秦国国君，任张仪为相，推行连横之策。

③ fecund, 富饶的，肥沃的。

④ annex, 吞并，兼并。

⑤ Shen Nong attacked Bu Sui, 神农伐补遂，据传说，这是最早的战争。

⑥ Chi You, 蚩尤，中华始祖之一。相传蚩尤面如牛首，背生双翅，是牛图腾和鸟图腾氏族的首领。约4 600年前，黄帝战胜炎帝后，在今河北涿鹿县境内，展开了与蚩尤部落的战争——涿鹿之战，蚩尤战死，东夷、九黎等部族融入了炎黄部族，形成了今天中华民族的最早主体。

⑦ Huan Dou, 驩兜，中国古代传说中的三苗族首领，传说因为与共工、鲧（gǔn）为非作乱而被舜流放至崇山。

⑧ San Miao, 三苗，中国传说中黄帝至尧舜禹时代的古族名，与驩兜、共工、鲧合称为"四罪"。

⑨ Gong Gong, 共工，氏族名，又称共工氏。共工氏是黄帝王朝时代的部落名。

⑩ Duke Huan of Qi, 齐桓公（前716—前643），春秋时齐国国君。在位时期任用管仲改革，选贤任能，加强武备，发展生产。晚年昏庸，信用易牙、竖刁等小人，最终在内乱中饿死。

⑪ Lianheng and Hezong, 连横，合纵，战国时期纵横家所宣扬并推行的外交和军事政策。战国时期，七雄并立，齐、秦两国最为强大。合纵就是南北纵列的国家联合起来，共同对付强国，阻止齐、秦两国兼并弱国；连横就是秦或齐拉拢一些国家，共

同进攻另外一些国家。

⑫ the Five Di-ancestors，五帝，一般是指中国上古传说中的五位圣明君主，即黄帝、颛顼、帝喾、尧、舜。

⑬ the Three King-ancestors，三王，夏、商、周三朝的第一位帝王大禹、商汤王、周武王、周文王的合称。

⑭ the Five Lord-protectors，五伯，即五霸，指春秋时期的齐桓公、宋襄公、晋文公、秦穆公和楚庄王。

⑮ muddle-headed，昏庸的，糊涂的。

⑯ *Yin Fu* written by Duke Tai，《太公阴符》，属道家一派之书，又叫《太公阴符经》，传说为姜太公所留。

⑰ stab his thigh with a wimble，引锥刺股，形容学习刻苦。

⑱ astute，机敏的，精明的。

⑲ Zou Ji，邹忌，战国时齐国大臣。以鼓琴游说齐威王，被任相国，劝说威王奖励群臣吏民进谏，主张革新政治，修订法律，选拔人才，奖励贤臣，处罚奸吏，并选荐得力大臣坚守四境，从此齐国渐强。

⑳ King Wei of Qi，齐威王，战国时期齐国国君。以善于纳谏用能，励志图强而名著史册。

㉑ remonstrate，抗议。

㉒ vie，竞争，较量。

㉓ Feng Xuan，冯谖，战国时齐国人，是薛国（今滕州市东南）国君孟尝君门下的食客之一，为战国时期一位高瞻远瞩、眼光颇为深远的战略家。

㉔ Lord Mengchang，孟尝君，名田文，战国时齐国贵族，战国四公子之一。因封于薛（今山东滕州市东南），又称薛公，号孟尝君。门下有食客数千。

㉕ hanger-on，食客，在古代寄食于贵族官僚家里，为主人策划、奔走的人。"食客"之风起于春秋战国之际，"客"者依附于主人，主人则负责"养客"，养客多者达三千余人。

㉖ jubilantly，欢欣地，喜气洋洋地。

㉗ fief，封地，采邑。

㉘ A sly hare digs three dens for itself，狡兔三窟，比喻隐蔽的地方或方法多，做好了充分的准备。

㉙ the Grand Tutor，太傅，中国古代官职。太傅处于专制统治者的核心位置，直接参与军国大事的拟定和决策，是皇帝统治四方的高级代言人。周代设置，汉代复置，春秋时期秦朝废止。西汉曾两度短暂复置该职位；东汉则长期设立。

Ⅳ. 问题思考

1. During the Warring States Period，talented people travelled from one state to another to satisfy self-interests under the name of serving the states they then worked for and bore no ideology on motherland or loyalty in their minds. What's your comment on their behavior?

2. To what extent do you agree with Su Qin on "Oh! When I was poor, my parents would not regard me as their son. But if I am rich and powerful, even my relatives will be afraid of me. How can one simply overlook power and wealth when he is alive?" Please reason your statement.

3. One needs courage and wisdom to put forward proposals to his superiors, and the superiors need much tolerance and a great mind to help accept proposals. Who do you admire, Zou Ji or King Wei of Qi? Why?

4. *Records on the Warring States Period* succeeded in narrating stories and portraying figures. Please give one or two examples.

5. In what sense were many of the thoughts manifested in *Records on the Warring States Period* against Confucianism?

Ⅴ. 经典导读

《战国策》（*Records on the Warring States Period*）是一部国别体史书。主要记述了战国时期纵横家的政治主张和策略，展示了战国时代的历史特点和社会风貌，是研究战国历史的重要典籍。《战国策》杂记东西周及秦、齐、楚、赵、魏、韩、燕、宋、卫、中山诸国之事，共33卷，约12万字，上接春秋，下至秦并六国，记事约两百四十年（前460—前220），西汉末刘向编定为33篇，并定名为"战国策"。北宋时已有缺失，由曾巩作了订补。南宋鲍彪改变原书次序，作新注。元代吴师道作《战国策校注》，其后各代都有众多研究《战国策》的著述。

从历史角度看，《战国策》是战国时期各国史官记载的策士们游说诸侯国的言论资料。全册书记载了战国时期各诸侯国发生的重大事件以及谋臣策士相互辩论时所提出的政治主张和斗争策略以及相互倾轧的阴谋诡计。它在一定程度上反映了上起三家分晋，下至楚汉之争两百多年中，各诸侯国之间和各国内部各阶级、阶层之间尖锐复杂的矛盾斗争，统治集团的争权夺利、相互倾轧、昏庸腐朽以及兼并战争给人民带来的痛苦和灾难。这些都为研究战国史提供了丰富的资料。《战国策》在很大程度上填补了《左传》、《国语》之后，《楚汉春秋》之前的史料空白，还是司马迁修《史记》的重要史料来源，但《战国策》的记事中有相当的虚构成分，这已经是后世的共识。

从文学角度看，《战国策》文思开阔，寓意深刻，语言风格辩丽恣肆，铺张扬厉，后人称赞它"文辞骎骎乎上薄六经，下绝来世"（宋代李文叔《书战国策后》）。在中国文学史上，它标志着中国古代散文发展的一个新时期，其文学性非常突出，尤其在人物形象的刻画、语言文字的运用、寓言故事等方面具有非常鲜明的艺术特色。人物刻画栩栩如生，有鲜明的个性。当详则尽情挥洒，不吝笔墨；当简则一字不多，惜墨如金。许多篇章成功描述了君王、后妃、谋臣、义士等不同类型的人物，把他们的性格特征、身份、处境都刻画得入木三分。如《秦策》写苏秦先以"连横"说秦王，转而又以"合纵"说六国，生动地描写出一个善于机变、惯于夸说，一切言行以利为转移，朝秦暮楚的纵横家形象。这些手法对后世传记文学的写作有很大影响。雄辩的论说、尖刻的讽刺、耐人寻味的幽默，构成了它独特的语言风格。书中主要记述谋臣策士们的说辞，他们为使听者接受自己的政治主张，尽量把话讲得严密雄辩，无懈可击，并努力抓住对方最关心之点，一语中的。

《战国策》长于通过讽喻的小故事说明道理，生动幽默、耐人寻味。例如"邹忌讽齐王纳谏"以邹忌借其妻、妾、朋友出于不同目的，赞美其"美于徐公"，说明"兼听则明，偏听则暗"（a clear head comes from on open-mind）的道理，劝诫齐王不应偏信宫妇近臣的话，而应广开言路，鼓励人民进谏。书中常见比喻、夸张、寓言等多样化修辞手段，增强散文的表达效果。这类寓言和比喻，写得饶有风趣，常隐寓着深刻的道理，耐人寻味，很多后来成了有名的典故，如"画蛇添足"、"狐假虎威"、

"惊弓之鸟"、"南辕北辙"、"鹬蚌相争"等。此外,《战国策》还多用工整的对偶和排比句法,使文章抑扬顿挫、气势贯通。

《战国策》对后代文学有深远的影响。汉初的散文家贾谊、晁错和司马迁,都受其影响。宋代苏洵、苏轼、苏辙的散文,也都得力于《战国策》。另外汉赋"铺张扬厉"的风格、工整的对偶和排比的句法都直接承自《战国策》;而赋中常见的主客对答、抑客申主的写法,也在《战国策》就已广为运用了。

《战国策》主体上体现了纵横家

《战国策》里的"南辕北辙"典故

的思想倾向,同时也反映出了战国时期思想活跃、价值观多元的历史特点。由于不受儒家正统观念的控制,没有"仁"、"义"、"礼"、"忠"、"信"等规范的束缚,人们得以展示比较真实的自我,而人类最原始的本能就是追求物质利益的最大化。

在《战国策》中,从国家到权臣,再到普通的小人物都赤裸裸地追求各自的私利。国家之间为了疆域、财宝,甚至是象征最高权力的重器(如九鼎)都可以发动战争;为了利益,设置骗局、愚弄盟国、背信弃义更是常见。国之重臣为了自己的权位,全无忠君的意识,甚至完全不顾国家利益。社会下层的小人物也可以用金钱收买。人们为了追求最大利益,往往不惜一切代价,不择任何手段。由此可见,战国时代是一个地地道道的追名逐利的时代。刘向在序中说:"战国之时,君德浅薄,为之谋策者,不得不因势而为资,据时而为画。故其谋扶急持倾,为一切之权,虽不可以临教化,兵革救急之势也。"国与国之间讲的是以势相争,以智谋相夺。那些活跃在政治舞台上的策士,也只是以自己的才智向合适的买主换取功名利禄,朝秦暮楚,毫不为怪。如苏秦始以连横之策劝说秦王并吞天下,后又以合纵之说劝赵王联合六国抗秦。他游秦失败归来时,受到全家人的蔑视;后富贵还乡,父母妻嫂都无比恭敬。于是他感慨道:"嗟夫,贫穷则父母不子,富贵则亲戚畏惧。人生世上,势位富贵,盖可忽乎哉!"这些在今天看来也许不值得赞赏,但在当时的历史条件下,原本受贵族压抑的平民的心理就是如此，这样比虚假的说教更富于真实性。

由于《战国策》在相当程度上背离了中国古代的正统思想，因此常常受到严厉的批评。与当时普遍追逐私利的社会风气相比较，儒家克己复礼、弘扬大义的观念的确代表着一种更为正义、无私的价值取向，也受到了同时代的义士的认同并影响到他们的价值判断与人生选择，从而在更大的范围内影响了更多的人。但以历史的眼光来看，《战国策》体现了战国时代活跃的思想氛围。

Ⅵ. 译本链接

1. 翟江月：《战国策》（中英对照），桂林：广西师范大学出版社 2008 年版。

2. James. I. Crump，《战国策读本》，伦敦：牛津大学出版社 1970 年版。

3. Burton Watson，*Han Fei Zi*，New York：Columbia University Press，1964.

4. http：lib. hku. hk/bonsall/zhanguoce/index1. html.

Unit Eleven
Records of the Historian(《史记》)

I. 背景简介

Born in a family of astrologers of the Western Han Dynasty (202 B. C. – 9 A. D.), Sima Qian, the author of the venerable *Records of the Historian*, was greatly inspired at his young age by the ambition of his father as the royal Grand Astrologer, and inherited his father's dying wish to accomplish the masterpiece from his thirties to fifties. Sima Qian lived during the reigns of Emperor Jing (r. 156 B. C. – 140 B. C.) and Emperor Wu (r. 140 B. C. – r. 86 B. C.), but no record of the dates of his birth and death can be found in the historical documents.

Sima Qian

(r. 145 **or** 135 **B. C.** – **r.** 87 **B. C.**)

Standing first among the Twenty-four Histories, the official chronicles of China from the remote antiquity to the Ming Dynasty (1368 – 1644), *Records of the Historian* was the first general history in the form of a series of biographies to appear in China. The book consists of 130 chapters, recording the history of China from the era of the legendary founder of the Chinese nation Huangdi (Yellow Emperor) in prehistoric times to the reign of Emperor Wu of the Western Han Dynasty (202

B. C. −9 A. D.). As the most representative and outstanding one of all historical books in the Chinese tradition, the monumental work presented an encyclopedic writing style by integrating literary creation with the historical record. Enjoying its reputation for accuracy, lofty style and vivid characterization, the book marked the start of biographical literature in China's history and had a profound influence on the literary works of later generations. Due to the original and ground-breaking writing style, *Records of the Historian* was ranked by Lu Xun, a China's literary giant of the 20th-century, as the country's leading work of history. With lofty personality, dogged perseverance and a strong sense of historical responsibility, Sima Qian accomplished the masterpiece under his sufferings due to a court intrigue in 98 B. C.. For over 2,000 years, the historical masterpiece has been known not only in China but also worldwide.

Sima Qian makes a clear intention of why to write *Records of the Historian* in the "Autobiographic Note" and "Letter to Ren An" as "to explore the relationship between the Way of Heaven and the Way of Man, having a thorough understanding of the course of historical development and the changes involved therein, expound my own opinions of the events of the past and present my own system of analysis". With these aims, Sima Qian drew extensively on the historical materials, coordinating varied texts from the previous Chinese classics and integrating different schools of thought. Therefore, over 4,000 historical figures appear in *Records of the Historian*, more than 100 of them with complete biographies. Centering on the historical figures, the historical dramas are unfold before readers. The literary techniques Sima Qian employed in the book include appearance description, detail description, psychological description, contrast, exaggeration and so on.

With a panoramic view of the social-economic conditions before and in Western Han dynasty, Sima Qian presented his views and opinions on wealth and the means and manners by which the merchant princes rose to wealth and fame from humble origin. As stated in the closing paragraph concluding that there is no fixed road to wealth and goods do not stay with the same master forever, wealth flows to those with ability but slips through the hands of incompetent men.

Spreading from mouth to mouth for centuries, the stories narrated in *Lian Po and Lin Xiangru* have been handed down due to its dramatic plots and contrastive descriptions contributing to the noble characters of a civil officer and a general. Once again you will have a taste of Lin's patriotism and loyalty to the throne in the story of the jade and Lian's sincere repentance by offering a humble apology to Lin when Lian woke up to his error.

Ⅱ. 文本选读

Lian Po and Lin Xiangru
(Excerpted)

Lian Po[①] was an able general of Zhao. In the 16th year of King Huiwen[②], he commanded the Zhao army against Qi and defeated its troops, taking the city of Yangjin[③]. Then he was made a chief minister and was known for his prowess[④] to all the states.

Lin Xiangru[⑤], a man of Zhao, was the steward[⑥] of Miao Xian[⑦] the chief eunuch[⑧].

King Huiwen had come into possession of the jade of Bian He[⑨], a man of Chu. When King Zhao of Qin[⑩] knew this, he sent an envoy with a letter to the king of Zhao, offering fifteen cities in exchange for the jade. The king took counsel with General Lian Po and his chief ministers, who feared that if the jade were sent to Qin they might be cheated and get no cities in return, yet if they refused the soldiers of Qin might attack. They could neither hit on a plan[⑪] nor find an envoy to take their answer to Qin.

Then Miao Xian the chief eunuch said, "My steward Lin Xiangru would make a good envoy."

"How do you know?" asked the king.

He replied, "Once I did something wrong and secretly planned to escape to Yan[⑫], but my steward stopped me, asking, 'How can you be sure of the king of Yan?' I answered, 'I met him at the frontier with our king, and he privately grasped my hand and offered me his friendship. That is how I know, and why I mean to go there.' Lin said, 'Zhao is strong and Yan is weak, and because you stood well with our lord the king of Yan desired your friendship. But if you now fly from Zhao to Yan, for fear of Zhao he will not dare to keep you and will have you sent back in chains. Your only possible out is to bare your shoulder and prostrate[13] yourself before the axe and block for punishment. ' I took his advice and Your Majesty pardoned me. To my mind he is a brave, resourceful[14] man, well fitted to be our envoy. "

The king thereupon[15] summoned Lin Xiangru and asked him, "Should I accept the king of Qin's offer of fifteen cities in exchange for my jade?"

"Qin is strong, we are weak," replied Lin Xiangru. "We cannot refuse. "

"What if he takes my jade but will not give me the cities?"

"If we refuse Qin's offer of cities in exchange for the jade, that puts us in the wrong[16]; but if we give up the jade and get no cities, that puts Qin in the wrong. Of these two courses, the better one is to agree and put Qin in the wrong. "

"Who can be our envoy?"

"If Your Majesty has no one else, I will gladly take the jade and go on this mission. If the cities are given to Zhao, the jade will remain in Qin. If no cities are given, I shall bring the jade back unscathed. "

So the king of Zhao sent Lin Xiangru with the jade west to Qin.

The king of Qin sat in his pleasure pavilion to receive Lin Xiangru, who presented the jade to him. The king, very pleased, had it shown to his ladies and attendants, and all his attendants cheered.

Seeing that the king had no intention of giving any cities to Zhao, Lin Xiangru stepped forward and said, "There is a blemish on the jade. Let me show it to you, sir. "

As soon as the king gave him the jade, Lin Xiangru retreated to stand with his back to a pillar. His hair bristling with fury[17], he said, "To get this jade, great king, you sent a letter to the king of Zhao. When our sovereign summoned his ministers to discuss the matter, they said, 'Qin is greedy and, relying on its strength, hopes to get our jade in return for empty promises. We are not likely to receive the cities. ' They were against giving you the jade. It seemed to me, however, that if even fellows in homespun[18] can trust each other, how much more can powerful states. Besides, how wrong it would be to offend mighty Qin for the sake of a piece of jade! So the king of Zhao, after fasting[19] for five days, sent me with a letter and the jade to your court. Why? To show the respect and awe in which we hold your great country. Yet on my arrival you received me in a pleasure pavilion and treated me with contempt. You took the jade and passed it among your ladies to make a fool of me. I can see you have no intention of giving Zhao those cities in return, so I have taken back the jade. If you use force against me, I will smash my head and the jade against this pillar."

With that, glancing at the pillar, he raised the jade and threatened to smash it.

To save the jade, the king of Qin apologized and begged him to stop, then ordered the officer in charge to look up the map and point out the boundaries of the fifteen cities to be given to Zhao.

Lin Xiangru, thinking this was a subterfuge[20] and that Zhao would never really get the cities, declared, "The jade of Bian He is a treasure known throughout the world, but for fear of Qin the king of Zhao dared not withhold it. Before parting with it he fasted for five days. So it is only right, great king, that you too should fast for five days and then prepare a grand court reception. Only then dare I hand it over."

Since he could not seize the jade by force, the king agreed to fast for five days, during which time Lin Xiangru should be lodged in the Guangcheng Hostel[21].

Lin Xiangru suspected that despite his fast the king would not keep his promise to give the cities. So, dressing one of his followers in rags and concealing the jade on his person, he made him hurry back to Zhao by paths and byways.

When the king of Qin had fasted for five days, he prepared a grand reception for Zhao's envoy.

Lin Xiangru, arriving, announced to the king, "Since the time of Duke Mu of Qin[22], not one of the twenty-odd princes of your state has kept faith. Fearful of being deceived by Your Majesty and letting my country down, I sent a man back with the jade. He should be in Zhao by now. Qin is strong and Zhao is weak. When you, great king, sent a single messenger to Zhao, we immediately brought the jade here. If your mighty state had first given us fifteen cities, we should not have dared offend you by keeping the jade. I know I deserve death for deceiving you and beg to be boiled in the cauldron[23]. Consider this well with your ministers, great king!"

The king and all his ministers gaped at each other. Some attendants prepared to drag Lin Xiangru away, but the king said, "Killing him now will not get us the jade but would spoil our relations with Zhao. Better treat him handsomely[24] and send him back. The king of Zhao dare not risk offending Qin for the sake of a piece of jade."

Thereupon he entertained Lin Xiangru in his court, dismissing him when the ceremony was over.

The king of Zhao was so pleased with the skill with which Lin Xiangru had saved the state from disgrace that he made him a high councillor[25] on his return. Neither did Qin give the cities to Zhao, nor Zhao give the jade to Qin.

After this, Qin attacked Zhao and took Shicheng[26].

The following year twenty thousand men of Zhao were killed in another attack. Then the king of Qin sent an envoy to the king of Zhao, proposing a friendly meeting at Mianchi south of Xihe[27]. The king of Zhao was loath to go, for fear of Qin. But Lian Po and Lin Xiangru reasoned with him saying, "Not to go, sir, would make our country appear weak and cowardly."

So the king went, accompanied by Lin Xiangru.

Lian Po saw them to the frontier, where he bade the king farewell[28] saying, "I reckon that Your Majesty's journey there, the meeting and the journey back should not take more than thirty days. If you fail to return in that time, I suggest that we set up the crown prince as king, to thwart the designs of Qin."

The king, having agreed, went to meet the king of Qin at Mianchi.

The king of Qin, merry after drinking, said, "I have heard that the king of Zhao is a good musician, Will you play the cithern[29] for me?"

The king of Zhao did as he asked. Then the Qin chronicler[30] stepped forward and recorded, "On such-and-such a day the king of Qin drank with the king of Zhao and ordered the king of Zhao to play the cithern."

Lin Xiangru then advanced and said, "The king of Zhao has heard that the king of Qin is a good hand at Qin music. Will you entertain us with a tune on the pitcher③?"

The king of Qin angrily refused. But Lin Xiangru went forward to present a pitcher and, kneeling down, requested him to play. Still the king refused.

"I am only five steps from you," cried Lin Xiangru. "I can bespatter② you, great king, with the blood from your throat!"

The attendants wanted to kill him, but he glared and shouted so fiercely that they shrank back. Then the king of Qin sullenly③ beat once on the pitcher, whereupon Lin Xiangru turned to bid the Zhao chronicler record, "On such-and-such a date, the king of Qin played the pitcher for the king of Zhao."

Then the ministers of Qin said, "We hope Zhao will present fifteen cities to the king of Qin."

Lin Xiangru retorted, "We hope Qin will present Xianyang④ to the king of Zhao!"

At this feast, then, the king of Qin was unable to get the better of⑤ Zhao. Nor dared he make any move because of the strong guard brought by the king of Zhao.

Upon their return to Zhao after this meeting, Lin Xiangru was appointed a chief minister for his outstanding service, taking precedence over⑥ Lian Po.

Lian Po protested, "As a general of Zhao I have served the state well in the field and stormed many cities. All Lin Xiangru can do is wag⑦ his tongue, yet now he is above me. I'd think shame to work under such a base-born⑧ fellow." He swore, "When I meet Lin Xiangru I shall humiliate him!"

When Lin Xiangru got word of this, he kept out of Lian Po's way and absented himself from court on grounds of illness, not wanting to compete for precedence. Once when he caught sight of Lian Po in the distance on the road he drove his carriage another way.

His stewards reproached⑨ him saying, "We left our kinsmen to serve you because we admired your lofty character, sir. Now you have the same rank as Lian Po, but when he insults you in public you try to avoid him and look abjectly afraid. This would disgrace even a common citizen, let alone generals and ministers! We are afraid we must beg to resign."

Lin Xiangru stopped them, asking, "Is General Lian Po as powerful in your eyes as the king of Qin?"

"Of course not," they replied.

"If, useless as I am, I lashed out⁣④⁰ at the mighty king of Qin in his court and insulted his ministers, why should I be afraid of General Lian Po? To my mind, however, were it not for the two of us, powerful Qin would not hesitate to invade Zhao. When two tigers fight, one must perish④¹. I behave as I do because I put our country's fate before private feuds④². "

When word of this reached Lian Po, he bared his shoulders, fastened a switch of thorns④³ to his back and had a protégé④⁴ conduct him to Lin Xiangru's gate. He apologized, "Contemptible boor④⁵ that I am, I could not understand your magnanimity④⁶, sir!"

They became close friends, ready to die for each other.

[…]

(Translated by Yang Xianyi and Gladys Yang)

The Money-makers
(Excerpted)

Lao Zi said, "When perfect government prevailed, although neighbouring states within sight of each other could hear the crowing of each other's cocks and the barking of each other's dogs, the people of each enjoyed their own food, admired their own clothing, were content with their ways and happy in their work, and would grow old and die without having any dealings with each other."④⁷ Yet if we tried to set the world right④⁸ today by stopping up the eyes and ears④⁹ of the people, it would prove well-nigh⁵⁰ impossible.

[…]

*The Book of Zhou*⁵¹ says, "Without farmers, food will be scarce; without artisans, goods will be scarce; without merchants, the three precious things will disappear; without men to open up the mountains and marshes, there will be a shortage of wealth." Here we have the four sources of men's food and clothing. When these sources are large there is prosperity; when small, there is scarcity. Above[52], they enrich a state; below, they enrich a family. The laws governing poverty and wealth are immutable[53], and the shrewd have plenty while the stupid go short.

When Patriarch Lü Shang[54] was given Yingqiu[55] as his fief[56], the land was swampy and brackish[57] and sparsely inhabited; but he encouraged the women to work, developed skilled occupations and opened up trade in fish and salt, so that men and goods poured in from every side. Soon the state of Qi was supplying the whole world with caps, belts, clothes and shoes, and the states between the Eastern Sea and Mount Tai paid respectful homage to it[58].

Later, Qi's power declined, but Guan Zhong[59] restored it by setting up a new currency and nine treasuries. As a result, Duke Huan of Qi[60] became an overlord and nine times summoned the other feudal lords to conferences, bringing order to the whole empire. Guan Zhong was rewarded with the fief of Sangui[61], and although his rank was only that of a servant's servant[62], he amasses greater wealth than the princes of other states. So Qi remained rich and powerful through the reigns of King Wei and King Xuan[63].

Thus it is said, "When the granaries are full, men learn propriety. When food and clothing are enough, men have a sense of honour and shame[64]." Ceremony is born of sufficiency and disappears in time of want. That is why when a gentleman is rich he delights in cultivating virtue, but when an inferior man is rich he will display his power. Just as fish multiply in deep lakes and wild beasts flock to deep mountains, humanity and justice follow riches. A wealthy man's influence is greater while he has power, but once he loses power his protégés have nowhere to go and there is an end of pleasure. This is even more true of the barbarians[65].

As the proverb justly says, "A man with a thousand pieces of gold will not die in the market-place." So it is said,

"How quickly after gain,

The whole world races!

How madly after gain,

The whole world chases![66]"

Even the king of a land with a thousand chariots, a marquis with a fief often thousand households, or a lord with a hundred households dreads poverty, much more so, then, the common citizens on the state register[67].

When King Goujian of Yue[68] was in desperate straits on Mount Kuaiji, he followed the advice of Fan Li and Ji Ran[69]. Ji Ran said, "One who knows how to compete prepares in advance; one who understands seasonal needs knows commodities; and a grasp of these two things enables him to understand the whole market. Each year is dominated by an element. Metal means a good harvest, water a flood, wood a crop failure, and fire a drought. In time of drought, invest in boats; in time of flood, invest in carriages. This is the principle to follow. Every six years there will be a good harvest, every six years a drought, every twelve years a great famine. When the price of grain is too low, the farmers suffer; when it is too high, the merchants and artisans suffer. When the merchants and artisans suffer, wealth is not forthcoming; when the farmers suffer, they stop weeding the fields. If the price of grain is neither too high nor too low, farmers and merchants and artisans will all profit. The right way to govern is to keep the price of grain steady so that there is no lack of goods and no shortage of taxes.

"The way to accumulate wealth is to produce goods and not let money stay idle[70]. Let there be an exchange of goods. Do not store up perishable commodities, or go in for those which are costly. By noting surpluses and shortages, you can tell what will be expensive and what cheap. When prices rise too high, they must fall again; when prices fall too low, they will rise again. When things are expensive, sell them off[71] as if they were dirt, and buy up[72] cheap goods as though they were jewels. Money should circulate like flowing water."

After King Goujian had observed these rules for ten years, his kingdom was so rich and his soldiers so well rewarded that they charged against arrows and stones like thirsty men rushing to drink. Then he took his revenge on the powerful state of Wu, demonstrate the might of his arms throughout the land and became one of the Five Overlords.

After the disgrace of Kuaiji was wiped out, Fan Li sighed and said, "By using five of

Ji Ran's seven precepts, Yue gained its ends. They have been applied in our states, and now I shall try them out for the benefit of my own family. "

He sailed in a small boat down rivers and across lakes and, having changed his name, went to Qi, where he was known as Chiyi Zipi[73], the Old Wine-skin. Then he went to Tao, where he was known as Lord Zhu[74].

Observing that Tao, at the hub of the realm, was a centre of communications and of barter, he acquired land property there, stored up commodities, and made a profit by biding his time without much exertion. He was a good manager, a sound judge of men, able to take advantage of the times. Three times in nineteen years he accumulated a thousand pieces of gold, and twice divided these between distant relatives and those in want. He was, in fact, a rich philanthropist. Later, when he grew old and infirm[75], he turned over his affairs[76] to his sons and grandsons, who carried on and developed his business until they had millions. Thus Lord Zhu of Tao became a byword for a rich man.

Zi Gong[77], after studying with Confucius, went to hold office in Wei (1024 B. C. – 209 B. C.). He made money by buying cheap and selling dear in the region of Cao and Lu. Of the seventy disciples of Confucius, he was the richest. While Yuan Xian[78] had not even husks enough to fill his belly and lived hidden in a wretched lane, Zi Gong travelled in a carriage drawn by four horses with an escort of riders bearing rolls of silk to present to the rulers of states. And wherever he went, the ruler received him as an equal. Indeed, it was thanks to Zi Gong that the fame of Confucius spread—a clear case of power increasing reputation.

Bai Gui[79], a native of Zhou, lived during the time of Marquis Wen of Wei[80], when Li Ke[81] was utilizing the land to the full. Bai Gui, however, enjoyed looking out for seasonal changes. What others spurned[82] he took, what others sought he supplied, at harvest time he bought in grain and sold silk and lacquer, when cocoons came on the market he bought in raw silk and sold grain.

When the Primal Female Principle[83] is in the sign of Cancer[84] there will be a good harvest, but a bad one the following year. When it is in the sign of Libra[85] there will be a drought, but a good harvest the next year. When it is in the sign of Capricorn[86], a good harvest will be followed by a failure the next year. When it is in the sign of Aries[87], there will be a serious drought followed by a good crop but also a flood the next year. When it returns to the sign of Cancer, the yearly store of grain will be doubled.

When he wanted more money, Bai Gui bought inferior grain; when he wanted to increase his stock, he bought good seeds. He spent little on food and drink, curbing his appetite and sharing the hardships and pleasures of his slaves, but seizing on any chance of grain as fiercely as some wild beast or bird of prey.

He said, "I do business in the same way that Yi Yin[88] and Lü Shang planned their policies, Sun Zi and Wu Qi[89] made war, and Lord Shang[90] applied the law. If men lack the intelligence to change with the times, the courage to make quick decisions, the magnanimity[91] to give things away and the strength to hold what they have, though they want to learn my art I will not teach them."

So all the world knows Bai Gui as the father of business management. He set a standard for those who wanted to learn from him, and accepted only those who came up to this standard. He did not teach everyone.

[…]

To sum up, the extensive region of Chu and Yue is sparsely inhabited. The people eat rice and fish, prepare the land for ploughing by burning, cultivate paddy-fields[92], and have a sufficiency of fruit, gourds and shellfish so that they need not resort to trade. Since there is an abundance of food and no fear of famine, the people are indolent[93] and easy-going. They do not store up wealth and many of them are poor. As a result, in the south of the Huai and Yangtse Rivers no one suffers from cold or hunger, but neither are there very wealthy families.

In the north of the Yi and Si Rivers[94], the land is suitable for grain, mulberries, hemp and livestock. The area is not large but densely populated and, owing to the frequency of floods and drought, the people store up provisions. Hence in Qin, Xia, Liang and Lu attention is paid to agriculture and most of the people are farmers. The same is true of

Sanhe, Wan and Chen, although the people also engage in trade. The people of Qi and Zhao are shrewd and resourceful⑤ and live by their wits, while those of Yan and Dai make a living by farming, cattle-breeding and sericulture⑥.

From this one thing becomes clear. For what purpose do able men try to plan ahead in affairs of state, dispute with each other at court, abide by their word and die for their principles? For what purpose do hermits in mountain caves try by every means to win fame? Their aim is wealth and comfort. So honest officials, remaining long at their posts, get rich in the end. Honest merchants, too, become wealthy.

Wealth is something all men desire instinctively without having to be taught. Brave soldiers scale a city wall⑦ ahead of their fellows, break through enemy lines, throw back the foe, kill his general, capture his flag and brave arrows, stones, boiling water and flames, all because of the prospect of a rich reward.

Young men from the byways set on passers-by and rob them, murder men and bury their bodies, kidnap people and plunder them, rob graves, coin counterfeit money, become local despots⑧, seize property, carry out personal vendettas⑨ and do dark and secret deeds, defying all laws and prohibitions and rushing headlong into danger⑩ — they do all this for the sake of money too.

The girls of Zhao and Zheng paint their faces, play clear lyres, flutter their long sleeves, mince about⑪ in pointed slippers, make eyes at men, flirt, and will gladly go a thousand li to find a lover regardless of his age, because they are after wealth and comfort too.

Idle young nobles wear splendid hats and swords and keep carriages and retinues of riders⑫, to flaunt their riches and rank. Some go hunting, shooting or fishing morning and night, braving frost and snow and riding through valleys where wild beats may spring out at them, so eager are they to get game. Gamblers and those who bet on horses, cock-fights and hounds grow angry or boastful and insist on winning, so reluctant are they to lose their wagers⑬. Men who devote all their skill and energy to medicine, cooking or other arts, do so for the sake of handsome payment⑭. Clerks who juggle with phrases⑮ twist the law⑯, fake seals and forge signatures[107] at the risk of decapitation[108] or being sawn asunder[109], do so because they have been bribed.

In the same way, peasants, artisans, merchants and cattle-breeders seek wealth and an increase of their possessions. Men of any intelligence spare no effort and will stop at nothing to achieve this, never letting slip a chance to make money.

There is a maxim: "Don't go a hundred li to sell firewood. Don't go a thousand li to deal in grain." If you are to be in a place for one year, sow grain; if for ten years, plant trees; if for a hundred years, rely on virtue—in other words on personal prestige. There are men with no government stipends[110], no revenue from fiefs, who live as well if they had these things and are called "nobles without titles". An enfeoffed noble[111] lives off taxes and levies an average of two hundred cash a year from each household. Thus the lord of a thousand households had an annual income of two hundred thousand cash, out of which he has to cover the expenses of his visits to court to pay homage, his gifts to other nobles and his sacrifices.

Common people such as farmers, artisans and merchants, who have ten thousand cash, can get a yearly interest of two thousand. This means that families with a million cash will also have an income of two hundred thousand, enough to buy themselves off conscript service[112], pay taxes and duties and still get all the fine clothes and food they want.

Thus it is said that a man's income equals that of a marquis with a fief of a thousand households if he has any of the following: pastures with fifty horses or a hundred and sixty-seven oxen, or two hundred and fifty sheep; swamps with two hundred and fifty pigs; ponds stocked with a thousand piculs[113] of fish; hills bearing a thousand timber trees; a thousand jujube trees in Anyi; a thousand chestnut trees in Yan or Qin; a thousand tangerine trees in Shu, Han or Jiangling; a thousand catalpas north of the Huai River, south of Changshan, or between the Yellow and Ji Rivers; a thousand mu of lacquer trees in Chen or Xia; a thousand mu of mulberries or hemp in Qi and Lu; a thousand mu of bamboos in Weichuan; a thousand mu of land producing sixty-four pecks a mu in the vicinity of cities[114] with ten thousand households in big provinces; a thousand mu of safflower; a thousand plots of ginger or scallion. Such men do not have to go to market or travel to other districts, but can sit at home waiting for the harvest, living as private gentlemen of means.

As for those paupers with old parents and an ailing wife and children who are not ashamed of being unable to sacrifice at the right season or to provide entertainment, food, drink, clothing and bedding, such men have no social standing. That is why, as a general rule, a man with no money works hard, one with a little money use his wits, and one who is well off⑪⑤ seizes every chance to better himself.

A good man should exert himself to make a living without waiting till he is in desperate straits. The best kind of wealth comes from farming, the next best from trade and handicrafts, the worst from evil practices. When, in spite of poverty and lowliness⑪⑥, one who is no hero or gentlemen of talent still talks about virtue and justice, he ought to be thoroughly ashamed of himself.

The ordinary citizen will abase himself before one ten times richer than he, fear one a hundred times richer, serve one a thousand times richer, and be the slave of one ten thousand times richer. This is the nature of things.

If a poor man wants to become rich, it is better to be an artisan than a farmer, better to be a merchant than an artisan, better to be a vender than work at embroidery⑪⑦. In other words, trade and handicrafts are the best way for a poor man to make money.

In centers of communications and large cities a man can live like the lord of a thousand chariots if each year he produces a thousand jars of wine, a thousand jars of vinegar or a thousand pots of sauce; if he slaughters a thousand oxen, sheep or pigs; if he sells a thousand zhong⑪⑧ of grain or a thousand cartloads of firewood; if he owns boats ten thousand feet long if set in a line, a thousand logs of timber, ten thousand bamboo poles, a hundred small carriages, a thousand oxcarts, a thousand varnished wood utensils⑪⑨, thirty thousand catties⑫⑩ of bronze, a thousand piculs of safflower, plain wooden vessels and iron implements, two hundred horses, two hundred and fifty oxen, two thousand sheep and swine, a hundred slaves, a thousand catties of tendons, horns and cinnabar, thirty thousand catties of silk floss, a thousand bolts of patterned silk, a thousand piculs of coarse cloth, skin or hide, a thousand *dou*[121] of lacquer, a thousand da of yeast, salt and salted beans; a thousand catties of large sea fish, a thousand piculs·of small fish, thirty thousand catties of salted fish, three thousand piculs of jujubes and chestnuts, a thousand fox or squirrel furs, a thousand piculs of sheep skins, a thousand carpets, or a thousand zhong of fruit and vegetables; or if he lends out a thousand strings of cash[122], demanding an interest of thirty percent from merchants who are greedy and fifty percent from those who are scrupulous[123]. This is the general rule. Various other trades which bring in a profit[124] of less than twenty percent are not worth pursuing.

Now let me speak briefly of how able men in recent times have made fortunes in different parts, so that later generations may profit by their example.

The ancestor of the Zhuo of Shu came from Zhao[125], where he made a fortune by smelting iron. When Qin conquered Zhao, the family was moved away and Zhuo and his wife as captives had to push a cart to the place assigned to them. Other captives who had little money asked the officers not to send them too far away, and were allowed to settle in Jiameng[126].

But Zhuo said, "That is a circumscribed[127] and barren region. I have heard that at the foot of Mount Wen[128] there is fertile land where taros[129] grow so well that no one need ever go hungry; and trade is easy in the local market."

So he asked to be sent far away and was assigned to Linqiong[130], to his great delight. Then he smelted iron ore from the mountain, contriving to[131] have workers sent there from Dian and Shu. He became so rich that he had a thousand slaves and could live like a lord, hunting and shooting among the fields and lakes.

Cheng Zheng[132], who was taken captive east of the mountains and forced to resettle, smelted iron too and traded with the people who wear their hair in cone-shaped knots[133]. He became as wealthy as Zhuo and also lived in Linqiong.

The ancestors of the Kong family of Wan[134] came from Wei (403 B. C. – 225 B. C.) where they had made a living by smelting iron. When Qin conquered Wei, the family was moved to Nanyang and carried on iron smelting on a large scale till Kong owned hills and lakes and a retinue of carriages and horses. He travelled through various states making money by trading, but had the name of a gentleman of leisure while he was making fabulous profits, far exceeding those of other tight-fisted merchants[135]. His family came to have thousands of pieces of gold, and all the travelling merchants of Nanyang imitated his easy manner.

The men of Lu are frugal and close-fisted[136], and the Bing family of Cao[137] was more so than most. Although they made tens of thousands by smelting iron, the whole family from the grandparents to the grandchildren by common accord seized every chance to make money. They engaged in usury[138] as well as trade in all the provinces and principalities. Indeed, it was owing to this family that so many people in Zou and Lu gave up the pursuit of learning to seek profit.

The men of Qi despise slaves, but Dao Jian[139] treated his well. And whereas other men mistrusted cunning slaves, he specially looked out for them and set them to trade in fish and salt to make a profit for him. Some of his slaves travelled about in carriages with mounted retainers[140] and made friends with provincial governors and ministers, but Dao Jian only trusted them the more, with the result that they helped him make tens of millions. Hence the saying, "An official title is not as good as working for Dao Jian." This was because he let his slaves become rich and powerful while utilizing their abilities to the full.

The men of Zhou are canny, and Shi Shi[141] more than most. With a few hundred cartloads of goods, he traded in every single province and principality. Luoyang lies at the center of Qi, Qin, Chu and Zhao, and the poor people in the city imitated the rich, priding themselves on making long business trips and passing their houses without time to cross the threshold[142]. By employing such men, Shi Shi succeeded in making seventy million.

The ancestor of the Ren family of Xuanqu[143] was a granary officer[144] at Dudao. When the Qin empire was overthrown and the chief citizens were scrambling for gold and jade, Ren's was the only family to store up grain. Soon the armies of Chu and Han (206 B. C. – 8 A. D.) were locked in combat at Xingyang, the peasants could not farm and the price of a picul of rice rose to ten thousand. Then gold and jade flowed from the others to the Rens, who made a fortune. Most rich men rival each other in extravagance, but the Rens lived simply and frugally, farming and raising cattle. Most farmers and cattle-breeders look out for bargains[145], but they bought only the best and most valuable. That is why they have remained rich for generations. The elder Ren has a rule that the family must not eat or wear anything not produced from their own fields and pastures, and must not drink wine or eat meat till their business is finished. As a result, they are an example to the whole district, rich and highly regarded by the emperor.

After the extension of the northern frontier, Qiao Yao[146] alone seized the opportunity to acquire a thousand horses, two thousand head of cattle, ten thousand sheep and ten thousand zhong of grain.

When Wu, Chu and the five other states revolted, the nobles in Chang'an joined the imperial army and tried to raise money for the expedition. But because their principalities lay east of the Pass and the outcome of the fighting there was uncertain, most of the money-lenders refused to make loans. Only the Wuyan family[147] lent them a thousand pieces of gold at an interest of nine hundred percent. When three months later the rebellion was crushed, Wuyan received a tenfold return on his money, becoming one of the richest men within the Passes.

Most of the wealthiest merchants within the Passes belong to the Tian family[148], such as Tian Se and Tian Lan. The Li family of Weijia and the Du families of Anling and Du[149] are also worth millions.

These are some of the most outstanding examples. None of these men had fiefs or government stipends, nor did they make money by evading the law or by sharp practice[150]. They simply acted intelligently and kept up with the times[151]. They made their fortunes in trade and handicrafts but preserved them through agriculture, seized their wealth in war but retained it by peaceful means. There was method in their rise to fortune which is worth studying.

Countless other cases might be cited of men who made money by working hard at farming, cattle-breeding, handicrafts, lumbering or trade, the greatest of them dominating provinces, the next counties, and the lesser ones villages⑬².

Thrift and hard work are the proper way to make a living, yet men always owe their wealth to some special gift. Farming is tough work, yet by it Qin Yang⑬³ became predominant in his province. Grave-robbing is evil, yet this gave Tian Shu⑬⁴ a start in his career. Gambling is bad, yet that is how Huan Fa⑬⁵ made his money. Pedding⑬⁹ is a low occupation, yet Le Cheng of Yong⑬⁷ became wealthy in this way. Selling animal fat is degrading, yet by so doing Yong Bo⑬⁸ made a thousand gold pieces. Hawking drinks is a poor trade, yet that is how the Zhang family⑬⁹ made ten million. Sharpening knives requires little skill, yet it enabled the Zhi family⑯⁰ to live like lords with food served in tripods⑯¹. Selling preserved tripe⑯² is lowly enough, yet in this way the Zhou family had a mounted retinue. A horse doctor is held cheap, yet Zhang Li⑯³ had bronze bells to make music. All these men achieved wealth through single-mindedness.

From this we can see that there is no fixed road to wealth, and goods do not stay with the same master forever. Wealth flows to those with ability as the spokes⑯⁴ of a wheel converge upon the axle⑯⁵, but it slips like a smashed tile⑯⁶ through the hands of incompetent men. A family with a thousand pieces of gold is comparable to the lord of a city; a man with millions can live like a king. Not for nothing⑯⁷ are such men called "nobles without fiefs⑯⁸".

(Translated by Yang Xianyi and Gladys Yang)

Ⅲ. 难点释义

① Lian Po，廉颇，战国时期赵国的名将。

② King Huiwen，赵惠文王。

③ Yangjin，阳晋，地名。

④ prowess，勇猛。

⑤ Lin Xiangru，蔺相如，战国时期赵国大臣，官至上卿，赵国宦官头目缪贤的家臣，战国时期政治家。

⑥ steward，即古书上所说的舍人或门客。

⑦ Miao Xian，缪贤，战国时期赵国的宦者令，蔺相如的举荐者。

⑧ eunuch，太监。

⑨ jade of Bian He，即著名的和氏璧。相传，春秋时期楚人卞和得一玉璞，先后献给楚厉王和楚武王，都被认为欺诈，先后受刑被砍去双脚。楚文王即位，他抱璞哭于荆山下，文王使人琢璞，得宝玉，名为"和氏璧"。

⑩ King Zhao of Qin，秦昭王。

⑪ hit on a plan，临时想到一个计策。

⑫ Yan，燕国。

⑬ prostrate，俯卧。

⑭ resourceful，足智多谋。

⑮ thereupon，副词，于是，随即。

⑯ puts us in the wrong，使我们成为过错方。

⑰ bristling with fury，怒发冲冠。

⑱ even fellows in homespun，穿着素衣的普通百姓。

⑲ fasting，斋戒，原形为 fast。

⑳ subterfuge，托词，借口。

㉑ Guangcheng Hostel，光程公馆。

㉒ Duke Mu of Qin，秦穆公。

㉓ cauldron，大锅。

㉔ treat him handsomely，对他宽厚相待。

㉕ councillor，上大夫，相当于如今的顾问。

㉖ Shicheng，石城，地名。

㉗ Mianchi south of Xihe，西河外的渑池。

㉘ bade the king farewell，与大王诀别。

㉙ cithern，瑟，古乐器。

㉚ chronicler，史官，御史。

㉛ pitcher，陶罐。

㉜ bespatter，溅污。

㉝ sullenly，脸色阴沉地，不高兴地。

㉞ Xianyang，咸阳，地名。

㉟ get the better of，占上风，打败。

㊱ taking precedence over，地位高于……。

㊲ wag，饶舌，摆动。

㊳ base-born，出身卑微的。

㊴ reproached，指责。

㊵ lashed out，猛烈抨击。

㊶ perish，消亡。

㊷ feuds，争斗，不合。

㊸ a switch of thorns，一根带刺的荆条。

㊹ protégé，门客，门徒。

㊺ contemptible boor，可鄙的粗人。

㊻ magnanimity，宽宏大量。

㊼ 这番话出自《道德经》第八十章，描述了老子理想中的小国寡民的世相。

㊽ set the world right，用方略来经世济国。

㊾ stopping up the eyes and ears，堵塞耳目。

㊿ well-nigh，几乎，相当于 almost。

(51) *The Book of Zhou*，即《周书》，又名《逸周书》、《周志》。

(52) above，用空间方位词来隐喻事理的程度，相当于“往大的方面说”，其后的 below 则表示“往小的方面说”。

(53) immutable，不变的。司马迁此处主要是指贫富有道，因人而异。

(54) Patriarch Lü Shang，即姜太公吕尚。

(55) Yingqiu，营丘，地名。

(56) fief，封地，采邑。

(57) swampy and brackish，沼泽多，盐碱重。

(58) paid respectful homage to it，（各诸侯国）向齐国表示敬意。

(59) Guan Zhong，即管仲，春秋时期齐国名相。

(60) Duke Huan of Qi，齐桓公。

(61) Sangui，三归，供游赏用的三座高台。

(62) a servant's servant，陪臣，春秋时诸侯的大夫对周天子自称为陪臣。

(63) King Wei and King Xuan，即齐威王与齐宣王。

(64) When the granaries...a sense of honour and shame，即著名的“仓廪实而知礼节，衣食足而知荣辱”，原语出自《管子·牧民》。

(65) barbarians，野蛮人。此处指中国古代的东部（夷）和北方（狄）落后的少数民族。

(66) 与这四行诗句对应的原文是：“天下熙熙，皆为利来；天下攘攘，皆为利往。”

(67) the common citizens on the state register，有户籍的民众。

(68) King Goujian of Yue，即越王勾践。

(69) Fan Li and Ji Ran，范蠡与计然。二人都是春秋时期越国谋士。

(70) let money stay idle，闲置钱财。

(71) sell them off，廉价出售。

(72) buy up，全部收购。

(73) Zhiyi Zipi，鸱夷子皮。范蠡经商时为自己取的名字。

(74) Lord Zhu，陶朱公。范蠡曾在陶这个地方经商，并成为巨富，后人因此对他以“陶朱公”相称，范蠡也由此成为民间财神的原型之一，被尊为“商圣”。下文对此有文字叙述。

(75) infirm，衰弱。

(76) turned over his affairs，移交事务。

(77) Zi Gong，子贡，即端木赐（前520－前446），春秋末年卫国人，孔子的得意门生，子贡利口巧辞，办事通达，善于经商，曾富致千金，为孔子弟子中首富。

(78) Yuan Xian，原宪，孔子弟子，出身贫寒，个性狷介，一生安贫乐道，不肯与世俗合流。

(79) Bai Gui，白圭，东周时期人，曾弃政从商，经营有方。

(80) Marquis Wen of Wei，魏文侯。

(81) Li Ke，李克，人名。

(82) spurned，唾弃，鄙视。

⑧ Primal Female Principle，太阴，八卦中的四象（太阴，少阴，太阳，少阳）之一。

⑧ Cancer，巨蟹座。

⑧ Libra，天秤座。

⑧ Capricorn，摩羯座。

⑧ Aries，白羊座。

⑧ Yi Yin，伊尹，夏末商初人，曾辅佐商汤王建立商朝。

⑧ Wu Qi，吴起，战国时期政治家、军事家。

⑨ Lord Shang，商鞅。

⑨ magranimity，宽宏大量，慷慨。

⑨ paddy-fields，水稻田。

⑨ indolent，懒散。

⑨ Yi and Si Rivers，沂水与泗水。

⑨ shrewd and resourceful，精明与机智。

⑨ sericulture，养蚕业。

⑨ scale a city wall，登攀城墙。

⑨ local despots，地方豪强。

⑨ carry out personal vendettas，替人仇杀。

⑩ rushing headlong into danger，末路狂奔。

⑩ mince about，碎步走。

⑩ retinues of riders，随从车骑。

⑩ wagers，赌注。

⑩ handsome payment，丰厚的报酬。

⑩ juggle with phrases，玩弄词句。

⑩ twist the law，枉法。

⑩ fake seals and forge signatures，私刻印章、伪造文书。

⑩ decapitation，斩首。

⑩ being sawn asunder，受刀锯之刑。

⑩ stipends，俸禄。

⑪ an enfeoffed noble，授予封地的贵族。

⑫ buy themselves off conscript service，雇人服兵役。

⑬ piculs，原形为 picul，石（容量单位）。

⑭ in the vicinity of cities，在城郊。

⑮ well off，富裕的。

⑯ lowliness，地位低贱。

⑰ embroidery，刺绣。

⑱ zhong，钟，古代计量单位。

⑲ varnished wood utensils，涂漆的木器。

⑳ catties，原形为 catty，斤（重量单位）。

㉑ dou，斗（容量单位）。

㉒ ends out a thousand strings of cash，放贷一千贯。

㉓ scrupulous，谨小慎微。

㉔ bring in a profit，产生（增加）利润。

㉕ Zhuo of Shu came from Zhao，赵国蜀郡的卓氏。

㉖ Jiameng，葭萌，地区名。

㉗ circumscribed，隔绝的。

㉘ Mount Wen，汶山。

㉙ taros，芋头。

㉚ Linqiong，临邛，地区名。

㉛ contriving to，设法做到。

㉜ Cheng Zheng，程郑，人名。

㉝ in cone-shaped knots，锥形发髻。

㉞ Kong family of Wan，宛这个地方的孔氏。

㉟ tight-fisted merchants，吝啬的商人。

㊱ frugal and close-fisted，节俭而吝啬。

㊲ Bing family of Cao，曹这个地方的邴氏。

㊳ usury，高利贷。

⑬⑨ Dao Jian，刀间，人名。

⑭⓪ carriages with mounted retainers，装备完好的马车。

⑭① Shi Shi，师史，人名。

⑭② passing their houses without time to cross the threshold，路过家门口却不入。

⑭③ Ren family of Xuanqu，宣曲这个地方的任氏。

⑭④ granary officer，管理粮仓的官员。

⑭⑤ look out for bargains，争相购买便宜货。

⑭⑥ Qiao Yao，桥姚，人名。

⑭⑦ Wuyan family，无盐氏。

⑭⑧ Tian family，田氏。

⑭⑨ Li family of Weijia and the Du families of Anling and Du，韦家的栗氏，安陵和杜县的杜氏。

⑮⓪ sharp practice，不正当的手段。

⑮① kept up with the times，与时俱进。

⑮② the next counties, and the lesser ones villages，在 counties 和 villages 之前，都承前省略了 dominating。意思是说，大的富甲一郡，中等的富盖一县，小的富盖乡里。

⑮③ Qin Yang，秦扬，人名。

⑮④ Tian Shu，田叔，人名。

⑮⑤ Huan Fa，桓发，人名。

⑮⑥ pedding，沿街叫卖。

⑮⑦ Le Cheng of Yong，雍这个地方的乐成（人名）。

⑮⑧ Yong Bo，雍伯，人名。

⑮⑨ Zhang family，张氏。

⑯⓪ Zhi family，郅氏。

⑯① in tripods，成三足鼎立的形式。主要是指衣食充足无忧。

⑯② preserved tripe，腌制的牛肚。

⑯③ Zhang Li，张里，人名。

⑯④ spokes，（车辆的）辐条。

⑯ axle，车轴。

⑯ smashed tile，破碎的瓦片。

⑯ not for nothing，不是没有道理的，是有原因的。

⑯ nobles without fiefs，素封者，指不靠官府封赏而靠自己的能力获得很高社会地位和经济地位的人。

Ⅳ. 问题思考

1. Wealth and trade were once restrained in China before the policy of Opening up and Reform was implemented in the late 1970s, but soon after, they were put on top agenda in the blueprint of economic growth. What is the significance of *The Money-makers* in modern China?

2. In traditional Chinese culture, wealth from trade is basically devalued and tradesmen are despised accordingly. But Sima Qian didn't seem to accord with the traditional view. Instead, he advocated material production and goods circulation, attaching great importance to trade and tradesmen. Try to demonstrate the concept of wealth held by Sima Qian.

3. In displaying distribution of natural products of different places and aspects of productive labour, Sima Qian mentioned repeatedly local customs and lifestyles. Why did Sima Qian keep in mind the possible influence of local customs on productive labour and business deals?

4. What makes the difference between nobles and "nobles without titles" in making fortunes?

5. Sima Qian revealed the law governing poverty and wealth and, as he said, the shrewd have plenty while the stupid go short. Can we safely conclude that wealth is accumulated by trickery or evil practices exclusively? Why or why not?

Ⅴ. 经典导读

太史公司马迁所著《史记》素以史料丰富翔实，文笔宏微俱秀而流芳百世。鲁迅先生誉之为"史家之绝唱，无韵之离骚"。作为中国第一部纪传体通史，《史记》

的历史和文学价值体现在后世在相关领域里不懈的探索、研究和学习中。可以毫不夸张地说，《史记》是知识的宝库，其影响是深远而广阔的。

《廉颇与蔺相如列传》是《史记》列传中的千古名篇，它是一部合传，不仅为廉、蔺两人立传，也为赵奢、李牧两位战国名将立传。篇幅上各占一半，可见司马迁对历史英雄人物的肯定与敬重。其中，"完璧归赵"、"渑池之会"、"负荆请罪"三个故事集中展现了廉颇、蔺相如两个人物，"赵奢治税"、"阏与之围"、"纸上谈兵"、"长平之战"、"廉颇之死"、"李牧之死"则主要体现赵奢和李牧两个人物。列传中的人物个个形象丰富饱满、生动鲜明，这一方面得力于司马迁对历史材料的取舍和安排，另一方面得力于作者的艺术创作手法，作者通过矛盾冲突、语言描写、动作描写、对比以及渲染铺垫和陪衬映托等手法，突显传记人物的个性特征，颂扬他们的历史功绩。

"完璧归赵"是每个中国人都很熟悉的故事。概括地讲，它沿着取璧、保璧、归璧的情节发展顺序行文，使蔺相如与和氏璧的命运紧密相连，前者的人格特征通过后者的命运发展得到充分的表现。还是因为和氏璧，廉颇与蔺相如的关系得以演变，两人的性格特征和人格魅力也进一步得到充分体现。列传开头只叙廉、蔺两人的身份、地位悬殊对比，为下文的人物矛盾作铺垫。接下来，在缪贤的举荐下，读者

"完璧归赵"故事情节连环画

以未见其人先闻其声的方式知晓了蔺相如"其人勇士，有智谋"的过人之处。面对秦王威慑，虚情假意以十五座城池求璧，赵国君臣举棋不定的艰难抉择，蔺相如首先提出"宁许以负秦曲"的外交方针，而后坚毅地"愿奉璧往使"。在秦王面前，蔺相如献璧取璧、保璧归璧、抗言秦廷，临危不惧，据理力争，大义凛然，智勇双全，捍卫了赵国的尊严与安全。

渑池之会显然是秦国出于对"秦亦不以城与赵，赵亦终不予秦璧"的不满意结局的报复行为。强秦假意示好，"赵王畏秦，欲勿行"。蔺相如晓之以理，并随行出访。面对秦王对赵王公然的侮辱，蔺相如针锋相对，机智勇敢，使得秦王"终不能

加胜于赵"，捍卫了赵王的威严，秦赵双方最终取得暂时的军事抗衡。司马迁运用细腻的文笔把大量的人物对话和人物动作的细节描写融入历史事件。例如，在应对赵王提问和氏璧"予"与"不予"秦国时，蔺相如力陈利弊，并主动请缨，语言描写相当简练深刻。在秦廷之上，蔺相如"持璧却立，倚柱，怒发上冲冠"，"睨柱"，"张目叱之"，动作描写准确入微。此外，通过大量对赵王、秦王的表情、语言和行为的细节描写来烘托蔺相如的人物形象，使其在重重矛盾冲突中栩栩如生，令人敬畏。

司马迁运用渲染的手法，将廉、蔺两人的矛盾写得剑拔弩张，摄人心魄。居功自傲的廉颇嫉恨有加，四处扬言见蔺相如"必辱之"。出人意料的是，以大局为重、不计个人恩怨的蔺相如对无理取闹的廉颇一再忍让退避。对比场景，一动一静，交相辉映。最终心胸宽阔的蔺相如令廉颇羞愧难当，负荆请罪，廉、蔺将相言和，结为刎颈之交。显然，司马迁刻画廉、蔺二人主次分明。以蔺相如为主，廉颇为次。司马迁丰富变换的创作手法为人物形象的刻画起到了至关重要的作用。这些都是读者在阅读中要特别注意的地方。

《货殖列传》是《史记》七十列传中独树一帜的名篇。简单地说，该文率先为富商大贾列传，首次展示了我国从春秋末期到西汉时期的自然条件、物产、人口、农业、工商业等政治、经济概况以及社会风俗习惯。因此，后人认为，《货殖列传》使司马迁成为我国具有经济学思想之第一人。

货殖，即经商，指货物的生产与流通。财富正是在货物的生产与流通过程中逐渐积累起来的。然而，货物不会凭空而至，财富不会坐等拥有。财富之于个人和国家，其重要性不言而喻。无论国家还是个人，只有结合实际情况，因人、因地、因时制宜，积极从事生产劳动，保障社会物资供应，把握时机，促进物资流通，发展商品贸易，才能创造发达的物质财富。这种朴素的劳动生产理论和社会经济思想在《货殖列传》一文中都有充分体现。无论是劳动生产、商品流通，还是经济发展，都是人们追求财富的社会体现。司马迁的"财富观"可以从以下三个方面予以说明。

第一，追求财富顺应自然，人之本性。司马迁说，自《诗》、《书》所记述的虞夏时代以来，人类就追求物质感官享受，追慕财富。为求衣食无忧，安居乐业，人们根据地方物产资源，竭尽所能，从事耕种、捕捞、开采、砍伐、制造、贸易等活动，求得各自所需，这是"道之所符"，"自然之验"，"人之情性，所不学而俱欲者也"，就像流水趋下，日夜无休一样自然。所谓"天下熙熙，皆为利来；天下攘攘，皆为利往"（How quickly after gain, the whole world races, How madly after gain, the whole world chases），都是财富驱动着人们为之奋力前往的结果。拥有千乘战车的君王也好，封有万户食邑的列侯也罢，无不如此，更何况平民百姓呢？司马迁认为，作为执政的统治阶级，顺应百姓的这种需求为上策，再次是因势利导，其次是教诲，再其次是整顿约束，下策是与民争斗。

第二，财富对于个人与国家具有根本的重要性。一人之事，基于衣食，度于仁义；一国之立，基于富强，安于仁治。财富无疑是安身立国的基本物质保障，也是上升到个人和国家精神意识层面的重要物质前提。"仓廪实而知礼节，衣食足而知荣辱"（When the granavies are full, men learns propriely; when food and clothing are enough, men have a sense of honor and share），司马迁借用春秋时期辅助齐桓公称霸的管仲之言，说明了财富对于富国强民的重要性。他说，君子富有了，才好施行他的仁德，小人富足了，就会发挥他的能力。就像水深了就有鱼存在，山深了就有野兽藏身，只有人富有了，仁义才会归附于他。司马迁例举子贡、原宪、白圭、猗顿、乌氏倮、巴寡妇清等诸多发财致富的历史名人轶事，广泛说明财富对于个人和国家的重要性。这些富有之人，多出身寒微，不名一文，后经商致富，以至富甲一方，得势显赫，有的甚至与君王分庭抗礼而名扬天下。列举这些事实，司马迁分明向后人昭示财富是存身之本，立人之道，人富则位高，国富则历久。

从现代马斯洛需求层次理论（Maslow's hierarchy of needs theory）看，司马迁肯定"仓廪实"、"衣食足"之于礼节荣辱的积极作用是符合客观事实的。同时，他肯定了富国裕民之道，这反映了他的进步的历史观。当然，作者在文中把人分成"君子"和"小人"，是依照当时统治阶级的标准来划分的；"人富而仁义附"的观点，过分强调了财富对人的品德形成的作用，而忽视了思想教育的意义，具有一定的历史局限性。

第三，致富有方。这是司马迁在《货殖列传》里所要表述的重要内容。从开篇否定老子所设想的"至老死不相往来"（People would grow old and die withoat having any dealings with each other）的理想社会开始，司马迁就开明宗义地表明了生产与流通之间的重要关系。从富国之策来讲，管仲设"轻重九府"，管理财物钱币治理齐国，使之强盛延绵数代。越王勾践采纳计然的富国之道，"平粜齐物，关市不乏"，"务完物，无息币"，"以物相贸，易腐败而食之货勿留，无敢居贵"，"贵出如粪土，贱取如珠玉"，"财币欲其行如流水"，凭借这些灵活机动的"贸易法"和"生意经"，越国逐渐强大，终于复仇吴国雪耻。从个人致富的角度看，范蠡"与时逐"，"择人而任时"，意思是说经商之道在于抓住时机追求利润，选择人力而把握时机。

文章悉数非因官爵封邑俸禄的"素封"之人，都是依靠审时度势，随机应变的"巧者"、"贤人"，他们靠工商末业发财，用农耕本业守财，勤劳节俭，诚心专一，终成富商巨贾。司马迁还不惜笔墨，关注了一些从事"末业"或"不务正业"的人，他们致富不问出身，出奇制胜，也获得了大的财富。

总而言之，《货殖列传》是中国文化典籍中首次为商人立传的文献。司马迁用他的千秋史笔为后世讲述了春秋至西汉时期的富商大贾的事迹，包括他们的经营思想、个人能力、经营风格等致富的个人主观条件，描绘了在那段历史时期内出现这些富商大贾的社会客观条件，包括他们的身世、发家致富的经过、财产的数量、经营的规模、活动的范围、社会地位，各地的自然条件、物产、人口、农工商业等经济发展情况和风俗习惯等。《货殖列传》被认为是研究司马迁经济思想的重要材料。全文史料丰富，据事论理，说服力强；结构严谨，层次分明；语言精美，明快畅达，亲切自然。

Ⅵ. 译本链接

1. 杨宪益、戴乃迭英译：《史记选》，北京：外文出版社 2008 年版。

2. 林语堂：《货殖列传·司马迁》，《伯夷列传·司马迁》，见《古文小品译英》，北京：外语教学与研究出版社，2009 年版。

3. Burton Watson：*Shiji*，New York：Columbia University Press，1968.

4. Http：//www.chinahistoryforum.com.（中国历史论坛网站）

Unit Twelve
Sun Zi: *The Art of War* (《孙子兵法》)

I. 背景简介

Sun Zi or Sun Tzu, the author of *The Art of War*, was a well-known Chinese military strategist and philosopher during the Spring and Autumn Period. There are scanty facts of his life. Some historians date his lifetime to 544 B. C. – 496 B. C.. According to *The Spring and Autumn Annals*, Sun Zi was born in Qi, while Sima Qian disagreed with this statement in the later *Records of the Grand Historian*. Sima Qian stated that Sun Zi was a native of Wu and served the King of Wu Helü as a general and strategist in the late sixth century B. C..

Sun Zi (544 **B. C.** – 496 **B. C.**)

The Art of War, the earliest known treatise on war and military science written by Sun Zi, is a masterpiece about the philosophy of war for managing conflicts and winning battles. It comprises 13 essays: "Making Assessments", "Waging War", "Attacking by Stratagem", "Disposition", "Momentum", "Weaknesses and Strengths", "Contest to Gain the Initiative", "Varying the Tactics", "Deploying the Troops", "The Terrain", "Nine Regions", "Attacking by Fire", and "Using Spies". These essays become a systematic guide to strategies and tactics of the war. They discuss how to make assessments of the weaknesses and strengths of two parties, stress the importance of using spies to get accurate information about the enemy's forces, and emphasize the unpredictability of battle and the need for varying tactics.

As it reveals the nature and important rules of warfare, *The Art of War* has been called a real "military classic", and its author Sun Zi a "military genius".

The Art of War is a condensation of Sun Zi's experience of warfare. Since the Spring and Autumn Period, it has had a tremendous influence on military, political and even philosophical thought in China. It was introduced into Japan in 760 A. D. and since the 17th century it has been translated into various languages. Nowadays, it has become one of the most popular military books in the world and influences many competitive endeavors in Southeast Asia and Western countries in various fields including politics, culture, business, and sports, as well as modern warfare.

Ⅱ. 文本选读

Making Assessments (Book One)

Sun Zi said:

War[①] is a question of vital importance to the state, a matter of life and death, the road to survival or ruin. Hence, it is a subject which calls for careful study.

To assess the outcome of a war, we need to examine the belligerent parties and compare them in terms of the following five fundamental factors:

The first is the way (*dao*); the second, heaven (*tian*); the third, earth (*di*); the fourth, command (*jiang*); and the fifth, rules and regulations (*fa*).

By "the way", I mean moral influence, or that which causes the people to think in line with their sovereign so that they will follow him through every vicissitude, whether to live or to die, without fear of mortal peril.

By "heaven", I mean the effects of night and day, of good and bad weather[②], of winter's cold and summer's heat; in short, the conduct of military operations in accordance with the changes of natural forces.

By "earth", I mean distance, whether it is great or small; the terrain, whether it is treacherous or secure; the land, whether it is open or constricted; and the place, whether it portends life or death.

By "command", I mean the wisdom, trust-worthiness, benevolence, courage and firmness of the commander.

By "rules and regulations", I mean the principles guiding the organization of army units[3], the appointment and administration of officers[4] and the management of military supplies and expenditures[5].

There is no general who has not heard of these five factors. Yet it is he who masters them that wins and he who does not that loses. Therefore, when assessing the outcome of a war, compare the two sides in terms of the above factors and appraise the situation accordingly.

Find out which sovereign possesses more moral influence, which general is more capable, which side has the advantages of heaven and earth, which army is better disciplined, whose troops are better armed and trained, which command is more impartial in meting out rewards and punishments, and I will be able to forecast which side will be victorious.

The general who employs my assessment methods is bound to win; I shall therefore stay with him. The general who does not heed my words will certainly lose; I shall leave him.

Having paid heed to my assessment of the relative advantages and disadvantages[6], the general must creates a favorable strategic situation which will help bring the victory to fruition. By this I mean being flexible and making the most of the advantages to gain the initiative in war.

War is a game of deception[7]. Therefore, feign incapability when in fact capable; feign inactivity when ready to strike; appear to be far away when actually nearby, and vice versa. When the enemy is greedy for gains, hand out a bait to lure him; when he is in disorder, attack and overcome him; when he boasts substantial strength, be doubly prepared against him; and when he is formidable, evade him. If he is given to anger, provoke[8] him. If he is timid and careful, encourage his arrogance. If his forces are rested, wear them down. If he is united as one, divide him. Attack where he is least prepared. Take action when he least expects you.

Herein lies a strategist's subtlety of command which is impossible to codify in hard-and-fast rules beforehand.

He who makes full assessment of the situation at the prewar council meeting in the temple (translator's note: an ancient Chinese practice) is more likely to win. He who makes insufficient assessment of the situation at this meeting is less likely to win. This being the case, what chance has he of winning if he makes no assessment at all? With my assessment method, I can forecast who is likely to emerge as victor.

(Translated by Lin Wusun)

Attacking by Stratagem (Book Three)

Sun Zi said:

Generally in war, the best policy is to take the enemy state whole and intact; to destroy it is not. To have the enemy's army surrender in its entirety⑨ is better than to crush it; likewise, to take a battalion⑩, a company⑪ or a five-man squad intact is better than to destroy it. Therefore, to fight a hundred battles and win each and every one of them is not the wisest thing to do. To break the enemy's resistance without fighting it.

Thus, the best policy in war is to thwart the enemy's strategy. The second best is to disrupt his alliance through diplomatic means. The third best is to attack his army in the field. The worst policy of all is to attack walled cities.

Attack a walled city only when there is no alternative. For it takes at least three months to get the mantelets⑫ and shielded vehicles⑬ ready and prepare the necessary arms and equipment; for it takes another three months to build the earthen mounds for soldiers to ascend the walls. The commander who loses his patience orders his troops to assault like swarming ants, with the result that one third of his men are slain and the city remains untaken. Such is the calamity of attacking walled cities.

Therefore, he who is skilled in war subdues the enemy without fighting. He captures the enemy's cities without assaulting them. He overthrows the enemy kingdom without prolonged operations in the field. By taking all under heaven with his "whole and intact strategy," he wins total victory without wearing out[14] his troops. This is the method of attacking by stratagem.

Consequently, the art of using troops is: when you outnumber the enemy ten to one, surround him; When five to one, attack him; when two to one, divide him; and if equally matched, stand up to him. If you are fewer than the enemy in number, retreat. If you are no match for him, try to elude him. For no matter how stubbornly a small force may fight, it must in the end succumb to greater strength and fall captive to it.

The commander is the country's bulwark. His proficiency in war can make the country strong, his deficiency make it weak.

There are three ways by which a sovereign may bring disaster to his army.

One, he arbitrarily orders his army to advance or retreat when in fact it should not, thus hampering the initiative of the army[15].

Two, he interferes with the administration of the army when he is ignorant of its internal affairs, thus causing confusing among the officers and men.

Three, he interferes with the officers' command, unaware of the principle that an army should adopt different tactics according to different circumstances. This will create misgivings in the minds of the officers and men.

When an army is confused and fraught with misgivings, neighboring states will take advantage of the situation and attack. This will disrupt the army and help the enemy to win.

Therefore, there are five factors to consider in anticipating which side will win, namely:

The side which knows when to fight and when not to will win;

The side which knows the difference between commanding a large army and a small army will win;

The side which has unity of purpose among its officers and men will win.

The side which engages enemy troops that are unprepared with preparedness on its own part will win;

The side which has a capable commander who is free of interference from the sovereign will win.

Bearing these points in mind, one is able to forecast victory in a war.

Therefore I say: Know your enemy and know yourself, and you can fight a hundred battles without peril. If you are ignorant of the enemy and know only yourself, you will stand equal chances of winning and losing. If you know neither the enemy nor yourself, you are bound to be defeated in every battle.

Using Spies（Book Thirteen）

Sun Zi said:

Now, when an army of 100,000 is raised and sent on a distant campaign, the expenses borne by the people, together with the disbursements of the treasury[16], will amount to a thousand pieces of gold daily. There will be continuous commotion at home and abroad. As many as 700,000[17] households will be unable to pursue their farm work, exhausted as they are by their toil on the roads. The two armies may confront each other for years before the day comes for the decisive battle. Therefore, a commander shows extreme lack of consideration for his people if he is too stingy to grant ranks, honors and a hundred pieces of gold to his spies and, as a result, loses the battle because he is ignorant of the enemy's situation. Such a person is no commander worthy of his soldiers, no counselor worthy of his sovereign, no master of victory.

The enlightened sovereign and the capable commander conquer the enemy at every move and achieve successes far surpassing those of ordinary people because they possess "foreknowledge". This "foreknowledge" cannot be obtained from ghosts or sprits, nor from gods, nor by analogy with past events[18], nor from events, nor from astrological calculations[19]. It can only come from men who know the enemy situation.

Hence the use of spies, of whom there are five kinds, namely, the native, the internal, the converted, the expendable and the surviving agents. When these five kinds of agents operate simultaneously and with total secrecy in their methods of operation, it can work miracles. This magical weapon constitutes a real treasure for the sovereign.

A native agent is the enemy's own countryman in your employ.

An internal agent is an enemy official whom you employ.

A converted agent, or double agent, is an enemy spy whom you employ.

An expendable agent is one who is deliberately given false information to mislead the enemy.

A surviving agent is one who returns with information from the enemy camp.

Of all those in the army close to the commander, none is more intimate than the agents; of all rewards, none more liberal than those given to agents; of all matters, none more confidential than those relating to secret operations. He who lacks wisdom cannot use agents; he who is not humane and generous cannot direct agents; he who is not sensitive and alert cannot get the truth out of them. So delicate and so secretive is espionage that there is nowhere you cannot put it into good use.

But if plans relating to secret operations are prematurely divulged, the agent and all those to whom he has leaked the secret should be put to death.

Generally, whether the object is to crush an army, to storm a city, or to assassinate an enemy official, it is always necessary to begin by finding out the identities of the garrison commander, his staff officers, retainers, gate-keepers and guards. The agents must be directed to obtain this information. It is essential to find out who the enemy agents are who have been sent to spy on you and to bribe them into serving you. Give them instructions and send them back home. This is how converted agents are recruited and used. It is through the information provided by the converted agents that native and internal agents are recruited and used, that the expendable agents can be sent to pass on false information to the enemy, and that the surviving agents can come back with the needed information as scheduled. The sovereign must be fully aware of the activities of all five kinds of agents. And it is the converted agent who is crucial to his obtaining the needed information. Therefore, he must treat the latter with the utmost generosity.

In ancient times, Yi Zhi[20], who had served the Xia Dynasty, was instrumental in the rise of the Yin (Shang) Dynasty over Xia. Likewise, Lü Ya[21], who had served the Yin Dynasty, had much to do with the rise of the succeeding Zhou Dynasty.

Therefore, only the enlightened sovereign and wise commanders who are capable of using the most intelligent people as agents are destined to accomplish great things. Secret operations are essential in war; upon them the army relies in deciding its every move.

(Translated by Lin Wusun)

Ⅲ. 难点释义

① war，兵，此处特指军事。

② good and bad weather，阴阳。阴阳是中国古代概括宇宙万象万物内在基本矛盾的一对范畴，但在此篇中专指气象和天象，如天气晴雨、天象昼夜的变化。

③ the principles guiding the organization of army units，曲制。曲，中国古代军队编制较小的单位，曲制，即军队编制的制度。

④ the appointment and administration of officers，官道，即对军队各级将领的职责划分和管埋形式、管理制度。

⑤ the management of military supplies and expenditures，主用。主，主持，这里可解释为掌管。用，费用，这里指军队的物资费用。主用，就是指对军队后勤军需的管理。

⑥ assessment of the relative advantage and disadvantages，计利。计，计较，这里引申为衡量。计利，指权衡利益。

⑦ a game of deception，诡道。诡，欺诈。道，这里引申为方法、计谋。诡道，指欺诈的方法和计谋。

⑧ provoke，挠，此处意为挑逗。

⑨ entirety，全军。军，春秋时期的军队编制，每军为 12 500 人。

⑩ battalion，旅。春秋时期军队的编制，每旅为 500 人。

⑪ company，卒。春秋时期军队的编制，每卒为 100 人。

⑫ mantlets，橹。一种用藤草制成的大盾牌。

⑬ shielded vehicles，辒，一种用桃木制成四周用牛皮遮蔽的大型攻城战车。

⑭ wearing out，顿，通"钝"，疲惫、挫折。

⑮ hampering the initiative of the army，縻军。"縻"，羁縻。指束缚军队的行动。

⑯ the disbursements of the treasury，公家之奉，国家开支的费用。

⑰ 700,000 households，七十万家。按曹操、李筌的注解，古代制度是一家从军，需要七家负担运输国粮等各种劳役。

⑱ nor by analogy with past events，不可象于事。象，比推、类比。不可象于事，不可能用对等相似事物的类比中去推想出敌情。

⑲ nor from astrological calculations，不可验于度。不可以用于主观机械的计度去体验所获得的敌情是否准确。

⑳ Yi Zhi，伊挚（在夏）。伊挚，指伊尹，原为夏桀的大臣以后归附商汤为相，在灭夏的过程中，伊尹发挥了很大的作用。

㉑ Lü Ya，吕牙（在殷）。吕牙，指姜尚，又名姜子牙，原是商纣时期的隐士，后归附于周武王。

Ⅳ. 问题思考

1. "War is a question of vital importance to the state, a matter of life and death, the road to survival or ruin." What do you think of Sun Zi's attitude towards the war according to this remark?

2. What are the five fundamental factors in assessing the outcome of a war? Discuss in details the importance of these factors in a war. How do you understand the first sentence "generally in war, the best policy is to take the enemy state whole and intact; to destroy it is not"?

3. Why the commander is called "the country's bulwark" by Sun Zi? What is the essence of Sun Zi's stratagem in the essay? Discuss with your classmates why Sun Zi put the "Using Spies" as the ending article of *The Art of War*?

4. How do you understand "[this] 'foreknowledge' cannot be obtained from ghosts or spirits, nor from gods, nor by analogy with past events, nor from astrological calculations. It can only come from men who know the enemy situation"?

5. What's the purpose of Sun Zi to mention Yi Zhi and Lü Ya in the concluding paragraph of "using spies"?

V. 经典导读

据司马迁《史记》记载，约前 515 至前 512 年间，（孙武）以兵法见于吴王阖闾。阖闾曰："子之十三篇，吾尽观之矣，可以小试勒兵乎?"说的是孙子带着所传《孙子兵法》十三篇晋见吴王，随即获得吴王重用的事迹。之后，孙子被封为吴国上将军，并为吴王立下了赫赫战功。

《孙子兵法》成书于春秋末期，是中国现存最早的最有价值的军事典籍，内含军事篇章十三篇，分别为《计篇》、《作战篇》、《谋攻篇》、《形篇》、《势篇》、《虚实篇》、《军争篇》、《九变篇》、《行军篇》、《地形篇》、《九地篇》、《火攻篇》和《用间篇》。该书语言简洁，内容富含哲理，总结了春秋时代的战争经验，揭示出战争的本质和一些重要规律。在书中探讨变化无穷的战略战术时，孙子运用了丰富的辩证法思想来阐述战争中系列矛盾的对立和转化，如敌我、主客、众寡、强弱、攻守、胜败、利害等，这当中体现的辩证思想在中国后世的辩证思维发展史中都占有重要地位，而他所强调的"知道"、"慎战"等军事思想更是对其后中国的政治和经济都

"知彼知己，百战不殆"成为千古名言

产生了重大影响。在孙子看来，最佳的胜利是不战而胜，即不通过正面战斗，而通过其他的方法来对敌军进行消耗，从而击溃敌人。日本的逢屋千村因此评价《孙子兵法》是教人和平的，并据此认为，孙子是一位和平主义者。无疑，《孙子兵法》中关于"慎战"的思想，对当今世界格局仍然具有积极的借鉴意义。

作为世界上第一部军事著作，《孙子兵法》中一些著名的革命性军事命题、基本思想和理论在世界范围内具有极大的影响力。美军前参谋长联席会议主席科林·鲍威

尔是这样评价《孙子兵法》的:"我读过中国的经典《孙子兵法》。这本书被研究了数百年,他对现在的政治家和士兵们都有鼓舞和指导作用。我们要求每个现役军人都要研读《孙子兵法》,所以每个美国大兵都知道这本书。"日本和朝鲜是世界上最早翻译和引入《孙子兵法》的两个国家。据考证,早在唐朝初期,该书就已传入朝鲜和日本,此后在这两个国家掀起了一股研究《孙子兵法》的浪潮。至18世纪,法国天主教耶稣会传教士阿米欧首次把《孙子兵法》翻译成法语引入欧洲,引起了欧洲公众的重视。到目前为止,《孙子兵法》已被译成英语、法语、俄语等数十种语言,在世界各地广为传播。而它的作用也不再仅仅局限于一本军事著作的范畴,它还为人们提供了许多思考问题和解决问题的方法,并在政治、经济、文化等各个领域不断发挥着重要作用。

《计篇》为《孙子兵法》的首篇,作为开篇,它对整本书所提出的军事战略起着提纲挈领的作用,它是孙子军事思想体系的代表,之后的十二篇都是在《计篇》的基本思想下延伸发展的。

在《计篇》中,孙子以"计"作为他军事战略思想研究的起点,"计"的意思是计算、估计,即战前的战略谋划,而"庙算"是《计篇》的中心战略预测思想和运筹理论。孙子所指的庙算包含了"五事七计":"五事"即"道、天、地、将、法",分别指作战双方的政治、天时、地利、将帅素质、军事体制这五个方面;"七计"由"五事"演绎而来,是指从七个方面即从双方政治清明、将帅才能、天时地利、法纪严明、武器优良、士卒训练有素、赏罚公正来分析敌我双方的情况,以探索战争胜负的情势("校之以计而索其情")。

《谋攻篇》为《孙子兵法》的第三篇,主要论述了如何以智谋进攻敌国、不专用武力的问题。归纳起来,孙子在《谋攻篇》中主要提出了以下五种军事主张:第一,"不战而屈人之兵。"(to break the enemy's resistance without fighting)孙子认为,作战的最高理想是不经交战而使敌人屈服,这样就达到了完整地保全自己又降服敌人的目的。第二,"上兵伐谋。"(The best policy in war is to thward the enemy's strategy)战争的最佳手段是以智谋取胜,以尽可能小的代价,取得战争的最大成功,即尽量做到不战而胜,不硬攻而夺取敌城,不久战而毁灭敌国。第三,"五则攻之、十则围之。"用兵应当遵守的法则是审时度势,在对敌我双方的兵力做了精确评估之后灵活应对,十倍于敌就包围敌人，五倍于敌就攻击敌人，两倍于敌就分散敌人，和敌人兵力相当时就与之对抗，实力弱于敌人时就退却。第五，"夫将者，国之辅也。"强调将帅是国家的辅佐，责任重大，辅助周密，国家就强盛，辅助有缺陷，国家就会衰弱。第五，"知己知彼，百战不殆。"（To know your enemy and yoursel, and you can fight a hundred boottles whithout peril）作战的关键是掌握信息。了解敌人又了解自己，历经百战都不会有危险；不了解敌人但了解自己，可能会胜利，也可能会失败；即不了解敌人，也不了解自己，那就每战必败。

《用间篇》为《孙子兵法》十三篇中的最后一篇。篇名中的"间"意即"间谍"，"用间"意为如何使用间谍之道，也就是现代人所说的情报战争。可以说，《用间篇》是中外战略思想史中最早把情报纳入战略思想体系的著作。

孙子在《用间篇》中提出了五种具体的"间"的形式，即"因间"、"内间"、"反间"、"死间"、"生间"。所谓"因间"，是指利用敌国的乡野之民充当间谍；所谓"内间"，是指利用敌国的官吏充当间谍；所谓"反间"，是指通过收买或利用敌方的间谍，为我所用；所谓"死间"，是指将假情报传播出去，让潜入敌方的我方间谍得知，再传给敌方；所谓"生间"，即能沽着回来报告情况的间谍。孙子强调，把以上"五间"合用，使敌方无从掌握我方用间的规律，是战争的制胜法宝。

Ⅳ. 译本链接

1. 林戊荪译：《孙子兵法·孙膑兵法》，北京：外文出版社 2011 年版。

2. Lionel Giles, M. A. . *Sun Tzu on the Art of War*. Leicester：Allandale Online Publishing，1910.

Unit Thirteen
Records of the Three Kingdoms &
Romance of the Three Kingdoms
(《三国志》 与 《三国演义》)

I. 背景简介

Chen Shou, style name Chengzuo, was the author of *Records of the Three Kingdom*. He was born in Anhan Prefecture, Baxi Commandery in Kingdom of Shu and lived in 233 A. D. – 297 A. D.. As a first-class historian living in the late Three Kingdoms period and early Western Jin Dynasty, he made a historical record on the Three Kingdoms of Wei, Shu and Wu with the form of a series of biographies in *Records of the Three Kingdoms*.

Chen Shou (233 A. D. – 297 A. D.)

The creation time of *Records of the Three Kingdoms* was in the second half of the 3rd century. The work comprises 65 volumes and about 360,000 Chinese characters which are divided into three books. The book *Wei* contains 30 volumes about the history of the Wei Kingdom; the book of *Shu*, 15 volumes of Shu Kingdom; the book of *Wu*, 20 volumes of Wu Kingdom. And each volume is composed of one or more biographies. In the work, Chen Shou offered an authoritative and official account of the important historical facts of the rival states Cao Wei, Shu Han and Eastern

Wu of the Three Kingdoms from 189 A. D. to 280 A. D. , which covers politics, military, economy, as well as academy, literature and science. In addition, it includes some histories of the ethnic minorities in China and of the neighboring countries of that age.

Although there are some imprecise and wrong information of historical events in the work and the account is plain and little more than a collection of historical facts due to its writing form of chronicle and biography, we can not deny its great historical value as it helped establish true history of the Three Kingdoms. It has been regarded as one of the early four historiographies of the Twenty-Four Histories canon with the other three works, *Records of the Grand Historian*, *Hanshu* (History of the [Former] Han Dynasty) and *Hou Han Shu* (History of the Later Han Dynasty).

Luo Guanzhong (1315 – 1400)

Luo Guanzhong, identified by historians to have lived in the late Yuan Dynasty and early Ming Dynasty, is the author of *Romance of the Three Kingdoms*. The facts about his life are scanty. It is believed now that he was born in Shangxi Province between 1315 to 1318 and died in Zhejiang province in 1400.

Romance of the Three Kingdoms is set in the chaotic years between 169 A. D. and 280 A. D. near the end of the Han Dynasty and the Three Kingdoms era of China. In fact, there have been many myths about the Three Kingdoms era as oral traditions during the Yuan Dynasty before Luo Guanzhong era. Until Ming Dynasty, more attempts to combine these myths into a written work were made as people showed more interests in this subject.

Romance of the Three Kingdoms comprises 120 chapters with 800,000 words, depicting nearly a thousand dramatic characters (mostly real in history). In the book, the author made use of some available historical records, including Chen Shou's chronicle book *Records of the Three Kingdoms* and some materials from Tang Dynasty poetic works and Yuan Dynasty operas. Additionally, the author fully exerted his own historical knowledge and imagination, enriching the stories well and creating hands of characters who are full of personalities. The artist achievements made in accounting the stories and portraying the characters are the greatest highlights of the work. As one of the four great classical novels of Chinese literature (the other three are *Dream of the Red Chamber*, *The Pilgrimage to the West* and *Water Margin*), *Romance of the Three Kingdoms* has become the most widely read novel in modern China and Southeast Asia.

Ⅱ. 文本选读
Reords of the Three kingdom：Zhuge Liang
(Excerpted)

[…]

Our late king① passed away before the great undertaking founded by him was half accomplished. Now China is divided into three kingdoms. Yizhou② is drained of its manpower and resources. This is a critical juncture of life or death for our country. Bearing the late king's special favor in hearts, the officials at court who guard Your Majesty dare not slacken in their vigilance and the devoted officers and soldiers at the front are fighting bravely disregarding their personal safety. They are now repaying to Your Majesty what they have received from the late king. It is advisable that Your Majesty should listen extensively to the counsels of officials in order to carry on the late king's lofty virtues, and heighten the morale of people with high aspirations. It is injudicious that Your Majesty should unduly humble yourself, and use metaphors with distorted meanings, lest you should block the way of sincere admonition.

The imperial court and the Prime Minister's Office are an integral whole. There should be impartiality in meting out rewards and punishments to officials from either administration. For both those who are treacherous and violate the law and those who are loyal and do some good deed, the same legally appointed officials③ should pass decision on how to punish or reward. This will make plain the equality and sagaciousness of Your Majesty's rule. There should be neither prejudice nor partiality in Your Majesty's attitude towards the officials inside and outside the court for fear that different laws be put into practice.

Shizhong④ Guo Youzhi⑤ and Fei Yi⑥ as well as Shilang⑦ Dong Yun⑧ are kind and honest men with a strong sense of loyalty. The late king appointed them for your sake, and I respectfully opine that all political affairs at court, regardless of magnitude, be first subjected to their inquiry before actions are taken. In this way can errors be amended, negligence avoided, and greater results attained.

General Xiang Chong⑨ is well versed in military affairs and is kind and just by nature. After evaluating his performance on a trial basis⑩, the late king praised his talent and ability. That is why officials have elected him to be commander-in-chief. I humbly suggest that military concerns, regardless of weight, be first met with his consultation. In this way will there be harmony among the troops, and men both capable and incapable will each find his proper place in the camp.

To be close to the virtuous and able officials, to keep away from the vile and mean persons, that was the reason that the Western Han Dynasty was prosperous. To be close to the vile and means persons, to keep away from the virtuous and able officials, that was the reason that the Eastern Han Dynasty collapsed. When the late king was alive and talked with me about these historical lessons, he used to heave a sigh in detestation for Emperor Huan and Emperor Ling⑪. Shizhong⑫, Shangshu⑬, Changshi and Canjun⑭ are faithful, upright, and ready to lay down their lives for honor and fidelity. As your humble servant, I hope that Your Majesty will retain close ties to them and trust them. Then can the prosperity of the Han Dynasty be soon realized.

I was originally a commoner who had to wear clothes made of hemp, and tilled land in Nanyang⑮. I merely managed to survive in times of turbulence and had no intention of seeking fame and position from princes. With an utter disregard of my low social status and meager fund of knowledge, the late king condescended to visit me at my thatched cottage three times to consult me about the current events of the country. I felt so grateful that I promised to serve him. Soon afterwards we suffered a military defeat⑯. Twenty-one years have passed since I received my assignment at the time of the setback and was dispatched as an envoy at the moment of crisis.

The late king knew my prudence, and entrusted me on his death bed with the duty of assisting Your Majesty in governing the country. Since then I have been worrying and sighing night and day lest I should do harm to the late king's illustrious fame if I fail to be effective. I was thus compelled to lead an army across the Lu River in May[17] and went deep into the barren district. Now the whole south is under our rule and we have plenty of fighters and armaments. It is time to reward our army men[18] and lead them northward to conquer the Central Plains. Although I am inferior in ability like a worn-out horse or a blunt knife, I would do my utmost to root out treacherous evildoers, rejuvenate the Han Dynasty, and move the capital back to the old city[19]. I owe this to the late king and wish to demonstrate my loyalty to Your Majesty. As for government affairs such as the augmentation or repeal of certain measures, or the broadening of the way to receive exhortations, they are the duties of Gou Youzhi, Fei Wei, and Dong Yun.

I hope Your Majesty would delegate to me the task of punishing the traitors and rejuvenating the Han Dynasty. If I should fail to achieve this, please punish me as to console the soul of the departed king. If Youzhi, Wei, and Yun fail to gather exhortations for the fostering of virtues, they should be held responsible for their negligence. Your Majesty should also make the most of your resources to solicit opinions on governing a country, to judge judiciously and accept good advices, and always bear in mind the imperial edict issued by the late king prior to his death. If this can be achieved, you will have my extreme gratitude.

I will be journeying far, and my eyes are full of tears in writing this memorial upon my departure. I can hardly express what else I should say.

(Translated by Luo Jingguo)

Preface of *Romance of the Three Kingdoms*
O so vast, O so mighty,

The Great River rolls to sea,

Flowers do waves thrash,

Heroes do sands smash,

When all the dreams drain,

Same are lose and gain.

Green mountains remain,

As sunsets ingrain,

Hoary fishers and woodcutters,

And some small rafts and calm waters,

In autumn moon, in spring winds,

By the wine jars, by porcelains,

Discuss talk and tale,

Only laugh and gale.

(Translated by C. H. Brewitt-Taylor)

Chapter 46 K'ung-ming Borrows Ts'ao Ts'ao's Arrows through a Ruse
(Excerpted)

[…]

By the fifth watch[20], K'ung-ming's little convoy[21] was nearing Ts'ao Ts'ao's river base. The vessels advanced in single file[22], their prows pointed west. The crew began to roar and pound their drums. Lu Su was alarmed. "What if they make a sally?" he asked. K'ung-ming smiled and replied, "I'd be very surprised if Ts'ao Ts'ao plunged into this fog. Let's pour the wine and enjoy ourselves. We'll go back when the fog lifts[23]."

As the clamor[24] reached Ts'ao Ts'ao's camp, the new naval advisers Mao Chieh and Yu Chin sent reports at once. Ts'ao Ts'ao issued an order: "The fog has made the river invisible. This sudden arrival of enemy forces must mean an ambush. I want absolutely no reckless movements. Let the archers and crossbowmen, however, fire upon the enemy at random." He also sent a man to his land headquarters calling for Chang Liao and Hsu

Huang to rush㉕ an extra three thousand crossbowmen to the shore. By the time Ts'ao's order reached Mao Chieh and Yu Chin, their men had already begun shooting for fear the southerners would penetrate their camp. Soon, once the marksmen from the land camp had joined the battle, ten thousand men were concentrating their shots toward the river. The shafts came down like rain.

K'ung-ming ordered the boats to reverse direction and press closer to shore to receive arrows while the crews continued drumming and shouting. When the sun climbed, dispersing the fog, K'ung-ming ordered the boats to hurry homeward. The straw bundles bristled with㉖ arrow shafts, for which K'ung-ming had each crew shout in unison㉗, "Thanks to the prime minister for the arrows!" By the time this was reported to Ts'ao Ts'ao, the light crafts, borne on swift currents㉘, were twenty tricents *li* downriver, beyond overtaking㉙. Ts'ao Ts'ao was left with the agony of having played the fool.

[…]

(Translated by Moss Roberts)

Ⅲ. 难点释义

① Our late king，先帝，指刘备。因刘备此时已死，故称先帝。

② Yizhou，益州，今四川省一带，这里指蜀汉政权。

③ appointed officials，有司，官吏，此指主管刑赏的官吏。

④ Shizhong，侍中，官名，皇帝的亲臣。

⑤ Guo Youzhi，郭攸之，南阳人，当时任刘禅的侍中。

⑥ Fei Yi，费祎（yī），字文伟，江夏人，刘备时任太子舍人，刘禅继位后，任费门侍郎，后升为侍中。

⑦ Shilang，侍郎，官名，皇帝的亲臣。

⑧ Dong Yun，董允，字休昭，南郡枝江人，刘备时为太子舍人，刘禅继位，升任黄门侍郎，诸葛亮出师时又提升为侍中。

⑨ Xiang Chong，向宠，三国襄阳宜城人，刘备时任牙门将，刘禅继位，被封为都亭侯，后任中部督。

⑩ After evaluating his performance on a trial basis，试用于昔日。据《三国志·蜀志·向朗传》记载，章武二年（222）刘备在秭归一带被东吴军队击败，而向宠的部队损失却甚少，试用于昔日指当此。

⑪ Emperor Huan and Emperor Ling，桓、灵，指桓帝刘志、灵帝刘宏。正是他们两位皇帝让东汉末年的皇帝政治腐败，使刘汉王朝倾覆。

⑫ Shizhong，侍中，指郭攸之、费祎、董允等人。

⑬ Shangshu，尚书，这里指陈震，南阳人，建兴三年（225）任尚书，后升为尚书令。

⑭ Changshi and Canjun，长史，这里指张裔，成都人，刘备时曾任巴湘乡人，当时任参军。诸葛亮出驻汉中，留下蒋琬、张裔来统管丞相府事，后又暗中上奏给刘禅："臣若不幸，后事宜以付琬。"

⑮ Nanyang，南阳，指隆中，在湖北省襄阳城西。隆中在当时属南阳郡管辖。

⑯ Soon afterwards we suffered a military defeat，意指以后遇到危难，此处指建安十二年（208）刘备在当阳长坂坡被曹操打败，退至夏口，派诸葛亮去联结孙权，共同抵抗曹操。

⑰ across the Lu River in May，五月渡泸，指建兴元年（223）云南少数民族的上层统治者发动叛乱，建兴三年（225）诸葛亮率师南征，五月渡泸水，直到秋天才平定了这次叛乱，下句"南方已定"即指此意。泸，泸水，即金沙江。

⑱ army men，三军，古代诸侯国的军队分上、中、下三军，三军即全军。

⑲ the old city，旧都，指东汉都城洛阳或西汉都城长安。

⑳ watch，夜晚的某个时段。

㉑ convoy，船队。

㉒ in single file，一列排开。

㉓ lifts，消失。

㉔ clamor，叫喊声。

㉕ rush，迅速出动。

㉖ bristled with，充满。

㉗ in unison，齐声。

㉘ borne on swift currents,顺流而行。

㉙ beyond overtaking,难以赶上。

Ⅳ. 问题思考

1. How many parts is *Records of the Three Kingdoms* made up of?

2. What, in the style of narrative, is the difference between *Records of the Three Kingdom* and *Romance of the Three Kingdoms*?

3. Why are there only 15 volumes of Shu Kingdom in *Records of the Three Kingdoms*?

4. What do you think the author Chen Shou's political view is reflected in the work? Discuss its influence on the development of later Chinese political system.

5. What's K'ung-ming's purpose to order the crew to roar and pound their drums?

6. Describe the mood of Ts'ao Ts'ao at the end of the text in your own words.

Ⅴ. 经典导读

西晋时期著名史学家陈寿（233—297）所写的《三国志》最初是以《魏志》、《吴志》、《蜀志》三书单独流传的，直到北宋咸平六年（1003），三书才合为一书。该书不仅是中国史学名著之一，同时也是"二十四史"中评价最高的"前四史"之一。

《三国志》一共六十五卷，分别为《魏书》三十卷，《蜀书》十五卷，《吴书》二十卷。主要记载了从魏文帝黄初元年（220）到晋武帝太康元年（280）六十年间魏、蜀、吴三国鼎立时期的纪传体国别史。"志"的意思为"记载"，《三国志》的意思是为魏、蜀、吴三国的纪传体正史，这有别于野史记载。因陈寿是晋朝朝臣，晋承魏而得天下，所以《三国志》中尊魏为正统，只为魏志有本纪，而列蜀、吴为传。《三国志》为曹操写了本纪，为曹操、曹丕、曹叡分别写了武帝纪、文帝纪、明帝纪，而刘备、孙权等都只有传，没有纪，如记刘备、刘禅为先主传、后主传，记孙权称吴主传。

《三国志》叙事简洁，文辞精练，剪裁得当，一出版就极受赞许，因此在其时就有"本书一出，其他三国诸史尽废"的说法。后人对该书也是推崇备至，认为在记载三国历史的所有史书中，只有陈寿的《三国志》可以同《史记》、《汉书》等相媲美，并有人把《三国志》和《史记》、《汉书》、《后汉书》并称为四大正史，指出读史的人必先读此四史。但后世对《三国志》仍有诸多诟病。首先，《三国志》中对于一些重要的历史人物和事件的记载过于简单，前人说其书"裁制有余，文采不足"。相较魏、蜀、吴三书，不难看出，《蜀书》比《魏书》、《吴书》更为简略，仅得十五卷，这是因为当时蜀国没有史官，后期也没有现成的蜀汉史书可借鉴，而王沈的《魏书》和韦昭的《吴书》中可供陈寿参考的关于魏、吴两国的史料已经较为完整，加上陈寿在对史实进行考证时认真考订、慎重择别，对可信度不高的资料都进行严格审核、取舍严谨，因此，《三国志》中的一些历史记录，尤其是《蜀书》中的许多重要人物的事迹，以及历史事件的记载都只有寥寥数笔，显得非常单薄简略。其次，受当时的历史条件所限，如部分史料未及披露，当时的政治条件以及作者本人的历史观的影响，陈寿在该书中的部分史实方面的记载有曲笔，甚至被指对部分人物的记载有严重背离，如《史通·直书》就曾批评《三国志》中的《魏书》对于司马家族对诸葛亮的作战不利不予置评，有失史家风范；清朝国学大师钱大昕先生也曾批评《三国志》中所记录的何晏不实，指出陈寿因何晏与司马懿有过节，所以在《三国志》中多有污蔑之言；而宋代唐庚则批评陈寿在《三国志》中为了显示魏晋的正统，故意以"蜀"称呼刘备、刘禅的政权，而不用其正式国号"汉"，据此种种，不一而足。此外，《三国志》虽然被后世称为"志"，但在内容方面，却完全是按人物排列的本纪和列传，没有撰述任何如地理、经济、典章制度等的志或表的内容，这不能不说是一种缺失。

尽管《三国志》有缺陷，但其"叙事隐晦而不失实录，扬善而不隐蔽缺点"，所以它仍被认为是是除《史记》、《汉书》、《后汉书》之外最好的纪传体史书，并对中国后世的史学及历史文学的发展都具有深远的影响。在《三国志》的基础上，南朝著名史学家裴松之（372—451）收集各家史料，弥补《三国志》记

诸葛亮草船借箭

载之不足，作《三国志注》，为后世了解三国历史提供了翔实的资料。至元末明初年间，由罗贯中根据《三国志》等史书改编的历史小说《三国演义》风靡全国，并经世代演绎，成为当今中国乃至东南亚地区最为畅销的历史演义艺术题材。可以说，《三国志》这部历史巨著就是记载三国这一传奇时代的本源之初。

本单元所选的《出师表》是三国时期蜀汉丞相诸葛亮两次北伐（227—228）曹魏前，上呈给后主刘禅的奏章。全文写得情真意切，感人肺腑，充分表达了诸葛亮对先帝刘备知遇之恩的真挚感情，以及挥师北伐的决心。与此同时，他还在该奏章中告诫后主"亲贤臣，远小人"，要继承先帝遗志，广开言路，严明赏罚，为兴复汉室而努力。

《三国演义》诞生于元末明初（约1310—1385），是罗贯中在借鉴前人关于三国时期的历史记录和杂记（如陈寿的《三国志》、裴松之的《三国志注》、匿名作品《三国志评话》）及大量吸取民间传说和戏曲的基础上，加入自己对社会人生的体悟加工创作而成的。全书共一百二十回，八十余万字，描写了自公元184年到280年近一百年间，从东汉末年至西晋初年间曹魏、蜀汉、孙吴三个统治集团之间的政治、军事、外交斗争，揭示了当时黑暗的社会现实和百姓生活的疾苦，表达了人民希冀社会安定、渴望明君仁政的强烈愿望。

《三国演义》代表了中国古代历史演义小说的最高艺术成就。小说无论在叙事技巧、人物刻画、结构安排、语言运用还是场面描写上都显示出作者极高的造诣。整部《三国演义》的出场人物众多，达1 798个，作者着重刻画的人物就有数十人之多，但每个人物都鲜明生动、独具特色，个个入木三分，令读者如闻其声，如见其人。所有情节的描写，突出了几个重要人物的性格特征，如诸葛亮的深谋远虑、济世爱民，周瑜的雄才大略但嫉贤妒能，曹操的多疑善变、精于谋略。

《三国演义》共描写了大大小小三百多场战争，每一场战争都写得独呈异彩，各具特色。作者在写战争的同时，兼写其他活动，如加入了对人物心理、语言和行为的细腻刻画，对整个战争外部环境如政治、外交等因素的描述，以及在具体战争条件下不同的战略战术的运用描写，每次战争的写法也根据战争的特点而有所不同，把史书中所没有的战争情节描写得细致逼真，使得每场战争都波澜起伏、跌宕跳跃，读来令人惊心动魄。这使《三国演义》中的战争描写达到了后人难以企及的高度。

本单元所选的《三国演义》开篇词，是明代三大才子之一的杨慎所作的《临江仙》。罗贯中将其录入《三国演义》后可谓家户晓，妇孺皆知。该词以滔滔长江水和巍巍青山为切入口，纵观历代兴亡盛衰，以英雄豪杰的成败得失抒发感慨，表现出一种旷达超脱乃至"大彻大悟"的历史观和人生观。

词的上阕透过历史现象来咏叹宇宙永恒，人生有限，江水不息，青山常在，而一代代的英雄人物无一不是转瞬即逝，这是不可抗拒的自然法则。尽管他们功绩卓著，到头来也只是"转头空"；尽管他们一生灿烂，最终也只能如同"夕阳红"一样昙花一现。

词的下阕主要寄托了作者高洁的情操和淡然的情怀。既然"是非成败"如过眼烟云，又何必耿耿于怀而一味斤斤计较呢？不如寄情山水，托趣渔樵，与秋月春风为伴，岂不怡然自得？

全词以古今沧桑入诗，以江山日月为画，把宇宙巨物作为"谈笑"之资、"浊酒"之佐，将"是非"、"成败"置之度外，豪放中有含蓄，高亢中蕴深沉，苍凉悲壮，意味深远。读来荡气回肠，令人感慨万千。作者试图在历史的长河中探索永恒的人生价值，在成败得失间寻找深刻的人生哲理。全词既有历史兴衰之感，更有人生沉浮之慨，成分表现了杨慎和罗贯中两位作者对历史和现实的透彻反思。

《三国演义》第四十六回也是家喻户晓的名篇，主要讲述周瑜因嫉妒诸葛亮的才华，想以十天造好十万支箭为由陷诸葛亮于死地的故事。然而，出乎周瑜所料的是，诸葛亮居然在三天之内用妙计从曹营"借"来十万支箭给周瑜。曹操由于不甘心如此蒙羞受辱，便派遣手下大将蔡中、蔡和去周瑜身边当奸细。结果被周瑜识破，周瑜与老将黄盖双双演出"苦肉计"以许降，再次蒙得曹军奸细的信任。这篇文章把诸葛亮、周瑜、黄盖等人塑造得鲜明生动。"借箭"故事意在表现周瑜刻意为难诸葛亮，借以凸显诸葛亮的神机妙算和胆识谋略；另一方面又描写了周瑜的杰出军事才能及其妒贤嫉能的狭窄心胸。赤壁大战时，周瑜曾布下迷阵，让蒋干盗走假文书，除掉曹操手下治理水军的大将蔡中兄弟，又利用黄盖许降，火烧战舰而大破曹军。

VI. 译本链接

1. 罗经国：《古文观止精选》，北京：外语教学与研究出版社 2005 年版。

2. 谢百魁：《中国历代散文选译》，北京：中国对外翻译出版公司 2008 年版。

3. Moss Roberts. *Three Kingdoms*, Los Angeles：University of California Press，2004.

Unit Fourteen
The Diamond Sutra (《金刚经》)

I. 背景简介

The Diamond Sutra is one of the most revered texts of Mahayana Buddhism and a jewel of the world's religious literature. It has fascinated Buddhists for centuries because of its insights into dualism and illusion. *The Diamond Sutra* illuminates how people's minds construct limited categories of thought. It offers people alternative ways to look at the world in its wholeness so that they can encounter a deeper reality, develop reverence for the environment and more harmonious communities, families, and relationships, and act in the world skillfully and effectively.

The Buddhism Music Performance

The Diamond Sutra is a brief text but defies literal interpretation. A typical English translation contains about 6,000 words, and an average reader could finish it in less than 30 minutes, easily. The sutra's title in Sanskrit, Vajracchedika Prajnaparamita Sutra, could be roughly translated as the "diamond-cutting perfection of wisdom sutra". It is also sometimes called *The Diamond Cutter Sutra*, or *the Vajra Sutra*. It is a part of a large canon of early Mahayana sutras called *The Prajnaparamita Sutras*. Prajnaparamita means "perfection of wisdom". In Mahayana Buddhism, the perfection of wisdom is the realization or direct experience of sunyata (emptiness). *The Heart Sutra* also is one of *The Prajnaparamita Sutras*. Sometimes these sutras are referred to as the "wisdom" literature. Mahayana Buddhist legend says that *the Prajnaparamita Sutras* were dictated by the historical Buddha to various disciples. However, scholars believe they were written in India beginning in the 1st century B. C.. For the most part, the oldest surviving versions of these texts are Chinese translations that date from the early first millennium.

The verses in *The Diamond Sutra* address the nature of reality and the activity of bodhisattvas. Throughout the sutra, the Buddha instructs us not to be bound by concepts, even concepts of "Buddha" and "dharma". *The Diamond Sutra*, like many Buddhist sutras, begins with the phrase "Thus have I heard". In the sutra, the Buddha has finished his daily walk with the monks to gather offerings of food, and he sits down to rest. Elder Subhuti comes forth and asks the Buddha a question. What follows is a dialogue regarding the nature of perception. The Buddha often uses paradoxical phrases and is generally thought to be trying to help Subhuti unlearn his preconceived, limited notions of the nature of reality and enlightenment. Emphasizing that all forms, thoughts and conceptions are ultimately illusory, he teaches that true enlightenment cannot be grasped through them; they must be set aside.

The four main points from the sutra are thought to be giving without attachment to self, liberating beings without notions of self and other, living without attachment, and cultivating without attainment. There is a common view that *The Diamond Sutra* primarily is about impermanence, because of a short verse in the last chapter that seems to be about impermanence and which often is mistaken as an explanation of the 31 enigmatic chapters that preceded it. However, to say that *The Diamond Sutra* is only about impermanence does not do it justice.

Ⅱ. 文本选读
The orthodox doctrine of the great vehicle 3

The Buddha told Subhuti①, "All Bodhisattvas②, Mahasattvas③, should subdue their minds thus: 'I must cause all living beings—those born from eggs, wombs, moisture, by transformation; those with form, those without form, those with thought, those without thought, those not totally endowed with thought, and those not totally without thought—to enter Nirvana④ without residue and be taken across to Cessation⑤. Yet of the immeasurable, numberless, boundless numbers of living beings thus taken across to Cessation, there is actually no living being taken across to Cessation.' Why? Subhuti, if a Bodhisattva has an appearance of self, others, living beings, or a life, he is not a Bodhisattva."

Wonderful practice is to not rely on anything 4

"Moreover, Subhuti, as to dharmas⑥, a Bodhisattva should not rely on anything when giving. That is to say, when giving, he should neither rely on forms, nor sounds, smells, tastes, tangible objects or dharmas. Subhuti, a Bodhisattva should give thus: he should not rely on appearances. Why? If a Bodhisattva does not rely on appearances when giving, his blessings and virtues are inconceivable and immeasurable." "Subhuti, what do you think, is space in the east conceivable or measurable?" "No, World Honored One." "Subhuti, is space in the south, west, north, or in the intermediate directions, above or below conceivable or measurable?" "No, World Honored One." "Subhuti, the blessings and virtues of a Bodhisattva who does not rely on appearances when giving, are just as inconceivable and immeasurable. Subhuti, a Bodhisattva should rely only on the teachings."

Leaving appearances and still cessation 14

At that time, upon hearing this sutra and deeply understanding its purport⑦, Subhuti wept and felt remorse⑧, and addressed the Buddha, "How rare, World Honored One, is this Sutra so profoundly explained by the Buddha. From the time I attained the eye of wisdom until the present, I have never heard such a Sutra. World Honored One, if someone listens to this Sutra with a mind of pure faith and can bring forth the Appearance of Reality[9], know that such a person has accomplished foremost and rare merit and virtue. World Honored One, the Appearance of Reality is without appearance. Therefore the Thus Come One[10] calls it the Appearance of Reality." "World Honored One, now as I listen to this Sutra, I believe, understand, accept and uphold it without difficulty. In the future, in the last five hundred years, if there are living beings who when they hear this Sutra, believe, understand, accept and uphold it, they will be outstanding and most rare. Why? Such people will be without the appearance of a self, the appearance of others, the appearance of living beings, and the appearance of a life. Why? The appearance of self is actually no appearance. The appearance of others, the appearance of living beings and the appearance of a life are actually not appearances. Why? All those who are called Buddhas have relinquished[11] all appearances." The Buddha told Subhuti, "So it is, so it is. If someone hears this Sutra and is not frightened, alarmed, or terrified, you should know such a person is most rare. Why? Subhuti, the foremost Paramita[12] spoken of by the Thus Come One is not the foremost Paramita. Therefore it is called the foremost Paramita. Subhuti, the Paramita of patience spoken of by the Thus Come One is not the Paramita of patience[13]. Therefore it is called the Paramita of patience. Why? Subhuti, in the past when the King of Kalinga[14] dismembered my body, I had no appearance of a self, of others, of living beings or of a life. Why? When I was cut limb from limb, if I had an appearance of a self, an appearance of others, an appearance of living beings or an appearance of a life, I would have been outraged." "Moreover Subhuti, I recall that in the past, for five hundred lives, I was the Patient Immortal[15]. During all those lives I was without the appearance of a self, others, living beings or a life. For that reason, Subhuti, a Bodhisattva should relinquish all appearances and bring forth the mind of Anuttarasamyaksambodhi[16]. He should bring forth thoughts which do not rely on forms or which do not rely on sounds, smells, tastes, tangible objects, or dharmas. He should bring forth thoughts which do not rely on anything.

Any relying of the mind is not relying." Therefore the Buddha says, "The Bodhisattva's mind should not rely on forms when he gives. Subhuti, because the Bodhisattva wishes to benefit all living beings, he should give in this way. The Thus Come One says that all appearances are actually not appearances, and that all living beings are actually not living beings. Subhuti, the Thus Come One speaks the truth. He speaks factually. He speaks of things as they really are. He never deceives nor are his words peculiar. Subhuti, the Dharma the Thus Come One obtained is neither true nor false. Subhuti, a Bodhisattva who gives with a mind relying on dharmas is like a person in the dark who sees nothing at all. A Bodhisattva who gives with a mind that does not rely on dharmas is like a person with eyes who can see all kinds of things in the bright sunlight. Subhuti, if in the future there is a good man or good woman who can accept, uphold, read or recite this Sutra, then the Thus Come One using his Buddha-wisdom will thoroughly know and thoroughly see such a person. That person will obtain immeasurable and boundless merit and virtue."

Responses and transformations are unreal 32

"Subhuti, suppose someone were to fill measureless asamkhyeyas⑰ of world systems with the seven precious jewels and give them as an offering. Further, if a good man or good woman who has resolved his mind on Bodhi were to receive, uphold, read or recite and extensively explain for others as little as four lines of verse from this Sutra, the latter person's blessings would surpass those of the former person. How should this Sutra be explained for others? By not grasping at appearances and being in unmoving thusness⑱. Why?" "All conditioned dharmas are like a dream, an illusion, a bubble or a shadow, Like dew or like a lightning flash. Contemplate them thus." After the Buddha spoke this Sutra, the Elder Subhuti, all the Bhikshus, Bhikshunis, upasakas and upasikas⑲, and all the gods, humans, and asuras⑳, and others from all the worlds, having heard what the Buddha had said, were extremely happy, faithfully accepted it, and put it into practice.

(Translated by the Buddhist Text Translation Society)

Ⅲ. 难点释义

① Subhuti，须菩提，意为善现、善吉、空生，古印度拘萨罗国舍卫城长者鸠留之子。佛陀十大弟子之一，有"解空第一"的称号。须菩提出生婆罗门教家庭，以"恒乐安定、善解空义、志在空寂"著称，每次化缘都去有钱人家里化缘。

② Bodhisattva，菩萨。

③ Mahasattva，大菩萨。

④ Nirvana，涅槃，超脱生死（佛教用语）。

⑤ Cessation，灭度，圆寂。

⑥ dharma，（佛教）宇宙法规；教规（包括自然法规，道德法规）。

⑦ purport，意义，要旨；目的，意图。

⑧ remorse，懊悔，自责。

⑨ the Appearance of Reality，实相，（佛教用语）原义为本体、实体、真相、本性等；引申指一切万法真实不虚之体相，或真实之理法、不变之理、真如、法性等。

⑩ the Thus Come One，如来佛，就是释迦牟尼佛，即如来佛祖，约前 624—前 544，又说前 564—前 484，原名悉达多·乔达摩，意为"一切义成就者"，佛教创始人。成佛后被称为释迦牟尼，尊称为佛陀，民间信徒称呼他为佛祖。

⑪ relinquish，放弃。

⑫ Paramita，波罗密，又作波罗密多。佛教认为，波罗密是所有菩萨行者必修的善德，是成就一切圣者的根本。在梵语中，"波罗"是"彼岸"的意思；"密多"是动词"到"的意思，当然佛经里也可以翻译成"度"。

⑬ the Paramita of patience，忍辱波罗密，大乘菩萨所必须实践之六种修行之一，意指全然忍耐。

⑭ the King of Kalinga，歌利王，佛陀本生谭中所出现之王名。佛陀于过去世为忍辱仙人时，此王恶逆无道。一日，率宫人出游，遇忍辱仙人于树下坐禅，随侍女见之，舍歌利王而至忍辱仙人处听法，王见之生恶心，遂割截仙人之肢体。歌利是残暴的意思，歌利王则是因为他的残暴而得名。

⑮ the Patient Immortal，忍辱仙人，指佛陀在过去世曾有一次是修忍辱的修行人，

住在山洞里修禅。

⑯ Anuttarasamyaksambodhi，阿耨多罗三藐三菩提，佛智名，意译为"无上正等正觉"，即是真正平等觉知一切真理的无上智慧。

⑰ asamkhyeyas，阿僧祇，新称阿僧企耶，译为无数，或译无央数，系印度数目的名辞。亦即是数目的极字。

⑱ thusness，（佛教用语）真如，意为不变的最高真理或本体。

⑲ Bhikshus，Bhikshunis，upasakas and upasikas，四众，全称为"佛弟子四众"，即比丘、比丘尼、优婆塞、优婆夷四种。比丘，指年满 20 岁的正式出家的男性佛教信徒。比丘尼，指年满 20 岁的正式出家的女性佛教信徒。优婆塞，在家修行的男性佛教信众。优婆夷，意思是在家修行的女性佛教信众。

⑳ asura，阿修罗，是梵文音译，汉译佛经中也有译为阿须罗、阿索罗、阿苏罗、阿素落、阿须伦、阿须轮等。意译为非天、非同类、不端正、不酒神。它们是佛国六道众之一。

Ⅳ. 问题思考

1. What are the most important teachings of *The Diamond Sutra*?

2. Does *The Diamond Sutra* make any practical sense for heathens?

3. *The Diamond Sutra* advocates "leaving appearances", but in daily life, people are encouraged to set up goals and to pursue it with all efforts. Is there any contradiction in it? Why or Why not?

4. How to interpret "All conditioned dharmas are like a dream, an illusion, a bubble or a shadow, Like dew or like a lightning flash. Contemplate them thus" in Section 32?

5. In your understanding, what led to the popularity of *The Diamond Sutra* in history?

Ⅴ. 经典导读

《金刚经》，全称《能断金刚般若波罗密经》，又称《金刚般若波罗密经》，一卷，印度大乘佛教般若系经典，后来经过鸠摩罗什的汉译。般若，梵语，意为智慧；波罗密，梵语，意为到彼岸。以金刚比喻智慧之锐利、顽强、坚固，能断一切烦恼，故名。此经采用对话体形式，说一切世间事物空幻不实，实相者即是非相；主张认识离一切诸相而无所住，即放弃对现实世界的认知和追求，以般若智慧契证空性，破除一切名相，从而达到不执着于任何一物而体认诸法实相的境地。《金刚经》是中国禅宗所依据的重要经典之一。《金刚经》成书于古印度，是如来世尊释迦牟尼在世时与长老须菩提等众弟子的对话记录，由弟子阿傩所记载。20世纪初出土于敦煌的《金刚经》，为世界最早的雕版印刷品之一，现存于大英图书馆。

释迦牟尼圣像

在传介到中国的大量佛教经典中，《金刚经》是译介最早、流传最广、影响最深的经典之一。历史上《金刚经》虽有多个译本，但最为流行的，还是鸠摩罗什的译本。在中国传统义化中，人们把《金刚经》与儒家的《论语》，道家的《道德经》、《南华经》并列视为释儒道三家的宗经宝典。

释迦牟尼认为："凡所有相皆是虚妄"，世上的一切事都如梦，如幻，如水面的气泡，如镜中的虚影，如清晨的露珠，日出即散，如雨夜的闪电，瞬息即逝。世上的一切都是因缘和合而成，并无自性，所谓"缘起性空"，因此，我们平时看到的一切事物的形相，实际都不是它们真正的形相，事物真正的形相是"无相"。这样，世界上一切都不值得执着，这就叫"无住"。能真正认识到无相之实相，能做到于世界万物都无念无系的"无住"，就可以得到真正的解脱。释迦牟尼通过否定摒弃事物的虚幻之相，揭示出世界的真实本质，即"实相者则是非相"。如果认识到一切事物都是虚幻无自性的，就认识到了世界的真实本质、真如实相，即"若见诸相非相，即见如来"。倘能如此，就能不"住色生心"，就能不执着于"我相"、"人相"、"众生相"、"寿者相"。修行者在扫去一切虚妄执着后，万法的真实情状、真如实相就会自然显示出来，即"信心清净，则生实相"。释迦牟尼要求人们扫相破执，甚至要求人们对"佛法"也不应执着，认为"说法者无法可说，是名说法"。经中以舟筏作喻，说明佛法只是方便设施，不应拘泥死守。该经的最后，佛说了一首偈子，作为该经思想的总结："一切有为法，如梦幻泡影，如露亦如电，应作如是观。"

《金刚经》具有破相破空破佛法，无住生心不染尘的大智慧、大境界，不仅为中国传统文化注入了活化因子，而且对现代人也有着诸多有益的启迪。《金刚经》对虚无的破除，避免了生命的沉空滞寂，对树立积极进取的人生观大有裨益。真正的悟者，应当培养谦和的心态，越是成功辉煌，越是超然宁静。在实际生活中，人们不知不觉中落入二元对立的思考，其实就是"有所住"，反之，则是"无所住"。好是由因缘而来，坏也是有因有缘，好会变坏，坏也可以变好，太固执好坏的观念，并不合乎事实的真相，执着"好"的观念，容易产生过度的期望，因为期望落空而失望，或者执着"坏"的观念，容易过度恐惧、忧虑，看不到好坏的因缘变化，从而变成用来逃避现实生活困境的借口。

《金刚经》可以说是佛教史上影响最大的经典，包含了大乘佛教般若学说的精华。其"性空幻有"、"扫相破执"为主要内容的般若思想是大乘佛教的理论基础。般若智慧实质上是大乘佛教所倡导的特殊的认知方式和思维方式，它要彻底地超越世俗的经验，否定或摆脱世俗的认识，从而认定尘世的感知都是虚幻不实的。只有把握"般若性空"之理，才能抛弃世俗的妄见妄念、妄想执着，才能体悟到佛门的真谛。对大乘佛教而言，《金刚经》及其思想有着无可替代的价值。

《金刚经》对中国社会文化的影响随处可见，直至近代和当代，寺院僧人日常课颂和讲经说法，都依此经。在民间，连目不识丁的妇孺也能随意背出一段或一句《金刚经》。在佛教施行扶世助化功德的过程中，各种各样的《金刚经》应验、感应故事成为中国民间社会劝善化导的重要形式。一方面让人们加强佛教信仰，一方面让人们在日常生活中努力止恶从善。

伴随着《金刚经》的传播，中国古代印刷、雕刻、绘画、文学、书法等文化艺术都不同程度地受其影响。世界现存最早的雕版印刷品是唐咸通九年（868）的《金刚经》木刻本；世界上最早的木刻版画是《金刚经》扉页的佛教绘画；现存规模最大、时间最早的石刻经文之一是山东泰山经石峪的石刻《金刚经》。此外，柳公权、赵孟頫等书法大家所书写的《金刚经》手迹也已成为珍贵的文化遗产，不少与《金刚经》相关的文学作品，以及《金刚经》论疏中的诗词美文等仍流传至今。

Ⅵ. 译本链接

1. Buddhist Text Translation Society, *The Diamond Sutra*. *http：//www.fodian.net/*

English/vajra. *sutra. htm*. 1998.

2. E. B. Cowell, F. Max Muller, J. Takakusu. *Buddist Mahayana Texts*. London: Routledge Curzon, 2001.

3. A. F. Price, Wong Mou-Lam. *The Diamond Sutra* and *the Sutra* of Hui-neng. Boston: Shambhala. 2005.

4. William Gemmell. *The Diamond Sutra* (Chin-Kang-Ching), or, *Prajna-Paramita*, New York: General Books, 2010.

Unit Fifteen
Huangdi Neijing (《黄帝内经》)

I. 背景简介

Huangdi Neijing, or the *Yellow Emperor's Canon of Medicine*, a monumental classic in Chinese medicine, is attributed to the great Huangdi, the Yellow Emperor, who reigned during the middle of the third century B. C. and is canonized as forefather by the Chinese and Taoists.

Huangdi, literally meaning Yellow Emperor, lived in China at the end of the Neolithic Age about 5,000 years ago. His family name was Gongsun and his courtesy names were Xuanyuan and Youxiong. He lived in the area of Loess Plateau of northern Shanxi Province, so his name is

Xuanyuan Huangdi,
B. C. 5,000

associated with the color of the earth. Later his tribe moved to an area near Zhuolu in Hebei Province and started to be engaged in stockbreeding and agriculture. After unifying many tribes and clans, Huangdi and his tribe settled in Qiaoshan of Shanxi Province and the areas surrounding the Loess Plateau in northern Shanxi Province. In the times of Huangdi's leadership, there were many inventions and creations, such as the raising of silkworms and reeling off of raw silk, building palaces and houses, invention of Chinese characters, music and rhythms, arithmetic, calendar, and making of coffins, vessels, ships and carts. According to Sima Qian, Chinese history began with Huangdi, who unified the tribes and ethnic groups in the Yellow River valley, hence promoting the cultural integration of the area which is considered to be the origin of China's prehistoric civilization.

Huangdi Neijing consists of two texts—*the Suwen*, ("Questions of Organic and Fundamental Nature") and *the Lingshu*, also called *the Zhenjing*, ("Classic of Acupuncture"). Each is in the form of a dialog between Huangdi and his ministers. *The Suwen* expounds the changes of the natural world while the Lingshu elaborates the theories of Zang-Fu and Jing-Luo.

A major component of *Huangdi Neijing*, the Yin-Yang (阳阳) theory elaborates physiology, pathology, disease and prevention, diagnosis and healthcare, integrating the exterior and the interior of the body by focusing on the system of the "Five Zang" (五脏) and "Six Fu" (六腑). In the system, the Jing-Luo is the channel through which exterior and interior, and Zang and Fu are linked up, while the Jing (精), Qi (气), Shen (神) are the mainstays that safeguard and dominate the whole system. And it also catalogs various diseases especially fever, malaria, cough, gout and paralysis, whose etiology, pathology, clinical symptoms and therapies are discussed, many of which remain as guiding principles for clinical practice today.

As a matter of fact, the theories of Yin-Yang and Wu-hsing came into being as early as the Pre-Qin Period and the most sophisticated forms were recorded in *Huangdi Neijing*.

The principle of Yin-Yang is applied to the Traditional Chinese Medicine (TCM) so as to interpret the complex correlations between parts of the body as well as between human life, nature and society. The Wu-hsing cycle (known as the five basic phases that explain changes in the cosmos, they are earth, wood, metal, fire, and water) serves as a principle in TCM that explains the functional correlations between the Five Zang Organs, the Six Fu Organs and the etiopathology upon the Zang-Fu imbalance. It also is useful in diagnosing and treating Zang-Fu diseases.

Huangdi Neijing detailed, for the first time in the history of Chinese medicine, the four diagnostic methods of TCM. They are Inspection, Listening and Smelling, Inquiry, and Pulse-taking and Palpation, which can catalogs various diseases especially fever, malaria, cough, gout and paralysis, whose etiology, pathology, clinical symptoms and therapies are discussed, many of which remain as guiding principles for clinical practice today.

Inspection means to observe the patient's outer appearance (especially the face) and his/her tongue, which are believed to reflect changes of the visceral functions in the human body so that a visceral disease can be detected.

Listening and Smelling involves two aspects: listening to the patient's voice in speaking, wheezing, coughing and vomiting to identify the pathological changes of the voice-related organs; smelling the patient's breath, and body odors (especially those of secretion and excrement) to diagnose diseases related to the internal organs, vital energy and blood, and body fluids.

Inquiry is to ask the patient or his/her company about the "when, where, why and how" of the disease, which was extended to "Ten Questions" such as hot and cold, sweat, head and body, stools and urine, food and drink, chest, hearing, thirst, persistent diseases and their causes, so as to distinguish between Yin and Yang, the interior and the exterior, chills and fever, asthenia and asthenia, which are characteristic of TCM dialectical treatment.

Pulse-taking and Palpation refers to touching or pressing the patient's pulse points or certain parts of the body to learn about the pathological changes which are reflected by the flow of Qi and blood throughout the body.

Huangdi Neijing, which embodies dialectical materialism, has become a landmark in the history of Chinese medicine. Rich in medical theories, this time-honored therapy resource has functioned as part of mainstream clinical practice in Chinese medicine for more than two millennia.

Ⅱ. 文本选读
Chapter 43 Yinxie Fameng: Dreams due to Invasion of Pathogenic Factors

43.1 Huangdi said, "I'd like to know what will happen if pathogenic factors overflow inside the body."

43.2 Qibo said, "When Zhengxie① (Normal-Evil) invades the body from the external, it does not aggress on a fixed place. [It penetrates through the viscera], flows together with Ying (Nutrient-Qi) and Wei (Defensive-Qi), floating with the Hun (Ethereal Soul) and Po (Corporeal Soul), making people restless in sleep and therefore frequently having dreams. [When] Qi^{②} invades the Fu-Organs, [Yangqi] will be excessive externally and [Yinqi] will be deficient internally. [When] Qi invades the Zang-Organs, [Yinqi] will be excessive internally and [Yangqi] will be deficient externally. "

43.3 Huangdi asked, "What are the manifestations of Shi (Excess) and Xu (Deficiency)?"

43.4 Qibo answered, " [If] Yinqi is superabundant, [people will] dream of walking across large river and feeling horrible; [if] Yangqi is superabundant, [people will] dream of flaming fire and feeling scorched; [if] both Yin and Yang are superabundant, [people will] dream [that they are] killing each other; [if pathogenic factors are] superabundant in the upper [part of the body, people will] dream of flying up; [if pathogenic factors are] superabundant in the lower [part of the body, people will] dream of falling down; extreme hunger will [make people] dream of asking [for food]; overeating will [make people] dream of offering [food to others]; [if] Liver-Qi is superabundant, [people will] dream of flaring into anger; [if] Lung-Qi is superabundant, [people will] dream of feeling fearful, crying and flying up; [if] Heart-Qi is superabundant, [people will] dream of repeatedly laughing, feeling fearful and scared; [if] Spleen-Qi is superabundant, [people will] dream of singing and rejoicing or feeling difficult to raising the body; [if] Kidney-Qi is superabundant, [people will] dream that the waist and the spine are separated. The twelve states of superabundance can be cured by reducing needling therapy. "

43.5 " [When] Reverse-Qi^{③} attacks the heart, [people will] dream of heavy smoke and fire in hills and mountains; [if it] attacks the lung, [people will] dream of flying up or seeing strange metal objects; [if it] attacks the liver, [people will] dream of mountains and trees; [if it] attacks the spleen, [people will] dream of hills, large lakes and houses broken by wind and rain; [if it] attacks the kidney, [people will] dream of approaching to an abyss and dropping into water; [if it] attacks the bladder, [people will] dream of wandering about④; [if it] attacks the stomach, [people will] dream of eating food; [if it] attacks the large intestine, [people will] dream of fields; [if it] attacks the small intestine, [people will] dream of gathering in a place of busy traffic; [if it] attacks the gallbladder, [people will] dream of fighting, lawsuit or committing suicide; [if it] attacks the external genitals, [people will] dream of sexual intercourse; [if it] attacks the neck, [people will] dream of being beheaded; [if it] attacks the shank, [people will] dream of difficulty in walking forwards or being trapped in a cellar or a garden; [if it] attacks the thigh, [people will] dream of performing the rite of kowtow; [if it] attacks the urethra and rectum, [people will] dream of urination and defecation. These fifteen states of insufficiency can be cured by reinforcing needling therapy. "

Chapter 63　Wuwei Lun: Discussion on Five Tastes⑤

63. 1 Huangdi asked Shaoyu, " [After] the five tastes are taken into the mouth, [they] enter [the viscera that they like] respectively and cause diseases differently. The sour [taste] enters the tendons, and excessive taking of sour [food] leads to difficulty to urinate; the salty [taste] enters the blood, and excessive taking of salty [food] leads to thirst; the acrid [taste] enters Qi, and excessive taking of acrid [food] leads to heart-burn; the bitter [taste] enters bones, and excessive taking of bitter [food] leads to vomiting; the sweet [taste] enters muscles, and excessive taking of sweet [food] leads to dysphasia⑥. I know this fact but I don't know the reason. Could you explain it for me?"

63. 2 Shaoyu said, " [When] the sour [taste] has entered the stomach, its Qi is austere and astringent. [It moves] upward to the Shangjiao (Upper Energizer) and Zhongjiao (Middle Energizer), but cannot come in and go out [along with the activity of Qi transformation]. [Since it] cannot go out, it just stays in the stomach. [If] the stomach is warm and normal [in function, it will] move downward into the bladder. The membrane of the bladder is thin and soft. When affected by sourness, it will shrink astringing [the orifice of the bladder] and causing difficult urination. The genital is the place where tendons converge. That is why the sour [taste] enters the tendons. "

62. 3 Huangdi said, "Why the salty [taste] enters the blood and excessive taking of salty [food] leads to thirst?"

63. 4 Shaoyu said, " [When] the salty [taste] has entered the stomach, its Qi flows to the Zhongjiao (Middle Energizer) and infuses into the Channels to mix up with the blood. [When] mixed up with the salty [taste], the blood will become astringent⑦. [When becoming] astringent, [the blood gets] fluid from the stomach to enrich it. [When the fluid] in the stomach is infused [into the blood], the stomach will be deficient in fluid. [When the stomach is] deficient [in fluid], the throat will feel dry. What is why the tongue is dry and frequently feels thirsty? The blood vessels are the routes of the Zhangjiakou (Middle Energizer) [to transport nutrients to the whole body]. That is why the salty [taste] enters the blood. "

63. 5 Huangdi said, "Why the acrid [taste] enters Qi and excessive taking of acrid [food] leads to heartburn?"

63. 6 Shaoyu said, " [When] the acrid [taste] has entered the stomach, its Qi moves to the Shangjiao (Upper Energizer). The Shangjiao (Upper Energizer) receives Qi [from the Zhongjiao (Middle Energizer)] and transports it to the entire Yang [phases in the whole body]. The taste of ginger and Chinese chives⑧ fumigates it; the Ying (Nutrient-Qi) and Wei (Defensive-Qi) frequently affect it and linger in the stomach. That is why there is heartburn. The acrid [taste tends to disperse and therefore] flows along with Qi. That is why [people] sweat [when they have] taken acrid [food]. "

63. 7 Huangdi said, "Why the bitter [taste] enters the bones and excessive taking of bitter [food] leads to vomiting?"

63. 8 Shaoyu said, " [When] the bitter [taste] has entered the stomach, it cannot be overcome by Qi of the five kinds of grains. [When] the bitter [taste] has descended to the lower part of the stomach, the passages of the Sanjiao (Triple Energizer) are all blocked. That is why there is vomiting. The teeth are the extension of the bones. That is why the bitter [taste] enters the bones after it has been taken [into the stomach]. So [when it] comes out after entering [into the body, it] indicates that it has moved into the bones. "

63. 9 Huangdi said，"Why the sweet［taste］enters the muscles and excessive taking of sweet［food］causes dysphasia?"

63. 10 Shaoyu said，"［When］the sweet［taste］has entered the stomach，its Qi is weak and soft.［So it］cannot flow to the Shangjiao（Upper Energizer），but stays in the stomach with the hod，making the stomach soft.［If］the stomach is soft，［it will become］relaxed.［If the stomach becomes］relaxed，［it will lead to］disturbance of parasites⑨.［When］disturbed by parasites，［the patient will feel］oppressed. The Qi［of sweet taste］runs externally to the muscles. That is why the sweet［taste］enters the muscles."

(Translated by Li Zhaoguo)

Ⅲ. 难点释义

① Zhengxie，正邪。正邪之气主要指刺激或干扰身心活动的一些因素，例如情感的变化，饥饿感，疲乏感等。

② Qi，气，指道家的养生之"气"。

③ Reverse-Qi，这里指的是"厥气"。按照《黄帝内经·素问》篇中的说法，厥气会侵入人的心脏，引起惊厥和恐慌。

④ wandering about，主要是指"梦游"的一种方式。

⑤ five tastes，此处主要是指酸、甜、苦、辣、咸五种味道。

⑥ dysphasia，心情烦闷不安。

⑦ astringent，血液浓稠。

⑧ Chinese chives，韭菜。

⑨ disturbance of parasites，扰动不安，心绪不宁。

Ⅳ. 问题思考

1. Internal alchemy is the most typical regimen for Taoism. Internal alchemy is a general term for promoting the circulation of "Qi"，guiding "Qi"，breathing and meditation. Do you think that Taoism has made great influence on the book of *Huangdi Neijing* in terms of "Jing"（精），"Qi"（气），and "Shen"（神）and the balance of "Yin" and

"Yang"? Why or Why not?

2. The TCM system includes four diagnostic methods: Inspection, Listening and Smelling, Inquiry, and Pulse-taking and Palpation, which holds that as the human body is an organic entity, its partial pathological changes may tell the conditions of the whole body, and the pathological changes of the internal organs may manifest themselves on the body surface. How does *Huangdi Neijing* exam this four diagnostic methods? Try to find some examples in the text for your understanding.

3. What is the relationship between "Five Tastes" and health of our human being?

4. *Huangdi Neijing* interprets dreams in terms of pathogenic factors while Sigmud Freud interprets dreams in terms of psychological factors, please find some examples to support your statements about the similarities and difference between the two interpretation of dreams.

5. Do you think that the balance between "Yin" and "Yang" is essential to the health and well-being of the body? How does it reflect our health according to the passage?

V. 经典导读

《黄帝内经》是古代医者托黄帝之名所作，具体的作者现已无从考据，大致成书于春秋战国至秦汉时期。《黄帝内经》之所以要冠以"黄帝"之名，意在溯源崇本，借以说明书中所述绝非妄言乱语。正如《淮南子》所言："世俗之人多尊古而贱今，故为道者必托之于神农黄帝而后能入说。"

《黄帝内经》共十八卷，分《灵枢》和《素问》两部分，各有九卷、八十一篇。全书以黄帝与岐伯，与雷公对话问答的形式阐述病理病机，主张"不治已病，而治未病"的原则，提出了养生、摄生、益寿、延年、阴阳、脏象、经络等许多医学论治之道。《素问》主要论述了自然界变化的规律、人与自然的关系等；《灵枢》的核心内容为脏腑经络学说。

历代医家用分类法对《黄帝内经》进行研究。其中分类最繁的是杨上善，分为十八类；最简的是沈又彭，分为四卷。各家认识较为一致的是脏象（包括经络）、病机、诊法、治则、养生等五大学说。这五大学说是《黄帝内经》理论体系的主要内容，这里简单述如下：

一、脏象学说

脏象学说主要包括脏腑、经络和精气神三部分。脏腑又由五脏、六腑和奇恒之腑组成。五脏，即肝、心、脾、肺、肾。六腑，即胆、胃、大肠、小肠、膀胱和三焦。奇恒之腑指脑、髓、骨、脉、胆和女子胞。经络系统可以分经脉、络脉和腧穴三部分。精气神为人身三宝。精，包括精、血、津、液；气，指宗气、荣气、卫气；神，指神、魂、魄、意、志。《灵枢·本脏》认为，"人之血气精神者，所以奉身而周于性命者也。"

二、病机学说

研究疾病发生发展、转归及变化等内在机理。

三、诊法学说

望、闻、问、切四诊源于《黄帝内经》，如《素问·阴阳应象大论》和《灵枢·邪气脏腑病形》都有详细论述。望诊包括观神色、察形态、辨舌苔；闻诊包括闻声和嗅气味；问诊主要是问讯患者的自觉症状以诊断病情；切诊包括切脉与切肤，主要有三部九候法；人迎寸口脉法；调息法；六纲脉法等许多种。

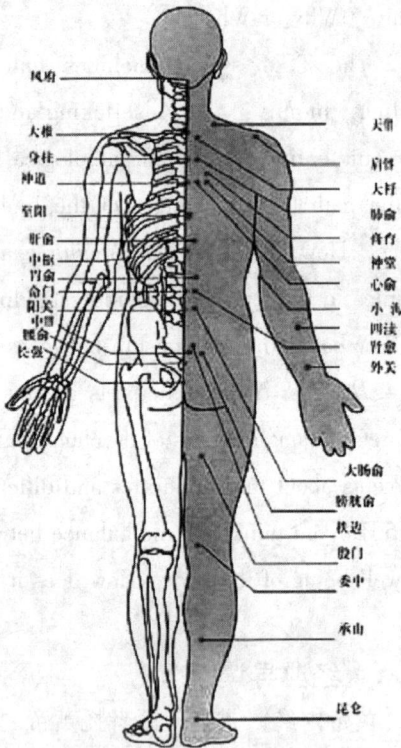

《灵枢》所述的人体经络系统

四、治则学说

《黄帝内经》对治疗法则是颇有研究的，至少包括十二个方面，即防微杜渐，未病先防，已病防变。因时、因地、因人制宜；因病之主次而先后施治；"治病必求于本。"因势利导，协调阴阳，正治反治，适事为度，"病为本，工为标。""辨证施治"，制方遣药，针刺灸祔，等等。

五、养生学说

《黄帝内经》强调四季养生、运动养生和气味养生。例如，《黄帝内经·素问》

中有言，"春三月，天地俱生，万物以荣。夜卧早起，广步于庭，被发缓行，以使志生"。强调顺应节气养生。"久视伤血，久坐伤肉，久力伤骨，久行伤筋"，强调劳逸结合的运动养生。"动"太过，则损伤机体形质；"逸"太多，又会阻塞气机，久之为病。因此，运动养生要遵循劳逸适度、张驰有度的原则。《黄帝内经·素问》呼吁人们应该根据春、夏、秋、冬四季的变化，在饮食起居和身心锻炼等方面要注意养生保健。做到慎起居，避风寒，调饮食，适运动，畅情志，以保持人体的阴阳平衡状态。具体而言，养生要做到四"宜"，即情志宜宣泄有度，起居宜节律有常，饮食宜寒热均衡，运动宜内外调和。气味养生主要包括臊味、焦味、香味、腥味、腐味等五种气味与五脏的关系。

臊味吸入人体以后影响肝脏，焦味影响到人的心脏，香味会影响到脾脏，腥味影响到肺脏，腐味则会影响人的肾脏。因此，气味养生时要注意浓淡的厚薄。微量或少量适中的气味可以把五脏的功能充分调动起来；反之，过浓过厚则会造成伤害。

《黄帝内经》被公认为中医学的奠基之作。它总结了战国以前的医学成就，在整体观、矛盾观、经络学、脏象学、病因病机学、养生和预防医学以及诊断治疗原则等各方面，都为中医学奠定了理论基础，历代著名医家在理论和实践方面的创新和建树都与本书密切相关。《黄帝内经》的部分内容曾被译成日、英、德、法等文字，对世界医学的发展产生了不可低估的影响。

本单元所选的第四十三篇《淫邪发梦》，主要阐述了邪气乘人体脏腑的虚弱而侵入脏腑，使魂魄不安而成梦的机理。列举了因各脏腑的盛衰，邪气的不同，出现十二种不同的梦境。阴气亢盛，梦见渡涉大水而感到恐惧；阳气亢盛，就会梦见大火烧灼的景象；阴气和阳气都亢盛，会梦见相互厮杀；人体上部邪气亢盛，梦见身体在天空飞腾；人体下部邪气亢盛，梦见身体向下坠堕；过度饥饿的时候，会梦见向人索取东西；过饱的时候，会梦见把东西送给别人；肝气亢盛，做愤怒的梦；肺气亢盛，做恐惧、哭泣和飞扬腾越的梦；心气亢盛，梦见好喜笑或恐惧畏怯；脾气亢盛，梦见歌唱奏乐或身体沉重不能举动；肾气亢盛，会梦见腰脊分离而不相连接。针对这十二种不同的梦境，书中提出了释梦诊断疾病的具体方法。第六十三篇的《五味论》，主要论述了酸、甜、咸、辣、苦等五味同人体经络、脏腑的关系，以及五味偏嗜太过时所出现的病理变化。文中强调，五味不能嗜食太过，否则会容易发生病变。正所谓"五味入于口，各有所走，各有所病"。饮食五味很显然地对人体既有其有利，又有其害，为此，要制订饮食五味的宜忌医嘱，从而提高疗效，保健养生。

VI. 译本链接

1. 李照国：《黄帝内经·素问》（汉英对照），上海：世界图书出版公司 2005 年版。

2. 李照国：《黄帝内经·灵枢》（汉英对照），上海：世界图书出版公司 2008 年版。

3. 朱明英：《黄帝内经》（英汉对照），北京：外文出版社 2001 年版。

4. Ilza Veith, *The Yellow Emperor's Classic of Internal Medicine*, Los Angels: University of California Press, 2002.

Unit Sixteen
The Classic of Tea（《茶经》）

Ⅰ. 背景简介

In ancient China there wasn't the Chinese word "cha" (tea). There was only the word "tu"（荼）, which was a bitter edible plant. The two words were used to refer to the same thing. The word "cha" came into being after the Tang Dynasty.

Originally tea was used as a kind of medicine instead of a drink. It was said that Shen Nong, the legendary ruler in ancient China, once tasted a lot of plants and got poisoned many times. It was tea that cured him of the poison. Later the ancient Chinese got to know more and more about tea. Instead of being regarded as a kind of medicine, it became a drink. Chinese tea culture was formed gradually.

Lu Yu（733 A. D. – 804 A. D.）

It was recorded that tea was drunk in the Western Hun Dynasty. During the period of the Three Kingdoms Period, drinking tea was very popular at least in the southern China.

During the Wei Dynasty, the Jin Dynasty and the Northern and Southern Dynasty, drinking tea already became a fashion for those people with high social status. Some literary writings concerning tea came into being, for example, in the Jin Dynasty's "Xiangmingfu" was the representative work of the tea literature of that time.

The Tang Dynasty was the mature period of Chinese tea culture. At that time it was customary to drink tea. People were fastidious about not only the tea production place, the picking and making of tea but also the drinking appliance and the way of drinking tea.

With the tea culture prevailing in the Tang Dynasty, tea was planted more widely in such provinces as Sichuan, Guangdong, Fujian, Guizhou, Hunan, Hubei, Zhejiang, Jiangsu, Jiangxi and Anhui. Moreover, tea trade became one of the main sources of royal government tax revenue. It was recorded that the law of tea taxation took effect in the Tang Dynasty and ever since tea tax was an important financial income for royal government.

Lu Yu (about 733A. D. – 804A. D.) had been abandoned in his early infancy to the causeway of Xihu Lake in a suburb of Jingling City (the present Tianmen County, Hubei Province). A Buddhist monk Zhiji, whose family name was Lu, brought him back to the Longgai Temple (the present Xita Temple) and named him Ji, with a courtesy name Jici, to show the delicate physique of the thin and weak baby. Later, Jici divined *The Book of Chan*, and received Hexagram 53, which reads: "The wild swan gracefully glides to the land and its feathers can be used for ceremonial ornament, indicating good luck and auspiciousness." Therefore, keeping the surname Lu (landing), he renamed himself Yu (plume), a courtesy name Hongjian (a gracefully landing swan), and a style name Jinglingzi (son of Jingling). During his lifetime, Lu Yu also used some other aliases such as Sangzhuweng (old man of mulberry, and ramie) and Donggangzi (son of the East Hill). As an industrious and insightful lad, Lu Yu read eagerly and mastered various techniques fast. Since his fostering father and teacher Zhiji had a keen interest in drinking tea, Lu Yu used to pluck, process brew the tea for him, building up an exquisite expertise and ability of tea appreciation. As he grew up, Lu Yu began to travel with his friends to where wonderful tea or superb water could be found. Hence, a lot of textual and field research had been conducted, and even richer knowledge accumulated.

In 755, Lu Yu returned to his hometown Jingling from his wide traveling and started to sort out his travelogue. The abundant ambition and enthusiasm for tea sparked Lu Yu's idea of condensing his experiences and perception of tea into a monograph. With this in mind,

Lu Yu again set off to major tea-growing areas to investigate experienced growers, performance in planting, plucking and making tea. His footprints had covered the middle and lower reaches of the Yangtze River up to all the areas around the Huai River. Those field trips were by no means light-hearted though. Most of the time, however, the determined tea master trudged along on his own, among steep mountains and deep valleys, braving all the roughness with his characteristic toughness. The philosophical belief that a cup of tea was a perfect harmony of all the sweetness in its bitterness remains .

In 760, Lu Yu arrived at Huzhou (the present Huzhou City, Zhejiang Province), where tea flavored the land. In order to concentrate on his monograph, Lu Yu stopped his migrating life to settle down in Shaoxi at the western suburb of the city. In seclusion he started to categorize, analyze and remember the information he had collected for his writing. After a long process of discarding the dross and maintaining the essence, Lu Yu finally succeed in accomplishing the first draft of *The Classic of Tea*. In 764, the revised version came into being, and in 775, adding Chapter Seven to his new edition. It was by then that the monumental works in the history of tea study, to which Lu Yu had devoted himself for decades, had finally received a real completion.

In 780, with the help of his close friend Jiaoran, Lu Yu managed to get the book printed. It received instant popularity and became the best seller of the time. Officials and tea merchants, as well as common citizens, could not wait to get a copy. In 783, Lu Yu migrated to his new abode in Shangrao City, which is now known as the Hongjian Residence, and Lu Yu Spring still flows briskly nearby. In the next ten years, Lu Yu compiled more works. In 799, in his 70s, the senior who had dedicated himself wholeheartedly to tea arts returned to his second homeland, Qingtang Residence in Huzhou City.

The Classic of Tea includes ten chapters in three volumes. Though with only about 7,000 Chinese characters, it carries with them a rich content going far beyond the number. The first volume covers the first three chapters: Chapter One illustrates the origin, characteristics, functions and different designations of tea; Chapter Two deals with an array of tools to pick and process tea; Chapter Three explains the time and methods for tea picking and processing. Volume Two is composed of the fourth and long chapter, elaborately illustrating 24 types of instruments for tea-making procedures. Volume Three includes the other five chapters. Chapter Five introduces the techniques for brewing tea and the quality of various waters. Chapter Six provides guidelines and codes for savoring tea. Chapter Seven records all the fates and legends of tea. Chapter Eight summarizes the distribution of the tea-producing regions during the Tang Dynasty. Chapter Nine analyzes some omissible apparatus for picking and processing tea under environment constraints. Chapter Ten offers a suggestion for tea-lovers who want to have a better understanding of the book.

The Classic of Tea has made a harmonious interdisciplinary crossing from botany, agronomy, ecology, pharmacology, hydrology, folklore to etymology and many other branches of learning, earning the fame of a true-to-name "encyclopedia of tea". Lu Yu has been recognized as the "Tea Sage", "Tea Saint", "Tea Ancestor", "Tea Predecessor", and even "Tea God". Chen Shidao of the Song Dynasty eulogized him in *Presence to the Tea Classic* as "the very first to write of tea in books and the very first to use the book for tea. Lu Yu has indeed contributed immensely to tea!"

Ⅱ. 文本选读
Chapter 3 Processing and Sorting Tea

The second, third and fourth months of the lunar year are a proper time for almost all sorts of tea to get harvested.

Tea sprouts shaped like chubby[①] bamboo shoots are usually found on fertile detritus soil. They normally stretch out four to five inches in length, resembling fern sprouts from a vernal land. The best picking time for such tea leaves is before daybreak, when dew is still glittering on them. Thinner leaves in the shape of germinating buds[②] are mostly found in bushes, each twig bearing only three, four or five pieces. Select fleshy ones to pluck.

When it comes to the proper weather for harvesting fresh tea, rains are definitely out of the question, and cloudiness should be excluded as well. Only clear and fine days allow for this activity. Following the initial step of plucking, the curing[3] then would go from steaming, pounding, molding, baking, stringing, all the way to packing in a row for fresh tea leaves to be processed ready.

The surface of caked tea could take on thousands of different looks. Here is an inkling of their appearances: some crease like the Tartars' leathern boots[4], others curl like buffalo's dewlap. Some unfold like a cluster of floating clouds from behind mountains, while others ripple almost audibly like a fiver being fondled by a breeze. Some look sleek and silky like pottery clay finely sifted and pasted with water, yet others feel rugged and rough like newly cultivated field eroded by pouring rains. All these are good teas in most cases.

Some tea leaves are tough as bamboo sheaths[5] with stiff stalks, making it hard to get them thoroughly steamed and finely pounded. The exterior of tea-cakes made of such leaves may often end up poriferous and natty like a coarse sieve. Some tea leaves are withered and blighted like frost-bitten lotus. Tea-cakes made from such baggy leaves would be sapless and shabby. Obviously, they fall into the category of inferior tea.

From picking to packing, the tea processing goes through seven procedures. From the "Tartars' boots" to the "frost-bitten lotus[6]," processed tea-cakes are sorted into eight quality grades. Judging by their looks, good comments tend to be given to those with smooth edge and in glossy black tint. However, such hasty judgment is often more prejudiced than precise. Assuming a tea to be good by its wrinkled or rugged[7] yellowish appearance is no more well-grounded. Justifiable opinions should offer the why in addition to the what.

Teas with the above-mentioned attributes[8] could be either good or bad. Here comes the explanation for why it is thus said. Tea with its juice pressed out to the surface will surely attain a glossy tint, while those without oozed juice[9] will look dull and rugged. Tea plucked and processed with a night in between would retain the nocturnal shade on the cakes, while intraday treatment will endow tea-cakes with a bright yellow. Tea-cakes tightly pressed in a gui after being steamed soft will be edged smoothly, while those slightly molded will look shapeless. In this aspect, tea is no different from any other foliaceous[10] plants. Whatsoever, the final assessment on the quality of any tea comes from actual sampling.

Chapter 5 Techniques for Brewing Tea

While parching a tea-cake, avoid doing it at places with a draught, for wind will make the flames flicker[①], causing the heat uneven. Hold the tea-cake close to the fire and turn it over constantly. When vesicles appear on the surface of the cake like papillae on the back of a toad, move it five inches away from the fire and keep on parching until the curled shell stretches out again. Then, repeat the whole procedure once more. The sign of sufficient parching is, for previously baked cakes, the fragrant smell emanating from them; and for previously sun-dried ones, thorough suppleness is the indication.

First of all, tender tea bullets have to be pounded while hot in a mortar after being steamed. The leaves will soon be smashed into paste, but the small bud stems may remain intact. Even Hercules[⑫] with a heavy pestle may find the pounding an awful task. Just as a muscular warrior might feel helpless pinching slippery lacquer seeds. Well-pounded tea paste for tea-cakes should be even and soft, with nothing stringy in it. The criterion for a properly parched tea-cake is its being pliable like a baby's chubby arm. At this stage, put the hot cake into a paper tea bag to prevent any loss of its fragrant[⑬] essence. To cook tea, roll the cake into powder after it cools down. [Note: Top-grade powder is in the shape of fine grain crumbs, whereas low-grade powder bears a resemblance to water chestnut flour.]

The fire to parch tea-cakes or boil tea water should be fueled with charcoal. Hard wood (such as mulberry tree, pagoda tree, tung, oak and the like) provides the next choice. Charcoal leftover from barbecue fire is soiled with odor and grease, which, if used to process tea, will spoil its pure flavor. Resinous wood (such as cypress, cassia-bark tree and juniper) and timbers of old wooden articles (worn or rotten house-hold items), too, will contaminate the tea, so they should be excluded from suitable fuel as well. "Labored firewood spoils its cooked food."[⑭] This old saying is proved to be true.

As to the aspect of cooking water, mountain springs always provide a preference. The next option is river water. Well water is but a less satisfactory choice. [Note: In Ode to Tea, it is said: "The best water runs from a mountain stream, clean and clear as a source of nice dreams."] Dripping trickles from stalactites[⑮] and slow creeks from rocks are the ideal waters for tea. However, attention should be paid never to using wild waters from falls, rapids and whirlpools, for long-term taking of such waters could result in neck ailments[16]. Stagnant water bodies in valleys are often infected by pests, snakes and poisonous vegetations during summer and autumn, clear as they may appear. When no other alternatives are available, breach a puddle to drain off the stale water and wait until fresh spring trickles in[17]. If river is the only accessible source, bail the water from a spot away from human habitation. Where well water has to be used, choose a well that is frequently drawn from.

The so-called simmer of water, or the initial boil, is a state when tiny fisheye-like bubbles appear with a low rustling sound. Seething is the second stage when strings of crystal beads gush out around the edge of the wok. The third and last stage refers to the ebullient state of water marked with lumpy waves[18] This draws the line. Exceeding this point, the water is assumed overdone, and should no longer be used for tea.

At the first boil, a small pinch of salt in proportion to the amount of water could be added to enhance the flavor. The water left in the spoon for sampling should be discarded. Never add too much salt. How can tea sipping be depreciated as salty soup savoring? At the second boil, take a ladle of water out of the wok and set it aside. Then use the measuring spoon to put a proper amount of tea powder in the middle of the boiling vortex while stirring the water with bamboo whipping chopsticks. When the soup starts to surge with foam, pour the ladled water atop to suppress the boil and preserve the essence.

Before the tea is served, be sure to let the pouring go evenly to each bowl to guarantee a fair share of the foam. Floating on top of the tea is the tea marrow. The thick cream is called "bo", and the thin spume of the marrow is called "mo". [Note: In both *Characters Book* (Zi Shu) and *Notes of Materia Medica* (Ben Cao Zhu), the best part of tea is termed as " mo and bo"]. "Hua" (literally meaning "flower") refers to even finer froth.

True to its name, "Hua" really resembles jujube flowers[19] drifting on the ripples of a pond. It may also be described as new duckweeds nestling over a winding pool, or follicular clouds curling in a serene sky. Metaphors to the thin marrow mo could be green duckweed floating on a river, or chrysanthemum petals perching on goblets and saucers. As for the thick cream called "bo", it displays a shining scene like clusters of white snow when thick tea is boiled. Such beauty is depicted in *Ode to Tea* "as splendid as silvery snow in winter; and as brilliant as white lilac in spring." This description gives a vivid image of the marrow.

At first boil, skim the thin layer of black mica-like coating on the surface of the water. It may result in a stained taste. The first bowl of tea from the wok is regarded as the pith, or prime, known as Juanyong, [Note: Juan means taste, and yong means lingering. In history, Juanyong is used as a metaphor to mean cultural quintessence surviving time and tide. Twenty pithy essays written by Kuai Tong were selected under the very title of Juanyong and included into *The History of the Former Han Dynasty*.] Save the juanyong in the hot-water calyx for later use, suppressing the surge and preserve the cream. The second and the third bowls are not so tasty. After the fourth or fifth bowls, the rest is no longer worth drinking, unless an urgent thirst needs to be quenched.

One liter of water is the fight amount for a wok of tea, which, having been brewed is adequate to serve about five persons. [Note: The count is from three to five bowls. If the batch of drinkers is larger than ten, boil two more woks.] Savor the tea while it is hot. Warm tea keeps the dregs to the bottom and the cream on the top, which, when cold, will be gone with its vapor. Perhaps "frugal"[20] is an appropriate word to describe the nature of tea. The quantity of water will cut into the quality of the drink. So care should be taken not to add undue amount of water. Even the latter half of the same bowl of tea may fade into insipid, let alone more diluted brew.

Good tea possesses a nice amber color, an aromatic fragrance and a savory taste. If sorted in more detail, tea can be specified like this: "jia" tasting sweet, "chuan" tasting bitter, and cha tasting bitter but with a lingering sweet after taste. [There are other sources of literature in which relevant definitions are given like this: "jia" is a kind of tea tasting bitter instead of sweet, while "chuan" tasting sweet rather than bitter.]

(Translated by Jiang Yi & Jiang Xin)

Ⅲ. 难点释义

① chubby，茂盛的，丰硕的。

② germinating buds，发芽。

③ curing，固化，梗化。

④ the Tartars' leathern boots，胡人的马皮靴子，这里比喻茶饼的形状。

⑤ bamboo sheaths，笋壳。

⑥ "frost-bitten lotus"，霜冻打过之后的莲花形状。

⑦ rugged，坚固的。

⑧ attributes，属性，标志。

⑨ oozed juice，渗出的茶汁。

⑩ foliaceous，叶状的。

⑪ flicker，闪烁。

⑫ Hercules，赫尔克里斯，大力神，是希腊神话中的主神宙斯之子。

⑬ fragrant，芬芳的，香气宜人的。

⑭ "Labored firewood spoils its cooked food." 唐朝时的一句古人谚语，"朽木坏器作烹柴，食染怪味随柴来"。意思是说，煮茶的材料对茶水的味道影响很大。陆羽建议用木炭煮茶为佳。

⑮ stalactites，钟乳石滴流。

⑯ neck ailments，颈部患病。

⑰ trickles in，涓涓地流淌，滴滴答答地流水。

⑱ lumpy waves，水波翻滚。

⑲ jujube flowers，枣花。

⑳ frugal，节俭的，少用量的。这里主要指泡茶时不宜多放水，否则就会味淡香薄。

Ⅳ. 问题思考

1. According to your own knowledge, what has formed the tea culture in ancient China?

2. Do you think tea drinking is an art or a technique? Why ?

3. Tea could be either good or bad, how does Lu Yu explain it? Find more examples in the passsage to support your statement?

4. Why does Lu Yu emphasize the importance of water for Brewing Tea?

5. Say something about the drinking etiquette in terms of tea-drinking and wine-drinking, in which someone will consider it as a kind of unique cultural symbol and a cultural consumption in China.

V. 经典导读

《茶经》（*The Classic of Tea*）是唐朝的陆羽在其余近 50 岁的时候完成的世界上第一部茶学专著。公元 756 年，年仅 24 岁的陆羽毅然决定与友人一起徒步去往各大茶区考察。他们经义阳、襄阳，往南漳，直到四川巫山，观察和学习茶农的经验和方法；公元 758 年，陆羽回到浙江湖州，对收集到的茶事资料进行分析整理，正式开始了《茶经》的著述工作。公元 765 年，陆羽根据他和朋友对 32 州、郡的实际考察资料及数年来的研究成果，完成了《茶经》的初稿。公元 780 年，陆羽在朋友的帮助下，呕心沥血数十载，反复增补修订，终于完成了《茶经》的著述，并正式刻印。这时的陆羽已 47 岁了，《茶经》的撰写总共耗去了陆羽二十七年的生命历程。

《茶经》全书共分三卷十节。约 7 000 字。上卷三节："一之源"，论述茶的起源、名称、品质，介绍茶树的形态特征、茶叶品质与土壤的关系，指出宜茶的土壤、茶地方位、地形，品种与鲜叶品质的关系，以及栽培方法，饮茶对人体的生理保健功能。还提到湖北巴东和四川东南发现的大茶树。"二之具"谈有关采茶叶的用具。详细介绍制作饼茶所需的 19 种工具名称、规格和使用方法。"三之造"讲茶叶种类和采制方法。指出采茶的重要性和采茶的要求，提出了适时采茶的理论。叙述了制造饼茶的6 道工序：蒸熟、捣碎、入模拍压成形、焙干、穿成串、封装，并将饼茶按外形的匀整和色泽分为 8 个等级。中卷一节："四之器"写煮茶饮茶之器皿。详细叙述了 28 种煮茶、饮茶用具的名称、形状、用材、规格、制作方法、用途，以及器具对茶汤品质的影响，还论述了各地茶具的好坏及使用规则。下卷六节："五之煮"写煮茶的方法和各地水质的优劣，叙述饼茶茶汤的调制，着重讲述烤茶的方法，烤炙、煮茶的燃料，泡茶用水和煮茶火候，煮沸程度和方法对茶汤色香味的影响。茶汤显现雪白而浓厚的泡沫是其精华所在。"六之饮"讲饮茶风俗，叙述饮茶风尚的起源、传播和饮茶习俗，提出饮茶的方式方法。"七之事"叙述古今有关茶的故事、产地和药效。记述了唐代以前与茶有关的历史资料、传说、掌故、诗词、杂文、药方等。"八之出"评各地所产茶之优劣。叙说唐代茶叶的产地和品质，将唐代全国茶叶生产区域划分成荆州之南、浙南、浙西、剑南、浙东、黔中、江西、岭南等八大茶区，每一茶区出产的茶叶按品质分上、中、下、又下四级。"九之略"谈哪些茶具茶器可省略以及在何种情况下可以省略哪些制茶过程、工具或煮茶、饮茶的器皿。如到深山茶地采制茶叶，随采随制，可简化七种工具。"十之图"指将采茶、加工、饮茶的全过程绘在绢素上，悬于茶室，品茶时可以亲眼领略茶经的风姿全貌。

　　根据《茶经》，我们知道，用水在煮茶环节中尤为重要。陆羽明确指出，用山水最好，其次是江河之水，井水最差。陆羽告诫饮者最好选喝乳泉山水，或石池漫流的山水，奔涌湍急的水不要饮用，常喝这种水会使人的颈部生病。溪流汇合处或停蓄于山谷的水也不宜用，因为水虽澄清，但不流动。热天到霜降前的

陆羽向孩童传授茶艺之道

水质污染有毒，饮用时应先挖开缺口，把污秽有毒的水放走，使新的泉水涓涓流来，然后饮用。要到远离尘嚣的地方去取江河之水，而井水则要从很多人打水的井里去汲取。

　　迄今为止，《茶经》是中国乃至世界最早、最完整、最全面的茶学专著，被誉为"茶叶百科全书"。陆羽因此而有"中国茶圣"之称。《茶经》是一部关于茶叶生产的历史、源流、现状、生产技术以及饮茶技艺，茶道原理的综合性茶学论著。它不仅是一部精辟的农学专著，同时又是一本阐述中国茶文化的学术论著书。它将普通茶事升格为一种美妙的文化艺能，弘扬了中国茶文化并推动其发展与传播。

Ⅵ. 译本链接

1. James Norwood Pratt, *The Art of Tea*, New York: Columbia University Press, 2001.

2. Vianney, Soeur Jean-Marie, *Le Classique Du the Par Lu Yu*, Paris: Morel, 1977.

3. Marco Ceresa, *The Tang Dynasty Monographs on Tea*, Naples: Istituto Universitario Orientale of Naples, 1990.

4. Olga Lomová, *The Classic of Tea*, Prague: Prague Milca Tea Association, 2002.

5. Alexander Kubuyefu, Llly Delisky, *The Classic of Tea*, Mosco: Mosco College of Human Science, 2007.

6. Okakura Kakuzo. *The Illustrated Book of Tea*, Chiang Mai: Cognoscenti Books, 2012.

7. Francis Ross, *The Classic of Tea*: *Origins & Rituals*, New York: Ecco Press, 1995.

8. 姜欣、姜怡,《茶经、续茶经》》(英汉对照), 长沙: 湖南人民出版社 2009 年版。

ENG

Appendix 1
Chinese Text（汉语文本原文）

第 1 单元　《诗经》

《关雎》
关关雎鸠，在河之洲。
窈窕淑女，君子好逑。

参差荇菜，左右流之。
窈窕淑女，寤寐求之。

求之不得，寤寐思服。
悠哉悠哉，辗转反侧。

参差荇菜，左右采之。
窈窕淑女，琴瑟友之。

参差荇菜，左右芼之。
窈窕淑女，钟鼓乐之。

《黍离》
彼黍离离，彼稷之苗。
行迈靡靡，中心摇摇。

知我者谓我心忧，
不知我者谓我何求。
悠悠苍天，此何人哉！

彼黍离离，彼稷之穗。
行迈靡靡，中心如醉。
知我者谓我心忧，
不知我者谓我何求。
悠悠苍天，此何人哉！

彼黍离离，彼稷之实。
行迈靡靡，中心如噎。
知我者谓我心忧，
不知我者谓我何求。
悠悠苍天，此何人哉！

《子衿》

青青子衿，悠悠我心。
纵我不往，子宁不嗣音？

青青子佩，悠悠我思。
纵我不往，子宁不来？

挑兮达兮，在城阙兮。
一日不见，如三月兮！

《伐檀 》

坎坎伐檀兮，置之河之干兮，河水清且涟猗。
不稼不穑，胡取禾三百廛兮？

不狩不猎，胡瞻尔庭有县狟兮？
彼君子兮，不素餐兮！

坎坎伐辐兮，置之河之侧兮，河水清且直猗。
不稼不穑，胡取禾三百亿兮？
不狩不猎，胡瞻尔庭有县特兮？
彼君子兮，不素食兮！

坎坎伐轮兮，置之河之漘兮，河水清且沦猗。
不稼不穑，胡取禾三百囷兮？
不狩不猎，胡瞻尔庭有县鹑兮？
彼君子兮，不素飧兮！

《蒹葭》
蒹葭苍苍，白露为霜。
所谓伊人，在水一方。
溯洄从之，道阻且长。
溯游从之，宛在水中央。

蒹葭凄凄，白露未晞。
所谓伊人，在水之湄。
溯洄从之，道阻且跻。
溯游从之，宛在水中坻。

蒹葭采采，白露未已。
所谓伊人，在水之涘。
溯洄从之，道阻且右。
溯游从之，宛在水中沚。

《采薇》

采薇采薇，薇亦作止。
曰归曰归，岁亦莫止。
靡室靡家，玁狁之故。
不遑启居，玁狁之故。
采薇采薇，薇亦柔止。
曰归曰归，心亦忧止。
忧心烈烈，载饥载渴。
我戍未定，靡使归聘。

采薇采薇，薇亦刚止。
曰归曰归，岁亦阳止。
王事靡盬，不遑启处。
忧心孔疚，我行不来！
彼尔维何？维常之华。
彼路斯何？君子之车。
戎车既驾，四牡业业。
岂敢定居？一月三捷。

驾彼四牡，四牡骙骙。
君子所依，小人所腓。
四牡翼翼，象弭鱼服。
岂不日戒？玁狁孔棘！
昔我往矣，杨柳依依。
今我来思，雨雪霏霏。
行道迟迟，载渴载饥。
我心伤悲，莫知我哀！

第 2 单元 《大学》

大学之道，在明明德，在亲民，在止于至善。

知止而后有定，定而后能静，静而后能安，安而后能虑，虑而后能得。物有本末，事有终始，知所先后，则近道矣。

古之欲明明德于天下者，先治其国；欲治其国者，先齐其家；欲齐其家者，先修其身；欲修其身者，先正其心；欲正其心者，先诚其意；欲诚其意者，先致其知；致知在格物。

物格而后知至，知至而后意诚，意诚而后心正，心正而后身修，身修而后家齐，家齐而后国治，国治而后天下平。自天子以至于庶人，壹是皆以修身为本。

其本乱而末治者否矣；其所厚者薄，而其所薄者厚，未之有也。

《康诰》曰："克明德。"《大甲》曰："顾諟天之明命。"《帝典》曰："克明峻德。"皆自明也。

汤之《盘铭》曰："苟日新，日日新，又日新。"《康诰》曰："作新民。"《诗》曰："周虽旧邦，其命维新。"是故君子无所不用其极。

《诗》云，"邦畿千里，惟民所止。"《诗》云，"缗蛮黄鸟，止于丘隅。"子曰："于止，知其所止，可以人而不如鸟乎？"

《诗》云，"穆穆文王，于缉熙敬止。"为人君，止于仁；为人臣，止于敬；为人子，止于孝；为人父，止于慈；与国人交，止于信。

《诗》云："瞻彼淇奥，菉竹猗猗。有斐君子，如切如磋，如琢如磨。瑟兮僴兮，赫兮喧兮。有斐君子，终不可谖兮！""如切如磋"者，道学也；"如琢如磨"者，自修也；"瑟兮僴兮"者，恂栗也；"赫兮喧兮"者，威仪也；"有斐君子，终不可喧兮"者，道盛德至善，民之不能忘也。

《诗》云："于戏，斐前王不忘！"君子贤其贤而亲其亲，小人乐其乐而利其利。此以没世不忘也。

子曰："听讼，吾犹人也。必也使无讼乎！"无情者不得尽其辞，大畏民志。此谓知本。

"程子补充"曰：所谓致知在格物者，言欲至吾之知，在即物而穷其理也。盖人心之灵，莫不有知，而天下之物，莫不有理。惟于理有未穷，故其知有不尽也。是以《大学》始教，必使学者即凡天下之物。莫不因其已知之理，而益穷之，以求至乎其极。至于用力之久，而一旦豁然贯通焉，则众物之表里精粗无不到，而吾心之全体大用无不明矣。此谓物格，此谓知之至也。

所谓诚其意者，毋自欺也。如恶恶臭，如好好色，此之谓自谦，故君子必慎其独也。小人闲居为不善，无所不至，见君子而后厌然，掩其不善，而著其善。人之视己，如见其肺肝然，则何益矣？此谓诚于中，形于外，故君子必慎其独也。曾子曰："十目所视，十手所指，其严乎。"富润屋，德润身，心广体胖，故君子必诚其意。

所谓修身在正其心者，身有所忿懥，则不得其正；有所恐惧，则不得其正；有所好乐，则不得其正；有所忧患，则不得其正。心不在焉，视而不见，听而不闻，食而不知其味。此谓修身在正其心。

所谓齐其家在修其身者，人之其所亲爱而辟焉，之其所贱恶而辟焉，之其所畏敬而辟焉，之其所哀矜而辟焉，之其所敖惰而辟焉。故好而知其恶，恶而知其美者，天下鲜矣！故谚有之曰："人莫知其子之恶，莫知其苗之硕。"此谓身不修，不可以齐其家。

所谓治国必先齐其家者，其家不可教而能教人者，无之。故君子不出家而成教于国。孝者，所以事君也；悌者，所以事长也；慈者，所以使众也。《康诰》曰："如保赤子。"心诚求之，虽不中，不远矣。未有学养子而后嫁者也！一家仁，一国兴仁；一家让，一国兴让；一人贪戾，一国作乱，其机如此。此谓一言偾事，一人定国。尧舜帅天下以仁，而民从之。桀纣帅天下以暴，而民从之。其所令反其所好，而民不从。是故君子有诸己而后求诸人；无诸己而后非诸人。所藏乎身不恕，而能喻诸人者，未之有也。故治国在齐其家。

《诗》云："桃之夭夭，其叶蓁蓁，之子于归，宜其家人。"宜其家人，而后可以教国人。《诗》云："宜兄宜弟。"宜兄宜弟，而后可以教国人。《诗》云："其仪不忒，正是四国。"其为父子兄弟足法，而后民法之也。此谓治国在齐其家。

所谓平天下在治其国者，上老老而民兴孝，上长长而民兴弟，上恤孤而民不倍。

是以君子有絜矩之道也。所恶于上，毋以使下。所恶于下，毋以事上；所恶于前，毋以先后；所恶于后，毋以从前。所恶于右，毋以交于左；所恶于左，毋以交于右。此之谓絜矩之道。

《诗》云："乐只君子，民之父母。"民之所好好之，民之所恶恶之。此之谓民之父母。《诗》云："节彼南山，维石岩岩。赫赫师尹，民具尔瞻。"有国者不可以不慎，辟则为天下僇矣。《诗》云："殷之未丧师，克配上帝。仪监于殷，峻命不易。"道得众则得国；失众则失国。是故君子先慎乎德。有德此有人；有人此有土；有土此有财；有财此有用。德者本也。财者末也。外本内末，争民施夺。是故财聚则民散。财散则民聚。是故言悖而出者，亦悖而入；货悖而入者，亦悖而出。

《康诰》曰："惟命不于常。"道善则得之，不善则失之矣。《楚书》曰："楚国无以为宝，惟善以为宝。"舅犯曰："亡人无以为宝，仁亲以为宝。"《秦誓》曰："若有一个臣，断断兮无他技，其心休休焉，其如有容焉。人之有技，若己有之；人之彦圣，其心好之，不啻若自其口出。实能容之，以能保我子孙黎民，尚亦有利哉！人之有技，媢疾以恶之；人之彦圣，而违之俾不通，实不能容。以不能保我子孙黎民，亦曰殆哉！唯仁人放流之，迸诸四夷，不与同中国。此谓"唯仁人为能爱人，能恶人。"见贤而不能举，举而不能先，命也；见不善而不能退，退而不能远，过也。好人之所恶，恶人之所好，是谓拂人之性，灾必逮夫身。是故君子大道，必忠信以得之，骄泰以失之。

生财有大道，生之者众，食之者寡，为之者疾，用之者舒，则财恒足矣。仁者以财发身。不仁者以身发财。未有上好仁，而下不好义者也。未有好义其事不终者也，未有府库财，非其财者也。孟献子曰："畜马乘不察于鸡豚；伐冰之家不畜牛羊；百乘之家不畜聚敛之臣。与其有聚敛之臣，宁有盗臣。"此谓国不以利为利，以义为利也。长国家而务财用者，必自小人矣。彼为善之，小人之使为国家，灾害并至。虽有善者，亦无如之何矣！此谓国不以利为利，以义为利也。

第 3 单元 《中庸》

【第 1 章】

天命之谓性，率性之谓道，修道之谓教。

道也者，不可须臾离也，可离非道也。是故君子戒慎乎其所不睹，恐惧乎其所不闻。莫见乎隐，莫显乎微，故君子慎其独也。

喜怒哀乐之未发谓之中，发而皆中节谓之和。中也者，天下之大本也；和也者，天下之达道也。致中和，天地位焉，万物育焉。

【第 2 章】

仲尼曰："君子中庸，小人反中庸。君子之中庸也，君子而时中；小人反之中庸也，小人而无忌惮也。"

【第 8 章】

子曰："回之为人也，择乎中庸，得一善，则拳拳服膺，而弗失之矣。"

【第 9 章】

子曰："天下国家，可均也；爵禄，可辞也；白刃，可蹈也；中庸不可能也。"

【第 10 章】

子路问强。子曰："南方之强与，北方之强与，抑而强与？宽柔以教，不报无道，南方之强也，君子居之。衽金革，死而不厌，北方之强也，而强者居之。故君子和而不流，强哉矫！中立而不倚，强哉矫！国有道，不变塞焉，强哉矫！国无道，至死不变，强哉矫！"

【第 14 章】

君子素其位而行，不愿乎其外。素富贵，行乎富贵；素贫贱，行乎贫贱；素夷狄，行乎夷狄；素患难，行乎患难。君子无入而不自得焉。在上位，不陵下；在下位，不援上；正己而不求于人，则无怨。上不怨天，下不尤人。故君子居易以俟命，小人行险以徼幸。子曰："射有似乎君子。失诸正鹄，反求诸其身。"

ENG

【第 20 章】

哀公问政。子曰："文武之政，布在方策。其人存，则其政举。其人亡，则其政息。人道敏政，地道敏树。夫政也者，蒲庐也。故为政在人，取人以身，修身以道，修道以仁。仁者，人也，亲亲为大；义者，宜也，尊贤为大。亲亲之杀，尊贤之等，礼所生也。在下位，不获乎上，民不可得而治矣。故君子不可以不修身。思修身，不可以不事亲；思事亲，不可以不知人，思知人，不可以不知天。天下之达道五，所以行之者三。曰：君臣也，父子也；夫妇也；昆弟也；朋友之交。五者，天下之达道也。知、仁、勇三者，天下之达德也。所以行之者一也。或生而知之；或学而知之；或困而知之。及其知之，一也。或安而行之；或利而行之；或勉强而行之；及其成功，一也。"子曰："好学近乎知，力行近乎仁，知耻近乎勇。知斯三者，则知所以修身，知所以修身，则知所以治人；知所以治人，则知所以治天下国家矣。"凡为天下国家有九经，曰："修身也，尊贤也，亲亲也，敬大臣也，体群臣也，子庶民也，来百工也，柔远人也，怀诸侯也。修身则道立，尊贤则不惑，亲亲则诸父昆弟不怨，敬大臣则不眩，体群臣则士之报礼重，子庶民则百姓劝，来百工则财用足，柔远人则四方归之，怀诸侯则天下畏之。齐明盛服，非礼不动，所以修身也。去谗远色，贱货而贵德，所以劝贤也。尊其位，重其禄，同其好恶，所以劝亲亲也。官盛任使，所以劝大臣也。忠信重禄，所以劝士也。时使薄敛，所以劝百姓也。日省月试，既禀称事，所以劝百工也。送往迎来，嘉善而矜不能，所以柔远人也。继绝世，举废国，治乱持危，朝聘以时，厚往而薄来，所以怀诸侯也。凡为天下国家有九经，所以行之者一也。凡事豫则立，不豫则废。言前定则不跲，事前定则不困，行前定则不疚，道前定则不穷。在下位不获乎上，民不可得而治矣。获乎上有道：不信乎朋友，不获乎上矣。信乎朋友有道，不顺乎亲，不信乎朋友矣。顺乎亲有道，反诸身不诚，不顺乎亲矣。诚身有道，不明乎善，不诚乎身矣。诚者，天之道也；诚之者，人之道也。诚者，不勉而中，不思而得，从容中道，圣人也。诚之者，择善而固执之者也。博学之，审问之，慎思之，明辨之，笃行之。有弗学，学之弗能，弗措也。有弗问，问之弗知，弗措也。有弗思，思之弗得，弗措也。有弗辨，弗之弗明，弗措也；有弗行，行之弗笃，弗措也。人一能之，己百之，人十能之，己千之。果能此道矣，虽愚必明，虽柔必强。"

第 4 单元　《论语》

1.《学而篇》　第一

1.1 子曰："学而时习之，不亦悦乎？有朋自远方来，不亦乐乎？人不知，而不愠，不亦君子乎？"

1.2 有子曰："其为人也孝悌，而好犯上者，鲜矣；不好犯上，而好作乱者，未之有也。君子务本，本立而道生。孝悌也者，其为仁之本与？"

1.3 子曰："巧言令色，鲜仁矣。"

1.4 曾子曰："吾日三省乎吾身——为人谋而不忠乎？与朋友交而不信乎？传不习乎？"

1.5 子曰："道千乘之国，敬事而信，节用而爱人，使民以时。"

1.6 子曰："弟子入则孝，出则悌，谨而信，汎爱众，而亲仁。行有余力，则以学文。"

1.7 子夏曰："贤贤易色；事父母，能竭其力；事君，能致其身；与朋友交，言而有信，虽曰未学，吾必谓之学矣。"

1.8 子曰："君子，不重则不威；学则不固。主忠信。无友不如己者。过则勿惮改。"

1.9 曾子曰："慎终，追远，民德归厚矣。"

1.10 子禽问于子贡曰："夫子至于是邦也，必闻其政，求之与？抑与之与？"子贡曰："夫子温、良、恭、俭、让以得之。夫子求之也，其诸异乎人之求之与？"

1.11 子曰："父在，观其志；父没，观其行；三年无改于父之道，可谓孝矣。"

1.12 有子曰："礼之用，和为贵。先王之道，斯为美；小大由之。有所不行，知和而和，不以礼节之，亦不可行也。"

1.13 有子曰："信近于义，言可复也。恭近于礼，远耻辱也。因不失其亲，亦可宗也。"

1.14 子曰："君子食无求饱，居无求安，敏于事而慎于言，就有道而正焉，可谓好学也已。"

1.15 子贡曰："贫而无谄，富而无骄，何如？"子曰："可也；未若贫而乐，富而好礼者也。"

子贡曰："《诗》云：'如切如磋，如琢如磨'，其斯之谓与？"子曰："赐也，始可与言《诗》已，告诸往而知来者。"

1.16 子曰："不患人之不己知，患不知人也。"

2.《为政篇》 第二

2.1 子曰："为政以德，譬如北辰居其所而众星共之。"

2.2 子曰："《诗》三百，一言以蔽之，曰：'思无邪'。"

2.3 子曰："道之以政，齐之以刑，民免而无耻；道之以德，齐之以礼，有耻且格。"

2.4 子曰："吾十有五而志于学，三十而立，四十而不惑，五十而知天命，六十而耳顺，七十而从心所欲，不逾矩。"

2.5 孟懿子问孝。子曰："无违。"樊迟御，子告之曰："孟孙问孝于我，我对曰，无违。"樊迟曰："何谓也？"子曰："生，事之以礼；死，葬之以礼，祭之以礼。"

2.6 孟武伯问孝。子曰："父母唯其疾之忧。"

2.7 子游问孝。子曰："今之孝者，是谓能养。至于犬马，皆能有养；不敬，何以别乎？"

2.8 子夏问孝。子曰："色难。有事，弟子服其劳；有酒食，先生馔，曾是以为孝乎？"

2.9 子曰："吾与回言终日，不违，如愚。退而省其私，亦足以发，回也不愚。"

2.10 子曰："视其所以，观其所由，察其所安。人焉廋哉！人焉廋哉？"

2.11 子曰："温故而知新，可以为师矣。"

2.12 子曰："君子不器。"

2.13 子贡问君子。子曰："先行其言而后从之。"

2.14 子曰："君子周而不比，小人比而不周。"

2.15 子曰："学而不思则罔，思而不学则殆。"

2.16 子曰:"攻乎异端,斯害也已。"

2.17 子曰:"由!诲汝知之乎!知之为知之,不知为不知,是知也。"

2.18 子张学干禄。子曰:"多闻阙疑,慎言其余,则寡尤;多见阙殆,慎行其余,则寡悔。言寡尤,行寡悔,禄在其中矣。"

2.19 哀公问曰:"何为则民服?"孔子对曰:"举直错诸枉,则民服;举枉错诸直,则民不服。"

2.20 季康子问:"使民敬、忠以劝,如之何?"子曰:"临之以庄,则敬;孝慈,则忠;举善而教不能,则劝。"

2.21 或谓孔子曰:"子奚不为政?"子曰:"《书》云:'孝乎惟孝,友于兄弟,施于有政。'是亦为政,奚其为为政?"

2.22 子曰:"人而无信,不知其可也。大车无輗,小车无軏,其何以行之哉!"

2.23 子张问:"十世可知也?"子曰:"殷因于夏礼,所损益,可知也;周因于殷礼,所损益,可知也。其或继周者,虽百世,可知也。"

2.24 子曰:"非其鬼而祭之,谄也。见义不为,无勇也。"

3.《阳货篇》 第十七

17.1 阳货欲见孔子,孔子不见,归孔子豚。孔子时其亡也,而往拜之。遇诸涂。谓孔子曰:"来!予与尔言。"曰:"怀其宝而迷其邦,可谓仁乎?"曰:"不可。"……好从事而亟失时,可谓知乎?"曰:"不可……日月逝矣,岁不我与。"孔子曰:"诺。吾将仕矣。"

17.2 子曰:"性相近也,习相远也。"

17.3 子曰:"唯上知与下愚不移。"

17.4 子之武城,闻弦歌之声。夫子莞尔而笑,曰:"割鸡焉用牛刀?"

子游对曰:"昔者偃也闻诸夫子曰:'君子学道则爱人,小人学道则易使也。'"

子曰:"二三子!偃之言是也。前言戏之耳。"

17.5 公山弗扰以费畔,召,子欲往。子路不悦,曰:"末之也已,何必公山氏之之也。"

子曰:"夫召我者,而岂徒哉?如有用我者,吾其为东周乎?"

17.6 子张问仁于孔子。孔子曰："能行五者于天下为仁矣。"

"请问之。"曰："恭、宽、信、敏、惠。恭则不侮，宽则得众，信则人任焉，敏则有功，惠则足以使人。"

17.7 佛肸召，子欲往。

子路曰："昔者由也闻诸夫子曰：'亲于其身为不善者，君子不入也。'佛肸以中牟畔，子之往也，如之何！"

子曰："然。有是言也。不曰坚乎，磨而不磷；不曰白乎，涅而不缁。吾岂匏瓜也哉？焉能系而不食？"

17.8 子曰："由也！女闻六言六蔽矣乎？"对曰："未也。"

"居！吾语女。好仁不好学，其蔽也愚；好知不好学，其蔽也荡；好信不好学，其蔽也贼；好直不好学，其蔽也绞；好勇不好学，其蔽也乱；好刚不好学，其蔽也狂。"

17.9 子曰："小子何莫学夫诗？诗，可以兴，可以观，可以群，可以怨。迩之事父，远之事君；多识于鸟兽草木之名。"

17.10 子谓伯鱼曰："女为《周南》、《召南》矣乎？人而不为《周南》、《召南》，其犹正墙面而立也与？"

17.11 子曰："礼云礼云，玉帛云乎哉？乐云乐云，钟鼓云乎哉？"

17.12 子曰："色厉而内荏，譬诸小人，其犹穿窬之盗也与？"

17.13 子曰："乡愿，德之贼也。"

17.14 子曰："道听而涂说，德之弃也。"

17.15 子曰："鄙夫可与事君也与哉？其未得之也，患得之。既得之，患失之。苟患失之，无所不至矣。"

17.16 子曰："古者民有三疾，今也或是之亡也。古之狂也肆，今之狂也荡；古之矜也廉，今之矜也忿戾；古之愚也直，今之愚也诈而已矣。"

17.17 子曰："巧言令色，鲜矣仁。"

17.18 子曰："恶紫之夺朱也，恶郑声之乱雅乐也，恶利口之覆邦家者。"

17.19 子曰："予欲无言。"子贡曰："子如不言，则小子何述焉？"子曰："天何言哉？四时行焉，百物生焉，天何言哉？"

17.20 孺悲欲见孔子，孔子辞以疾。将命者出户，取瑟而歌。使之闻之。

17.21 宰我问："三年之丧，期已久矣。君子三年不为礼，礼必坏；三年不为乐，乐必崩。旧谷既没，新谷既升，钻燧改火，期可已矣。"

子曰："食夫稻，衣夫锦，于女安乎？"曰："安。"

"女安，则为之！夫君子之居丧，食旨不甘，闻乐不乐，居处不安，故不为也。今女安，则为之！"

宰我出。子曰："予之不仁也！子生三年，然后免于父母之怀。夫三年之丧，天下之通丧也。予也有三年之爱于其父母乎！"

17.22 子路曰："饱食终日，无所用心，难矣哉！不有博弈者乎？为之，犹贤乎已。"

17.23 子路曰："君子尚勇乎？"子曰："君子义以为上，君子有勇而无义为乱，小人有勇而无义为盗。"

17.24 子贡曰："君子亦有恶乎？"子曰："有恶。恶称人之恶者，恶居下流而讪上者，恶勇而无礼者，恶果敢而窒者。"

曰："赐也亦有恶乎？""恶徼以为知者，恶不孙以为勇者，恶讦以为直者。"

17.25 子曰："唯女子与小人为难养也，近之则不孙，远之则怨。"

17.26 子曰："年四十而见恶焉，其终也已。"

第5单元　《孟子》

公孙丑章句　上

……

3.3 孟子曰："以力假仁者霸，霸必有大国。以德行仁者王，王不待大。汤以七十里，文王以百里。以力服人者，非心服也，力不赡也。以德服人者，中心悦而诚服也。如七十子之服孔子也。诗云：'自西自东，自南自北，无思不服。'此之谓也。"

3.4 孟子曰："仁则荣，不仁则辱。今恶辱而居不仁，是犹恶湿而居下也。如恶之，莫如贵德而尊士。贤者在位，能者在职，国家闲暇，及是时明其政刑，虽大国必畏之矣。诗云：'迨天之未阴雨，撤彼桑土，绸缪牖户，今此下民，或敢侮予。'孔子曰：'为此诗者，其知道乎？能治其国家，谁敢侮之？'今国家闲暇，及是时，般乐怠敖，是自求祸也。祸福无不自己求之者。诗云：'永言配命，自求多福。太甲曰：天作孽，犹可违，自作孽，不可活。'此之谓也。"

3.5 孟子曰："尊贤使能，俊杰在位，则天下之士，皆悦而愿立于其朝矣。市廛而不征，法而不廛，则天下之商，皆悦而愿藏于其市矣。关讥而不征，则天下之旅，皆悦而愿出于其路矣。耕者助而不税，则天下之农，皆悦而愿耕于其野矣。廛无夫里之布，则天下之民，皆悦而愿为之氓矣。信能行此五者，则邻国之民，仰之若父母矣。率其子弟，攻其父母，自生民以来，未有能济者也。如此，则无敌于天下。无敌于天下者，天吏也，然而不王者，未之有也。"

3.6 孟子曰："人皆有不忍人之心。先王有不忍人之心，斯有不忍人之政矣。以不忍人之心，行不忍人之政，治天下可运之掌上。所以谓人皆有不忍人之心者，今人乍见孺子将入于井，皆有怵惕恻隐之心，非所以纳交于孺子之父母也，非所以要誉于乡党朋友也，非恶其声而然也。由是观之，无恻隐之心，非人也；无羞恶之心，非人也；无辞让之心，非人也；无是非之心，非人也。恻隐之心，仁之端也；羞恶之心，义之端也；辞让之心，礼之端也；是非之心，智之端也。人之有是四端也，犹其有四体也。有是四端而自谓不能者，自贼者也。谓其君不能者，贼其君者也。凡有四端于我者，知皆扩而充之矣。若火之始燃，泉之始达。苟能充之，足以保四海，苟不充之，不足以事父母。"

3.7 孟子曰："矢人岂不仁与函人哉？矢人唯恐不伤人，函人唯恐伤人，巫匠亦然。故术不可不慎也。孔子曰：'里仁为美，择不处仁，焉得智？'夫仁，天之尊爵也，人之安宅也。莫之御而不仁，是不智也。不仁不智，无礼无义，人役也。人役而耻为役，由弓人而耻为弓，矢人而耻为矢也。如耻之，莫如为仁。仁者如射，射者正己而后发，发而不中，不怨胜己者。反求诸己而已矣。"

3.8 孟子曰："子路，人告之以有过则喜。禹，闻善言则拜。大舜有大焉，善与人同，舍己从人，乐取于人以为善，自耕稼陶渔以至为帝，无非取于人者。取诸人以为善，是与人为善者也。故君子莫大乎与人为善。"

3.9 孟子曰："伯夷，非其君不事，非其友不友，不立于恶人之朝，不与恶人言。立于恶人之朝，与恶人言，如以朝衣朝冠坐于涂炭。推恶恶之心，思与乡人立，其冠不正，望望然去之，若将浼焉。是故诸侯虽有善其辞命而至者，不受也。不受也者，是亦不屑就已。柳下惠，不羞污君，不卑小官，进不隐贤，必以其道。遗佚而不怨，扼穷而不悯。故曰：'尔为尔，我为我，虽袒裼裸裎于我侧，尔焉能浼我哉？'故由由然与之偕而不自失焉，援而止之而止。援而止之而止者，是亦不屑去已。"孟子曰："伯夷隘，柳下惠不恭。隘与不恭，君子不由也。"

告子章句　上

……

11.2 告子曰："性犹湍水也，决诸东方则东流，决诸西方则西流。人性之无分于善不善也，犹水之无分于东西也。"

孟子曰："水信无分于东西。无分于上下乎？人性之善也，犹水之就下也。人无有不善，水无有不下。今夫水，搏而跃之，可使过颡（sǎng）；激而行之，可使在山。是岂水之性哉？其势则然也。人之可使为不善，其性亦犹是也。"

……

11.4 告子曰："食、色，性也。仁，内也，非外也；义，外也，非内也。"孟子曰："何以谓仁内义外也？"曰："彼长而我长之，非有长于我也；犹彼白而我白之，从其白于外也，故谓之外也。"曰："异于白马之白也，无以异于白人之白也；不识长马之长也，无以异于长人之长欤？且谓长者义乎？长之者义乎？"曰："吾弟则爱之，秦人之弟则不爱也，是以我为悦者也，故谓之内。长楚人之长，亦长吾之长，是以长为悦者也，故谓之外也。"曰："耆秦人之炙，无以异于耆吾炙，夫物则亦有然者也，然则耆炙亦有外欤？"

11.5 孟季子问公都子曰："何以谓义内也？"曰："行吾敬，故谓之内也。""乡人长于伯兄一岁，则谁敬？"曰："敬兄。""酌则谁先？"曰："先酌乡人。""所敬在此，所长在彼，果在外非由内也。"公都子不能答，以告孟子。

孟子曰："敬叔父乎？敬弟乎？彼将曰：'敬叔父。'曰：'弟为尸，则谁敬？'彼将曰：'敬弟。'子曰：'恶在其敬叔父也？'彼将曰：'在位故也。'子亦曰：'在位故也。庸敬在兄，斯须之敬在乡人。'"季子闻之，曰："敬叔父则敬，敬弟则敬，果在外非由内也。"

公都子曰："冬日则饮汤，夏日则饮水，然则饮食亦在外也？"

11.6 公都子曰："告子曰：'性无善无不善也。'或曰：'性可以为善，可以为不善；是故文武兴，则民好善；幽厉兴，则民好暴。'或曰：'有性善，有性不善。是故以尧为君而有象，以瞽（gǔ）瞍（sǒu）为父而有舜，以纣为兄之子，且以为君，而有微子启、王子比干。'今曰'性善'，然则彼皆非欤？"

孟子曰："乃若其情，则可以为善矣，乃所谓善也。若夫为不善，非才之罪也。恻隐之心，人皆有之；羞恶之心，人皆有之；恭敬之心，人皆有之；是非之心，人皆有之。恻隐之心，仁也；羞恶之心，义也；恭敬之心，礼也；是非之心智也。仁义礼智，非由外铄我也，我固有之也，弗思耳矣。故曰：'求则得之，舍则失之。'或相倍蓰（xǐ）而无筭者，不能尽其才者也。《诗》曰：'天生蒸民，有物有则。民之秉彝，好是懿德。'孔子曰：'为此诗者，其知道乎！故有物必有则；民之秉彝也，故好是懿德。'"

11.7 孟子曰："富岁，子弟多赖；凶岁，子弟多暴，非天之降才尔殊也，其所以陷溺其心者然也。今夫麰（móu）麦，播种而耰（yóu）之，其地同，树之时又同，浡然而生，至于日至之时，皆熟矣。虽有不同，则地有肥硗，雨露之养、人事之不齐也。故凡同类者，举相似也，何独至于人而疑之？圣人，与我同类者。故龙子曰：'不知足而为屦，我知其不为蒉（kuì）也。'屦之相似，天下之足同也。口之于味，有同耆也。易牙先得我口之所耆者也。如使口之于味也，其性与人殊，若犬马之与我不同类也，则天下何耆皆从易牙之于味也？至于味，天下期于易牙，是天下之口相似也。惟耳亦然。至于声，天下期于师旷，是天下之耳相似也。惟目亦然。至于子都，天下莫不知其姣也。不知子都之姣者，无目者也。故曰，口之于味也，有同耆焉；耳之于声也，有同听焉；目之于色也，有同美焉。至于心，独无所同然乎？心之所同然者何也？谓理也，义也。圣人先得我心之所同然耳。故理义之悦我心，犹刍豢（huàn）之悦我口。"

11.8 孟子曰："牛山之木尝美矣，以其郊于大国也，斧斤伐之，可以为美乎？是其日夜之所息，雨露之所润，非无萌蘖（niè）之生焉，牛羊又从而牧之，是以若彼濯濯也。人见其濯濯也，以为未尝有材焉，此岂山之性也哉？虽存乎人者，岂无仁义之心哉？其所以放其良心者，亦犹斧斤之于木也，旦旦而伐之，可以为美乎？其日夜之所息，平旦之气，其好恶与人相近也者几希，则其旦昼之所为，有梏亡之矣。梏之反复，则其夜气不足以存；夜气不足以存，则其违禽兽不远矣。人见其禽兽也，而以为未尝有才焉者，是岂人之情也哉？故苟得其养，无物不长；苟失其养，无物不消。孔子曰：'操则存，舍则亡；出入无时，莫知其乡。'惟心之谓与？"

11.9 孟子曰："无或乎王之不智也。虽有天下易生之物也，一日暴之，十日寒之，未有能生者也。吾见亦罕矣，吾退而寒之者至矣，吾如有萌焉何哉？今夫弈之为数，小数也；不专心致志。则不得也。弈秋，通国之善弈者也。使弈秋诲二人弈，其一人专心致志，惟弈秋之为听。一人虽听之，一心以为有鸿鹄将至，思援弓缴而射之，虽与之俱学，弗若之矣，为是其智弗若与？曰：非然也。"

11.10 孟子曰："鱼，我所欲也，熊掌亦我所欲也；二者不可得兼，舍鱼而取熊掌者也。生亦我所欲也，义亦我所欲也；二者不可得兼，舍生而取义者也。生亦我所欲，所欲有甚于生者，故不为苟得也；死亦我所恶，所恶有甚于死者，故患有所不辟也。如使人所欲莫甚于生，则凡可以得生者，何不用也？使人之所恶莫甚于死者，则凡可以辟患者，何不为也？由是则生而有不用也，由是则可以辟患而有不为也。是故所欲有甚于生者，所恶有甚于死者。非独贤者有是心也，人皆有之，贤者能勿丧耳。一箪食，一豆羹，得之则生，弗得则死，嘑尔而与之，行道之人弗受；蹴尔而与之，乞人不屑也。万钟则不辩礼义而受之。万钟于我何加焉？为宫室之美、妻妾之奉、所识穷乏者得我与？乡为身死而不受，今为宫室之美为之；乡为身死而不受，今为妻妾之奉为之；乡为身死而不受，今为所识穷乏者得我而为之，是亦不可以已乎？此之谓失其本心。"

11.11 孟子曰："仁，人心也；义，人路也。舍其路而弗由，放其心而不知求，哀哉！人有鸡犬放，则知求之；有放心而不知求。学问之道无他，求其放心而已矣。"

第 6 单元 《易经》

《乾卦》 第一

乾：元亨，利贞。

初九，潜龙，勿用。

九二，见龙在田，利见大人。

九三，君子终日乾乾，夕惕若，厉无咎。

九四，或跃在渊，无咎。

九五，飞龙在天，利见大人。

上九，亢龙，有悔。

用九，见群龙无首，吉。

《坤卦》 第二

坤：元亨，利牝马之贞。君子有攸往，先迷，后得主，利。西南得朋，东北丧
朋。安贞吉。

初六，履霜，坚冰至。

六二，直，方，大，不习，无不利。

六三，含章，可贞，或从王事，无成有终。

六四，括囊，无咎无誉。

六五，黄裳，元吉。

上六，龙战于野，其血玄黄。

用六，利永贞。

《需卦》 第五

需：有孚，光亨。贞吉，利涉大川。

初九，需于郊，利用恒，无咎。

九二，需于沙，小有言，终吉。

九三，需于泥，致寇至。

六四，需于血，出自穴。

九五，需于酒食，贞吉。

上六，入于穴，有不速之客三人来，敬之，终吉。

《比卦》 第八

比：吉。原筮，元永贞，无咎。不宁方来，后夫凶。

初六，有孚，比之，无咎。有孚，盈缶，终来有它，吉。

六二，比之自内，贞吉。

六三，比之匪人。

六四，外比之，贞吉。

九五，显比，王用三驱，失前禽，邑人不诫，吉。

上六，比之无首，凶。

《谦卦》 第十五

谦：亨。君子有终。

初六，谦谦君子，用涉大川，吉。

六二，鸣谦，贞吉。

九三，劳谦，君子有终，吉。

六四，无不利，伪谦。

六五，不富以其邻，利用侵伐，无不利。

上六，鸣谦，利用行师，征邑国。

《随卦》 第十七

随：元亨，利贞，无咎。

初九，官有渝，贞吉，出门交有功。

六二，系小子，失丈夫。

六三，系丈夫，失小子。随有求得，利居贞。

九四，随有获，贞凶。有孚在道，以明，何咎？

九五，孚于嘉，吉。

上六，拘系之，乃从维之。王用亨于西山。

《观卦》 第二十

观：盥而不荐，有孚颙若。

初六：童观，小人无咎，君子吝。

六二，窥观，利女贞。

六三，观我生，进退。

六四，观国之光，利用宾于王。

九五，观我生，君子无咎。

上九，观其生，君子无咎。

《益卦》 第四十二

益：利有攸往。利涉大川。

初九，利用为大作，元吉，无咎。

六二，或益之十朋之龟，弗克违，永贞吉。王用亨于帝，吉。

六三，益之用凶事，无咎。有孚，中行，告公用圭。

六四，中行，告公从，利用为依迁国。

九五，有孚，惠心，勿问，元吉。有孚，惠我德。

上九，莫益之，或击之，立心勿恒，凶。

第 7 单元　《道德经》

【第一章】

道可道，非常道；名可名，非常名。

无名天地之始；有名万物之母。

故常无欲以观其妙；

常有欲以观其徼。

此两者同出而异名，同谓之玄。

玄之又玄，众妙之门。

【第二章】

天下皆知美之为美，斯恶矣；皆知善之为善，斯不善已。

有无相生，难易相成，长短相形，高下相盈，音声相和，前后相随，恒也。

是以圣人处无为之事，行不言之教；万物作而弗始，生而弗有，为而弗恃，功成而弗居。夫唯弗居，是以不去。

【第八章】

上善若水。水善利万物而不争，处众人之所恶，故几于道。

居善地，心善渊，与善仁，言善信，政善治，事善能，动善时。

夫唯不争，故无尤。

【第九章】

持而盈之，不如其已；

揣而锐之，不可长保。

金玉满堂，莫之能守；

富贵而骄，自遗其咎。

功遂身退，天之道也。

【第十三章】

宠辱若惊，贵大患若身。

何谓宠辱若惊？宠为下，得之若惊，失之若惊，是谓宠辱若惊。

何谓贵大患若身？吾所以有大患者，为吾有身，及吾无身，吾有何患？

故贵以身为天下，若于寄天下；爱以身为天下，若可托天下。

【第十六章】

致虚极，守静笃。

万物并作，吾以观复。

夫物芸芸，各复归其根。

归根曰静，静曰复命。

复命曰常，知常曰明。

不知常，妄作凶。

知常容，容乃公，

公乃全，全乃天，

天乃道，道乃久，

没身不殆。

【第二十二章】

曲则全，枉则直，

洼则盈，敝则新，

少则得，多则惑。

是以圣人抱一为天下式。

不自见，故明；

不自是，故彰；

不自伐，故有功；

不自矜，故长。

夫唯不争，故天下莫能与之争。

古之所谓"曲则全"者，

岂虚言哉！

诚全而归之。

【第二十五章】

有物混成，先天地生。

寂兮寥兮，

独立而不改，

周行而不殆，

可以为天地母。

吾不知其名，

强字之曰道，

强为之名曰大。

大曰逝，逝曰远，远曰反。

故道大，

天大，地大，人亦大。

域中有四大，

而人居其一焉。

人法地，地法天，天法道，道法自然。

【第四十二章】

道生一，

一生二，

二生三，

三生万物。

万物负阴而抱阳，

冲气以为和。

人之所恶，

唯孤、寡、不谷，

而王公以为称。

故物或损之而益，

或益之而损。

人之所教，

我亦教之。

强梁者不得其死,

吾将以为教父。

第 8 单元 《庄子》

1.《逍遥游》

北冥有鱼,其名为鲲,鲲之大,不知其几千里也;化而为鸟,其名为鹏,鹏之背,不知其几千里也。怒而飞,其翼若垂天之云。是鸟也,海运则将徙于南冥。南冥者,天池也。

《齐谐》者,志怪者也。《谐》之言曰:"鹏之徙于南冥也,水击三千里,抟扶摇而上者九万里,去以六月息者也。"野马也,尘埃也,生物之以息相吹也。天之苍苍,其正色邪?其远而无所至极邪?其视下也,亦若是则已矣。且夫水之积也不厚,则其负大舟也无力。覆杯水于坳堂之上,则芥为之舟;置杯焉则胶,水浅而舟大也。风之积也不厚,则其负大翼也无力。故九万里,则风斯在下矣,而后乃今培风;背负青天而莫之夭阏者,而后乃今将图南。蜩与学鸠笑之曰:"我决起而飞,抢榆枋,时则不至,而控于地而已矣,奚以之九万里而南为?"适莽苍者,三餐而反,腹犹果然;适百里者,宿舂粮;适千里者,三月聚粮。之二虫又何知!小知不及大知,小年不及大年。奚以知其然也?朝菌不知晦朔,蟪蛄不知春秋,此小年也。楚之南有冥灵者,以五百岁为春,五百岁为秋;上古有大椿者,以八千岁为春,八千岁为秋,此大年也。而彭祖乃今以久特闻,众人匹之,不亦悲乎?

汤之问棘也是已。"穷发之北有冥海者,天池也。有鱼焉,其广数千里,未有知其修者,其名曰鲲。有鸟焉,其名为鹏,背若太山,翼若垂天之云;抟扶摇羊角而上者九万里,绝云气,负青天,然后图南,且适南冥也。斥鷃笑之曰:'彼且奚适也?我腾跃而上,不过数仞而下,翱翔蓬蒿之间,此亦飞之至也。而彼且奚适也?'"此小大之辩也。

故夫知效一官,行比一乡,德合一君而征一国者,其自视也亦若此矣。而宋荣子犹然笑之。且举世誉之而不加劝,举世非之而不加沮,定乎内外之分,辩乎荣辱之境，斯已矣。彼其于世，未数数然也。虽然，犹有未树也。夫列子御风而行，泠然善也，旬又五日而后反。彼于致福者，未数数然也。此虽免乎行，犹有所待者也。若夫乘天地之正，而御六气之辩，以游无穷者，彼且恶乎待哉！故曰：至人无己，神人无功，圣人无名。

尧让天下于许由，曰："日月出矣，而爝火不息，其于光也，不亦难乎！时雨降矣，而犹浸灌，其于泽也，不亦劳乎？夫子立而天下治，而我犹尸之，吾自视缺然。请致天下。"许由曰："子治天下，天下既已治也。而我犹代子，吾将为名乎？名者，实之宾也。吾将为宾乎？鹪鹩巢于深林，不过一枝；偃鼠饮河，不过满腹。归休乎君，予无所用天下为！庖人虽不治庖，尸祝不越樽俎而代之矣！"

肩吾问于连叔曰："吾闻言于接舆，大而无当，往而不反。吾惊怖其言。犹河汉而无极也；大有径庭，不近人情焉。"连叔曰："其言谓何哉？"曰："藐姑射之山，有神人居焉，肌肤若冰雪，淖约若处子，不食五谷，吸风饮露，乘云气，御飞龙，而游乎四海之外。其神凝，使物不疵疠而年谷熟。吾以是狂而不信也。"连叔曰："然！瞽者无以与乎文章之观，聋者无以与乎钟鼓之声。岂唯形骸有聋盲哉？夫知亦有之。是其言也，犹时女也。之人也，之德也，将磅礴万物以为一，世蕲乎乱，孰弊弊焉以天下为事！之人也，物莫之伤，大浸稽天而不溺，大旱金石流、土山焦而不热。是其尘垢秕穅，将犹陶铸尧舜者也，孰肯以物为事！"宋人资章甫而适诸越，越人断发文身，无所用之。尧治天下之民，平海内之政，往见四子藐姑射之山，汾水之阳，窅然丧其天下焉。

惠子谓庄子曰："魏王贻我大瓠之种，我树之成，而实五石，以盛水浆，其坚不能自举也；剖之以为瓢，则瓠落无所容。非不呺然大也，吾为其无用而掊之。"庄子曰："夫子固拙于用大矣。宋人有善为不龟手之药者，世世以洴澼絖为事。客闻之，请买其方以百金。聚族而谋曰：'我世世为洴澼絖，不过数金；今一朝而鬻技百金，请与之。'客得之，以说吴王。越有难，吴王使之将，冬与越人水战，大败越人，裂地而封之。能不龟手，一也；或以封，或不免于洴澼絖，则所用之异也。今子有五石之瓠，何不虑以为大樽而浮于江湖，而忧其瓠落无所容？则夫子犹有蓬之心也夫！"

惠子谓庄子曰："吾有大树，人谓之樗。其大本拥肿而不中绳墨，其小枝卷曲而不中规矩，立之涂，匠者不顾。今子之言，大而无用，众所同去也。"庄子曰："子独不见狸狌乎？卑身而伏，以候敖者；东西跳梁，不辟高下；中于机辟，死于罔罟。今夫斄牛，其大若垂天之云。此能为大矣，而不能执鼠。今子有大树，患其无用，何不树之于无何有之乡，广莫之野，彷徨乎无为其侧，逍遥乎寝卧其下。不夭斤斧，物无害者，无所可用，安所困苦哉！"

2. 《秋水》（节选）

秋水时至，百川灌河。泾流之大，两涘渚崖之间，不辩牛马。于是焉河伯欣然自喜，以天下之美为尽在己。顺流而东行，至于北海，东面而视，不见水端。于是焉河伯始旋其面目，望洋向若而叹曰："野语有之曰：'闻道百，以为莫己若'者，我之谓也。且夫我尝闻少仲尼之闻而轻伯夷之义者，始吾弗信；今吾睹子之难穷也，吾非至于子之门则殆矣。吾长见笑于大方之家。"

北海若曰："井蛙不可以语于海者，拘于虚也；夏虫不可以语于冰者，笃于时也；曲士不可以语于道者，束于教也。今尔出于崖涘，观于大海，乃知尔丑，尔将可与语大理矣。天下之水，莫大于海，万川归之，不知何时止而不盈；尾闾泄之，不知何时已而不虚；春秋不变，水旱不知。此其过江河之流，不可为量数。而吾未尝以此自多者，自以比形于天地，而受气于阴阳，吾在天地之间，犹小石小木之在大山也。方存乎见少，又奚以自多！计四海之在天地之间也，不似礨空之在大泽乎？计中国之在海内，不似稊米之在大仓乎？号物之数谓之万，人处一焉；人卒九州，谷食之所生，舟车之所通，人处一焉；此其比万物也，不似豪末之在于马体乎？五帝之所连，三王之所争，仁人之所忧，任士之所劳，尽此矣！伯夷辞之以为名，仲尼语之以为博。此其自多也，不似尔向之自多于水乎？"

河伯曰："然则吾大天地而小豪末，可乎？"

北海若曰："否。夫物，量无穷，时无止，分无常，终始无故。是故大知观于远近，故小而不寡，大而不多，知量无穷；证曏今故。故遥而不闷，掇而不跂，知时无止；察乎盈虚，故得而不喜，失而不忧，知分之无常也；明乎坦涂，故生而不说，死而不祸，知终始之不可故也。计人之所知，不若其所不知；其生之时，不若未生之时。以其至小，求穷其至大之域，是故迷乱而不能自得也。由此观之，又何以知毫末之足以定至细之倪？又何以知天地之足以穷至大之域？"

河伯曰："世之议者皆曰：'至精无形，至大不可围。'是信情乎？"

北海若曰："夫自细视大者不尽，自大视细者不明。夫精，小之微也；垺，大之殷也。故异便，此势之有也。夫精粗者，期于有形者也；无形者，数之所不能分也；不可围者，数之所不能穷也。可以言论者，物之粗也；可以意致者，物之精也。言之所不能论，意之所不能察致者，不期精粗焉。是故大人之行：不出乎害人，不多仁恩；动不为利，不贱门隶；货财弗争，不多辞让；事焉不借人，不多食乎力，不贱贪污；行殊乎俗，不多辟异；为在从众，不贱佞谄；世之爵禄不足以为劝，戮耻不足以为辱；知是非之不可为分，细大之不可为倪。闻曰：'道人不闻，至德不得，大人无己。'约分之至也。"

河伯曰："若物之外，若物之内，恶至而倪贵贱？恶至而倪小大？"

北海若曰："以道观之，物无贵贱。以物观之，自贵而相贱。以俗观之，贵贱不在己。以差观之，因其所大而大之，则万物莫不大；因其所小而小之，则万物莫不小。知天地之为稊米也，知毫末之为丘山也，则差数睹矣。以功观之，因其所有而有之，则万物莫不有；因其所无而无之，则万物莫不无。知东西之相反而不可以相无，则功分定矣。以趣观之，因其所然而然之，则万物莫不然；因其所非而非之，则万物莫不非。知尧、桀之自然而相非，则趣操睹矣。昔者尧、舜让而帝，之、哙让而绝；汤、武争而王，白公争而灭。由此观之，争让之礼，尧桀之行，贵贱有时，未可以为常也。梁丽可以冲城，而不可以窒穴，言殊器也；骐骥骅骝一日而驰千里，捕鼠不如狸狌，言殊技也；鸱鸺夜撮蚤，察毫末，昼出瞋目，而不见丘山，言殊性也。故曰：'盖师是而无非，师治而无乱乎？'是未明天地之理，万物之情者也。是犹师天而无地，师阴而无阳，其不可行明矣。然且语而不舍，非愚则诬也。帝王殊禅，三代殊继。差其时、逆其俗者，谓之篡夫；当其时、顺其俗者，谓之义徒。默默乎河伯！女恶知贵贱之门，小大之家！"

河伯曰："然则我何为乎？何不为乎？吾辞受趣舍，吾终奈何？"

北海若曰："以道观之，何贵何贱？是谓反衍；无拘而志，与道大蹇。何少何多？是谓谢施；无一而行，与道参差。严乎若国之有君，其无私德；繇繇乎若祭之有社，其无私福。泛泛乎其若四方之无穷，其无所畛域。兼怀万物，其孰承翼？是谓无方。万物一齐，孰短孰长？道无终始，物有死生，不恃其成。一虚一满，不位乎其形。年不可举，时不可止。消息盈虚，终则有始。是所以语大义之方，论万物之理也。物之生也，若骤若驰，无动而不变，无时而不移。何为乎，何不为乎？夫固将自化。"

河伯曰："然则何贵于道邪？"

北海若曰："知道者必达于理，达于理者必明于权，明于权者不以物害己。至德者，火弗能热，水弗能溺，寒暑弗能害，禽兽弗能贼。非谓其薄之也，言察乎安危，宁于祸福，谨于去就，莫之能害也。故曰：天在内，人在外，德在乎天。知天人之行，本乎天，位乎得，蹢躅而屈伸，反要而语极。"

……

第 9 单元　《文心雕龙》

《神思》第二十六

26.1 古人云："形在江海之上，心存魏阙之下。"神思之谓也。文之思也，其神远矣。故寂然凝虑，思接千载，悄焉动容，视通万里；吟咏之间，吐纳珠玉之声；眉睫之前，卷舒风云之色：其思理之致乎？故思理为妙，神与物游，神居胸臆，而志气统其关键；物沿耳目，而辞令管其枢机。枢机方通，则物无隐貌；关键将塞，则神有遁心。

26.2 是以陶钧文思，贵在虚静，疏瀹五藏，澡雪精神；积学以储宝，酌理以富才，研阅以穷照，驯致以怿辞，然后使元解之宰，寻声律而定墨；独照之匠，窥意象而运斤：此盖驭文之首术，谋篇之大端。

26.3 夫神思方运，万涂竞萌，规矩虚位，刻镂无形。登山则情满于山，观海则意溢于海，我才之多少，将与风云而并驱矣。方其搦翰，气倍辞前，暨乎篇成，半折心始。何则？意翻空而易奇，言征实而难巧也。是以意授于思，言授于意，密则无际，疏则千里：或理在方寸而求之域表，或义在咫尺而思隔山河：是以秉心养术，无务苦虑，含章司契，不必劳情也。

26.4 人之禀才，迟速异分，文之制体，大小殊功。相如含笔而腐毫，扬雄辍翰而惊梦，桓谭疾感于苦思，王充气竭于思虑，张衡研京以十年，左思练都以一纪。虽有巨文，亦思之缓也。淮南崇朝而赋骚，枚皋应诏而成赋，子建援牍如口诵，仲宣举笔似宿构，阮瑀据案而制书，祢衡当食而草奏。虽有短篇，亦思之速也。

26.5 若夫骏发之士，心总要术，敏在虑前，应机立断；覃思之人，情饶歧路，鉴在疑后，研虑方定：机敏故造次而成功，虑疑故愈久而致绩。难易虽殊，并资博练。若学浅而空迟，才疏而徒速，以斯成器，未之前闻。是以临篇缀虑，必有二患：理郁者苦贫，辞溺者伤乱。然则博见为馈贫之粮，贯一为拯乱之药，博而能一，亦有助乎心力矣。

26.6 若情数诡杂，体变迁贸，拙辞或孕于巧义，庸事或萌于新意，视布于麻，虽云未贵，杼轴献功，焕然乃珍。至于思表纤旨，文外曲致，言所不追，笔固知止。至精而后阐其妙，至变而后通其数，伊挚不能言鼎，轮扁不能语斤，其微矣乎！

26.7 赞曰：神用象通，情变所孕。物以貌求，心以理应。刻镂声律，萌芽比兴。结虑司契，垂帷制胜。

《情采》第三十一

31.1 圣贤书辞，总称文章，非采而何！夫水性虚而沦漪结，木体实而花萼振：文附质也。虎豹无文，则鞟同犬羊；犀兕有皮，而色资丹漆：质待文也。若乃综述性灵，敷写器象，镂心鸟迹之中，织辞鱼网之上，其为彪炳，缛采名矣。

31.2 故立文之道，其理有三：一曰形文，五色是也；二曰声文，五音是也；三曰情文，五性是也。五色杂而成黼黻，五音比而成韶夏，五情发而为辞章，神理之数也。

31.3 孝经垂典，丧言不文；故知君子常言，未尝质也。老子疾伪，故称"美言不信"，而五千精妙，则非弃美矣。庄周云"辩雕万物"，谓藻饰也。韩非云"艳乎辩说"，谓绮丽也。绮丽以艳说，藻饰以辩雕，文辞之变，于斯极矣。

31.4 研味孝老，则知文质附乎性情；详览庄韩，则见华实过乎淫侈。若择源于泾渭之流，按辔于邪正之路，亦可以驭文采矣。夫铅黛所以饰容，而盼倩生于淑姿；文采所以饰言，而辩丽本于情性。故情者文之经，辞者理之纬；经正而后纬成，理定而后辞畅：此立文之本源也。

31.5 昔诗人什篇，为情而造文；辞人赋颂，为文而造情。何以明其然？盖风雅之兴，志思蓄愤，而吟咏情性，以讽其上，此为情而造文也；诸子之徒，心非郁陶，苟驰夸饰，鬻声钓世，此为文而造情也。故为情者要约而写真，为文者淫丽而烦滥。而后之作者，采滥忽真，远弃风雅，近师辞赋，故体情之制日疏，逐文之篇愈盛。

31.6 故有志深轩冕，而泛咏皋壤；心缠几务，而虚述人外。真宰弗存，翩其反矣。夫桃李不言而成蹊，有实存也；男子树兰而不芳，无其情也。夫以草木之微，依情待实；况乎文章，述志为本，言与志反，文岂足征？

31.7 是以联辞结采，将欲明经，采滥辞诡，则心理愈翳。固知翠纶桂饵，反所以失鱼。"言隐荣华"，殆谓此也。是以"衣锦褧衣"，恶文太章；贲象穷白，贵乎反本。夫能设谟以位理，拟地以置心，心定而后结音，理正而后摛藻，使文不灭质，博不溺心，正采耀乎朱蓝，间色屏于红紫，乃可谓雕琢其章，彬彬君子矣。

31.8 赞曰：言以文远，诚哉斯验。心术既形，英华乃赡。吴锦好渝，舜英徒艳。繁采寡情，味之必厌。

第 10 单元　《战国策》

《苏秦始将连横》（秦策）

苏秦始将连横，说秦惠王曰："大王之国，西有巴、蜀、汉中之利，北有胡貉、代马之用，南有巫山、黔中之限，东有崤、函之固。田肥美，民殷富，战车万乘，奋击百万，沃野千里，蓄积饶多，地势形便，此所谓天府，天下之雄国也。以大王之贤，士民之众，车骑之用，兵法之教，可以并诸侯，吞天下，称帝而治。愿大王少留意，臣请奏其效。"

秦王曰："寡人闻之，毛羽不丰满者，不可以高飞；文章不成者，不可以诛罚；道德不厚者，不可以使民；政教不顺者，不可以烦大臣。今先生俨然不远千里而庭教之，愿以异日。"

苏秦曰："臣固疑大王不能用也。昔者神农伐补遂，黄帝伐涿鹿而禽蚩尤，尧伐驩兜，舜伐三苗，禹伐共工，汤伐有夏，文王伐崇，武王伐纣，齐桓任战而伯天下。由此观之，恶有不战者乎？古者使车毂击驰，言语相结，天下为一；约从连横，兵革不藏；文士并饬，诸侯乱惑，万端俱起，不可胜理；科条既备，民多伪态；书策稠浊，百姓不足；上下相愁，民无所聊；明言章理，兵甲愈起；辩言伟服，战攻不息；繁称文辞，天下不治；舌弊耳聋，不见成功；行义约信，天下不亲。于是，乃废文任武，厚养死士，缀甲厉兵，效胜于战场。夫徒处而致利，安坐而广地，虽古五帝、三王、五伯，明主贤君，常欲佐而致之，其势不能，故以战续之。宽则两军相攻，迫则杖戟相撞，然后可建大功。是故兵胜于外，义强于内；威立于上，民服于下。今欲并天下，凌万乘，诎敌国，制海内，子元元，臣诸侯，非兵不可！今之嗣主，忽于至道，皆于教，乱于治，迷于言，惑于语，沉于辩，溺于辞。以此论之，王固不能行也。"

说秦王书十上，而说不行。黑貂之裘弊，黄金百斤尽。资用乏绝，去秦而归。羸縢履蹻，负书担橐，形容枯槁，面目黎黑，状有归色。归至家，妻不下纴，嫂不为炊，父母不与言。苏秦喟叹曰："妻不以我为夫，嫂不以我为叔，父母不以我为子，是皆秦之罪也！"乃夜发书，陈箧数十，得《太公阴符》之谋，伏而诵之，简练以为揣摩。读书欲睡，引锥自刺其股，血流至足。曰："安有说人主不能出其金玉锦绣，取卿相之尊者乎？"期年，揣摩成，曰："此真可以说当世之君矣！"

于是乃摩燕乌集阙，见说赵王于华屋之下，抵掌而谈。赵王大悦，封为武安君，受相印。革车百乘，绵绣千纯，白璧百双，黄金万溢，以随其后，约从散横，以抑强秦。故苏秦相于赵而关不通。

当此之时，天下之大，万民之众，王侯之威，谋臣之权，皆欲决苏秦之策。不费斗粮，未烦一兵，未战一士，未绝一弦，未折一矢，诸侯相亲，贤于兄弟。夫贤人在而天下服，一人用而天下从。故曰："式于政，不式于勇；式于廊庙之内，不式于四境之外。"当秦之隆，黄金万溢为用，转毂连骑，炫熿于道，山东之国，从风而服，使赵大重。且夫苏秦特穷巷掘门、桑户枢之士耳，伏轼撙衔，横历天下，廷说诸侯之王，杜左右之口，天下莫之能伉。

将说楚王，路过洛阳。父母闻之，清宫除道，张乐设饮，郊迎三十里。妻侧目而视，倾耳而听；嫂蛇行匍伏，四拜自跪而谢。苏秦曰："嫂，何前倨而后卑也？"嫂曰："以季子之位尊而多金。"苏秦曰："嗟乎！贫穷则父母不子，富贵则亲戚畏惧。人生世上，势位富贵，盖可忽乎哉！"

《邹忌讽齐王纳谏》（齐策）

邹忌修八尺有余，身体昳丽。朝服衣冠窥镜，谓其妻曰："我孰与城北徐公美？"其妻曰："君美甚，徐公何能及公也！"城北徐公，齐国之美丽者也。忌不自信，而复问其妾曰："吾孰与徐公美？"妾曰："徐公何能及君也！"旦日，客从外来，与坐谈，问之客曰："吾与徐公孰美？"客曰："徐公不若君之美也。"

明日，徐公来。孰视之，自以为不如；窥镜而自视，又弗如远甚。暮，寝而思之曰："吾妻之美我者，私我也；妾之美我者，畏我也；客之美我者，欲有求于我也。"

于是入朝见威王曰："臣诚知不如徐公美，臣之妻私臣，臣之妾畏臣，臣之客欲有求于臣。皆以美于徐公。今齐地方千里，百二十城，宫妇左右，莫不私王；朝廷之臣，莫不畏王；四境之内，莫不有求于王。由此观之，王之蔽甚矣！"王曰："善。"乃下令："群臣吏民，能面刺寡人之过者，受上赏；上书谏寡人者，受中赏；能谤议于市朝，闻寡人之耳者，受下赏。"

令初下，群臣进谏，门庭若市。数月之后，时时而间进。期年之后，虽欲言及，无可进者。燕、赵、韩、魏闻之，皆朝于齐。此所谓战胜于朝廷。

《冯谖客孟尝君》（齐策）

齐人有冯谖者，贫乏不能自存，使人属孟尝君，愿寄食门下。孟尝君曰："客何好？"曰："客无好也。"曰："客何能？"曰："客无能也。"孟尝君笑而受之曰："诺。"左右以君贱之也，食以草具。

居有顷，倚柱弹其剑，歌曰："长铗归来乎！食无鱼。"左右以告。孟尝君曰："食之，比门下之鱼客。"居有顷，复弹其铗，歌曰："长铗归来乎！出无车。"左右皆笑之，以告。孟尝君曰："为之驾，比门下之车客。"于是乘其车，揭其剑，过其友，曰："孟尝君客我。"后有顷，复弹其剑铗，歌曰："长铗归来乎！无以为家。"左右皆恶之，以为贪而不知足。孟尝君问："冯公有亲乎？"对曰："有老母。"孟尝君使人给其食用，无使乏。于是冯谖不复歌。

　　后孟尝君出记，问门下诸客："谁习计会，能为文收责于薛乎？"冯谖署曰："能。"孟尝君怪之，曰："此谁也？"左右曰："乃歌夫'长铗归来'者也。"孟尝君笑曰："客果有能也，吾负之，未尝见也。"请而见之，谢曰："文倦于事，愦于忧，而性懧愚，沉于国家之事，开罪于先生。先生不羞，乃有意欲为收责于薛乎？"冯谖曰："愿之。"于是约车治装，载券契而行，辞曰："责毕收，以何市而反？"孟尝君曰："视吾家所寡有者。"

　　驱而之薛，使吏召诸民当偿者，悉来合券。券遍合，起，矫命以责赐诸民，因烧其券，民称万岁。

　　长驱到齐，晨而求见。孟尝君怪其疾也，衣冠而见之，曰："责毕瓶乎？来何疾也！"曰："收毕矣。""以何市而反？"冯谖曰："君云'视吾家所寡有者。'臣窃计，君宫中积珍宝，狗马实外厩，美人充下陈，君家所寡有者以义耳！窃以为君市义。"孟尝君曰："市义奈何？"曰："今君有区区之薛，不拊爱子其民，因而贾利之。臣窃矫君命，以责赐诸民，因烧其券，民称万岁，乃臣所以为君市义也。"孟尝君不说，曰："诺，先生休矣！"

　　后期年，齐王谓孟尝君曰："寡人不敢以先王之臣为臣。"孟尝君就国于薛，未至百里，民扶老携幼，迎君道中。孟尝君顾谓冯谖："先生所为文市义者，乃今日见之。"冯谖曰："狡兔有三窟，仅得免其死耳。今君有一窟，未得高枕而卧也。请为君复凿二窟。"孟尝君予车五十乘，金五百斤，西游于梁，谓惠王曰："齐放其大臣孟尝君于诸侯，诸侯先迎之者，富而兵强。"于是，梁王虚上位，以故相为上将军，遣使者，黄金千斤，车百乘，往聘孟尝君。冯谖先驱，诫孟尝君曰："千金，重币也；百乘，显使也。齐其闻之矣。"梁使三反，孟尝君固辞不往也。齐王闻之，君臣恐惧，遣太傅赍黄金千斤，文车二驷，服剑一，封书谢孟尝君，曰："寡人不祥，被于宗庙之祟，沉于谄谀之臣，开罪于君。寡人不足为也，愿君顾先王之宗庙，姑反国统万人乎？"冯谖诫孟尝君曰："愿请先王之祭器，立宗庙于薛。"庙成，还报孟尝君曰："三窟已就，君姑高枕为乐矣。"

　　孟尝君为相数十年，无纤介之祸者，冯谖之计也。

ENG

第 11 单元 《史记》

《廉颇蔺相如列传》（节选）

廉颇者，赵之良将也。赵惠文王十六年，廉颇为赵将，伐齐，大破之，取阳晋，拜为上卿，以勇气闻于诸侯。

蔺相如者，赵人也。为赵宦者令缪贤舍人。

赵惠文王时，得楚和氏璧。秦昭王闻之，使人遗赵王书，愿以十五城请易璧。赵王与大将军廉颇诸大臣谋：欲予秦，秦城城恐不可得，徒见欺；欲勿予，即患秦兵之来。计未定，求人可使报秦者，未得。

宦者令缪贤曰："臣舍人蔺相如可使。"王问："何以知之？"对曰："臣尝有罪，窃计欲亡走燕。臣舍人相如目臣曰：'君何以知燕王？'臣语曰，臣尝从大王与燕王会境上，燕王私握臣手曰，'愿结友'，以此知之，故欲往。相如谓臣曰：'夫赵强而燕弱，而君幸于赵王，故燕王欲结于君。今君乃亡赵走燕，燕畏赵，其势必不敢留君，而束君归赵矣。君不如肉袒伏斧质请罪，则幸得脱矣。'臣从其计，大王亦幸赦臣。臣窃以为其人勇士，有智谋，宜可使。"

于是王召见，问蔺相如曰："秦王以十五城请易寡人之璧，可予不？"相如曰："秦强而赵弱，不可不许。"王曰："取吾璧，不予我城，奈何？"相如曰："秦以城求璧而赵不许，曲在赵；赵予璧而秦不予赵城，曲在秦。均之二策，宁许以负秦曲。"王曰："谁可使者？"相如曰："王必无人，臣愿奉璧往使。城入赵而璧留秦；城不入，臣请完璧归赵。"赵王于是遂遣相如奉璧西入秦。

秦王坐章台见相如。相如奉璧奏秦王。秦王大喜，传以示美人及左右，左右皆呼万岁。相如视秦王无意偿赵城，乃前曰："璧有瑕，请指示王。"王授璧。相如因持璧却立，倚柱，怒发上冲冠，谓秦王曰："大王欲得璧，使人发书至赵王，赵王悉召群臣议，皆曰：'秦贪，负其强，以空言求璧，偿城恐不可得。'议不欲予秦璧，臣以为布衣之交尚不相欺，况大国乎？且以一璧之故逆强秦之欢，不可。于是赵王乃斋戒五日，使臣奉璧，拜送书于庭。何者？严大国之威以修敬也。今臣至，大王见臣列观，礼节甚据，得璧，传之美人，以戏弄臣。臣观大王无意偿赵王城邑，故臣复取璧。大王必欲急臣，臣头今与璧俱碎于柱矣！"

相如持其璧睨柱，欲以击柱。秦王恐其破璧，乃辞谢，固请，召有司案图，指从此以往十五都予赵。

相如度秦王特以诈佯为予赵城，实不可得，乃谓秦王曰："和氏璧，天下所共传宝也，赵王恐，不敢不献。赵王送璧时斋戒五日。今大王亦宜斋戒五日，设九宾于廷，臣乃敢上璧。秦王度之，终不可强夺，遂许斋五日，舍相如广成传舍。

相如度秦王虽斋，决负约不偿城，乃使其从者衣褐，怀其璧，从径道亡，归璧于赵。

秦王斋五日后，乃设九宾礼于廷，引赵使者蔺相如。相如至，谓秦王曰："秦自缪公以来二十余君，未尝有坚明约束者也。臣诚恐见欺于王而负赵，故令人持璧归，间至赵矣。且秦强而赵弱，大王遣一介之使至赵，赵立奉璧来。今以秦之强而先割十五都予赵，赵岂敢留璧而得罪于大王乎？臣知欺大王之罪当诛，臣请就汤镬。唯大王与群臣孰计议之。"

秦王与群臣相视而嘻。左右或欲引相如去，秦王因曰："今杀相如，终不能得璧也，而绝秦赵之欢。不如因而厚遇之，使归赵。赵王岂以一璧之故欺秦邪？"卒廷见相如，毕礼而归之。

相如既归，赵王以为贤大夫，使不辱于诸侯，拜相如为上大夫。

秦亦不以城予赵，赵亦终不予秦璧。

其后秦伐赵，拔石城。明年复攻赵，杀二万人。秦王使使者告赵王，欲与王为好，会于西河外渑池。赵王畏秦，欲毋行。廉颇、蔺相如计曰："王不行，示赵弱且怯也。"赵王遂行。相如从。廉颇送至境，与王决曰："王行，度道里会遇之礼毕，还，不过三十日。三十日不还，则请立太子为王，以绝秦望。"王许之。遂与秦王会渑池。

秦王饮酒酣，曰："寡人窃闻赵王好音，请奏瑟。"赵王鼓瑟。秦御史前书曰："某年月日，秦王与赵王会饮，令赵王鼓瑟。"蔺相如前曰："赵王窃闻秦王善为秦声，请奉盆缻秦王，以相娱乐。"秦王怒，不许。于是相如前进缻，因跪请秦王。秦王不肯击缻。相如曰："五步之内，相如请得以颈血溅大王矣！"左右欲刃相如，相如张目叱之,左右皆靡。于是秦王不怿,为一击缻。相如顾召赵御史书曰:"某年月日,秦王为赵王击缻。"秦之群臣曰:"请以赵十五城为秦王寿。"蔺相如亦曰:"请以秦之咸阳为赵王寿。"

秦王竟酒,终不能加胜于赵。赵亦盛设兵以待秦,秦不敢动。

既罢,归国,以相如功大,拜为上卿,位在廉颇之右。

廉颇曰:"我为赵将,有攻城野战之大功,而蔺相如徒以口舌为劳,而位居我上。且相如素贱人,吾羞,不忍为之下!"宣言曰:"我见相如,必辱之。"相如闻,不肯与会。相如每朝时,常称病,不欲与廉颇争列。已而相如出,望见廉颇,相如引车避匿。

于是舍人相与谏曰:"臣所以去亲戚而事君者,徒慕君之高义也。今君与廉颇同列,廉君宣恶言,而君畏匿之,恐惧殊甚。且庸人尚羞之,况于将相乎!臣等不肖,请辞去。"蔺相如固止之,曰:"公之视廉将军孰与秦王?"曰:"不若也。"相如曰:"夫以秦王之威,而相如廷叱之,辱其群臣。相如虽驽,独畏廉将军哉?顾吾念之,强秦之所以不敢加兵于赵者,徒以吾两人在也。今两虎共斗,其势不俱生。吾所以为此者,以先国家之急而后私仇也。"

廉颇闻之,肉袒负荆,因宾客至蔺相如门谢罪,曰:"鄙贱之人,不知将军宽之至此也!"

卒相与欢,为刎颈之交。

……

《货殖列传》(节选)

《老子》曰:"至治之极,邻国相望,鸡狗之声相闻,民各甘其食,美其服,安其俗,乐其业,至老死不相往来。"必用此为务,挽近世涂民耳目,则几无行矣。

……

《周书》曰:"农不出则乏其食,工不出则乏其事,商不出则三宝绝,虞不出则财匮少。"财匮少而山泽不辟矣。此四者,民所衣食之原也。原大则饶,原小则鲜。上则富国,下则富家。贫富之道,莫之夺予,而巧者有余,拙者不足。故太公望封于营丘,地潟卤,人民寡,于是太公劝其女功,极技巧,通鱼盐,则人物归之,襁至而辐凑。故齐冠带衣履天下，海岱之间敛袂而往朝焉。其后齐中衰，管子修之，设轻重九府，则桓公以霸，九合诸侯，一匡天下；而管氏亦有三归，位在陪臣，富於列国之君。是以齐富强至于威、宣也。

故曰："仓廪实而知礼节，衣食足而知荣辱。"礼生于有而废于无。故君子富，好行其德；小人富，以适其力。渊深而鱼生之，山深而兽往之，人富而仁义附焉。富者得势益彰，失势则客无所之，以而不乐。夷狄益甚。谚曰："千金之子，不死于市。"此非空言也。故曰："天下熙熙，皆为利来；天下攘攘，皆为利往。"夫千乘之王，万家之侯，百室之君，尚犹患贫，而况匹夫编户之民乎？

昔者越王勾践困于会稽之上，乃用范蠡、计然。计然曰："知斗则修备，时用则知物，二者形则万货之情可得而观已。故岁在金、穰；水、毁；木、饥；火、旱。旱则资舟，水则资车，物之理也。六岁穰，六岁旱，十二岁一大饥。夫粜，二十病农，九十病末。末病则财不出，农病则草不辟矣。上不过八十，下不减三十，则农末俱利。平粜齐物，关市不乏，治国之道也。积著之理，务完物，无息币。以物相贸，易腐败而食之货勿留，无敢居贵。论其有余不足，则知贵贱。贵上极则反贱，贱下极则反贵。贵出如粪土，贱取如珠玉。财币欲其行如流水。"修之十年，国富，厚赂战士，士赴矢石，如渴得饮，遂报强吴，观兵中国，称号"五霸"。

范蠡既雪会稽之耻，乃喟然而叹曰："计然之策七，越用其五而得意。既已施於国，吾欲用之家。"乃乘扁舟浮於江湖，变名易姓，适齐为鸱夷子皮，之陶为朱公。朱公以为陶天下之中，诸侯四通，货物所交易也。乃治产积居。与时逐而不责於人。故善治生者，能择人而任时。十九年之中三致千金，再分散与贫交疏昆弟。此所谓富好行其德者也。後年衰老而听子孙，子孙脩业而息之，遂至巨万。故言富者皆称陶朱公。

子赣既学於仲尼，退而仕於卫，废著鬻财於曹、鲁之间，七十子之徒，赐最为饶益。原宪不厌糟糠，匿於穷巷。子项结驷连骑，束帛之帛以聘享诸侯，所至，国君无不分庭与之抗礼。夫使孔子名布扬於天下者，子贡先後之也。此所谓得埶而益彰者乎？

白圭，周人也。当魏文侯时，李克务尽地力，而白圭乐观时变，故人弃我取，人取我与。夫岁孰取谷，予之丝漆；茧出取帛絮，予之食。太阴在卯，穰；明岁衰恶。至午，旱；明岁美。至酉，穰；明岁衰恶。至子，大旱；明岁美，有水。至卯，积著率岁倍。欲长钱，取下谷；长石斗，取上种。能薄饮食，忍嗜欲，节衣服，与用事僮仆同苦乐，趋时若猛兽挚鸟之发。故曰："吾治生产，犹伊尹、吕尚之谋，孙吴用兵，商鞅行法是也。是故其智不足与权变，勇不足以决断，仁不能以取予，彊不能有所守，虽欲学吾术，终不告之矣。"盖天下言治生祖白圭。白圭其有所试矣，能试有所长，非苟而已也。

……

总之，楚越之地，地广人希，饭稻羹鱼，或火耕而水耨，果隋蠃蛤，不待贾而足，地势饶食，无饥馑之患，以故呰窳偷生，无积聚而多贫。是故江淮以南，无冻饿之人，亦无千金之家。沂、泗水以北，宜五谷桑麻六畜，地小人众，数被水旱之害，民好畜藏，故秦、夏、梁、鲁好农而重民。三河、宛、陈亦然，加以商贾。齐、赵设智巧，仰机利。燕、代田畜而事蚕。

由此观之，贤人深谋于廊庙，论议朝廷，守信死节隐居岩穴之士设为名高者安归乎？归于富厚也。是以廉吏久，久更富，廉贾归富。富者，人之情性，所不学而俱欲者也。故壮士在军，攻城先登，陷阵却敌，斩将搴旗，前蒙矢石，不避汤火之难者，为重赏使也。其在闾巷少年，攻剽椎埋，劫人作奸，掘冢铸币，任侠并兼，借交报仇，篡逐幽隐，不避法禁，走死地如骛者，其实皆为财用耳。今夫赵女郑姬，设形容，揳鸣琴，揄长袂，蹑利屣，目挑心招，出不远千里，不择老少者，奔富厚也。游闲公子，饰冠剑，连车骑，亦为富贵容也。弋射渔猎，犯晨夜，冒霜雪，驰坑谷，不避猛兽之害，为得味也。博戏驰逐，斗鸡走狗，作色相矜，必争胜者，重失负也。医方诸食技术之人，焦神极能，为重糈也。吏士舞文弄法，刻章伪书，不避刀锯之诛者，没于赂遗也。农工商贾畜长，固求富益货也。此有知尽能索耳，终不余力而让财矣。

谚曰："百里不贩樵，千里不贩籴。"居之一岁，种之以谷；十岁，树之以木；百岁，来之以德。德者，人物之谓也。今有无秩禄之奉，爵邑之入，而乐与之比者。命曰"素封"。封者食租税，岁率户二百。千户之君则二十万，朝觐聘享出其中。庶民农工商贾，率亦岁万息二千，百万之家则二十万，而更徭租赋出其中。衣食之欲，恣所好美矣。故曰陆地牧马二百蹄，牛蹄角千，千足羊，泽中千足彘，水居千石鱼陂，山居千章之材；安邑千树枣；燕、秦千树栗；蜀、汉、江陵千树橘；淮北、常山已南，河济之间千树萩，陈、夏千亩漆，齐、鲁千亩桑麻，渭川千亩竹，及名国万家之城，带郭千亩亩锺之田，若千亩卮茜，千畦姜韭。此其人皆与千户侯等。然是富给之资也，不窥市井，不行异邑，坐而待收，身有处士之义而取给焉。若至家贫亲老，妻子软弱，岁时无以祭祀进醵，饮食被服不足以自通，如此不惭耻，则无所比矣。是以无财作力，少有斗智，既饶争时，此其大经也。今治生不待危身取给，则贤人勉焉。是故本富为上，末富次之，奸富最下。无岩处奇士之行，而长贫贱，好语仁义，亦足羞也。

凡编户之民，富相什则卑下之，伯则畏惮之，千则役，万则仆，物之理也。夫用贫求富，农不如工，工不如商，刺绣文不如倚市门。此言末业，贫者之资也。通邑大都，酤一岁千酿，醯酱千瓨，浆千甔，屠牛羊彘千皮，贩谷粜千钟，薪稿千车，船长千丈，木千章，竹竿万个，其轺车百乘，牛车千两，木器髤者千枚，铜器千钧，素木铁器若卮茜千石，马蹄躈千，牛千足，羊彘千双，僮手指千，筋角丹沙千斤，其帛絮细布千钧，文采千匹，榻布皮革千石，漆千斗，蘗麴、盐、豉千荅，鲐鮆千斤，鲰千石，鲍千钧，枣栗千石者三之，狐、貂裘千皮，羔羊裘千石，旃席千具，它果菜千钟，子贷金钱千贯，节驵会，贪贾三之，廉贾五之，此亦比千乘之家，其大率也。它杂业不中什二，则非吾财也。

请略道当世千里之中，贤人所以富者，令后世得以观择焉。

蜀卓氏之先，赵人也，用铁冶富。秦破赵，迁卓氏。卓氏见虏略，独夫妻推辇，行诣迁处。诸迁虏少有余财，争与吏，求近处，处葭萌。唯卓氏曰："此地狭薄。吾闻汶山之下，沃野，下有蹲鸱，至死不饥。民工于市，易贾。"乃求远迁。致之临邛，大喜，即铁山鼓铸，运筹策，倾滇蜀之民，富至僮千人。田池射猎之乐，拟于人君。

程郑，山东迁虏也，亦冶铸，贾椎髻之民，富埒卓氏，俱居临邛。

宛孔氏之先，梁人也，用铁冶为业。秦伐魏，迁孔氏南阳。大鼓铸，规陂池，连车骑，游诸侯，因通商贾之利，有游闲公子之赐与名。然其赢得过当，愈于纤啬，家致富数千金，故南阳行贾尽法孔氏之雍容。

鲁人俗俭啬，而曹邴氏尤甚，以铁冶起，富至巨万。然家自父兄子孙约，俯有拾，仰有取，贳贷行贾遍郡国。邹、鲁以其故多去文学而趋利者，以曹邴氏也。

　　齐俗贱奴虏，而刀间独爱贵之。桀黠奴，人之所患也，唯刀间收取，使之逐渔盐商贾之利。或连车骑，交守相，然愈益任之。终得其力，起富数千万。故曰"宁爵毋刀"，言其能使豪奴自饶而尽其力。

　　周人既纤，而师史尤甚，转毂以百数，贾郡国，无所不至。洛阳街居在齐秦楚赵之中，贫人学事富家，相矜以久贾，数过邑不入门，设任此等，故师史能致七千万。

　　宣曲任氏之先，为督道仓吏。秦之败也，豪杰皆争取金玉，而任氏独窖仓粟。楚汉相距荥阳也，民不得耕种，米石至万，而豪杰金玉尽归任氏，任氏以此起富。富人争奢侈，而任氏折节为俭，力田畜。田畜人争取贱贾，任氏独取贵善。富者数世。然任公家约，非田畜所出弗衣食，公事不毕则身不得饮酒食肉。以此为闾里率，故富而主上重之。

　　塞之斥也，唯桥姚已致马千匹，牛倍之，羊万头，粟以万钟计。吴楚七国兵起时，长安中列侯封君行从军旅，赍贷子钱，子钱家以为侯邑国在关东，关东成败未决，莫肯与。唯无盐氏出捐千金贷，其息什之。三月，吴楚平，一岁之中，则无盐氏之息什倍，用此富埒关中。

　　关中富商大贾，大抵尽诸田，田啬、田兰。韦家栗氏，安陵、杜杜氏，亦巨万。

　　此其章章尤异者也。皆非有爵邑奉禄弄法犯奸而富，尽椎埋去就，与时俯仰，获其赢利，以末致财，用本守之，以武一切，用文持之，变化有概，故足术也。若至力农、畜、工、虞、商贾，为权利以成富，大者倾郡，中者倾县，下者倾乡里者，不可胜数。

　　夫纤啬筋力，治生之正道也，而富者必用奇胜。田农，掘业，而秦扬以盖一州。掘冢，奸事也，而田叔以起。博戏，恶业也，而桓发用富。行贾，丈夫贱行也，而雍乐成以饶。贩脂，辱处也，而雍伯千金。卖浆，小业也，而张氏千万。洒削，薄技也，而郅氏鼎食。胃脯，简微耳，浊氏连骑。马医，浅方，张里击锺。此皆诚壹之所致。

　　由是观之，富无经业，则货无常主，能者辐凑，不肖者瓦解。千金之家比一都之君，巨万者乃与王者同乐。岂所谓"素封"者邪？非也？

第 12 单元 《孙子兵法》

《计篇》（一）

孙子曰：兵者，国之大事，死生之地，存亡之道，不可不察也。

故经之以五事，校之以计，而索其情：一曰道，二曰天，三曰地，四曰将，五曰法。道者，令民于上同意，可与之死，可与之生，而不危也；天者，阴阳、寒暑、时制也；地者，远近、险易、广狭、死生也；将者，智、信、仁、勇、严也；法者，曲制、官道、主用也。凡此五者，将莫不闻，知之者胜，不知之者不胜。故校之以计，而索其情，曰：主孰有道？将孰有能？天地孰得？法令孰行？兵众孰强？士卒孰练？赏罚孰明？吾以此知胜负矣。将听吾计，用之必胜，留之；将不听吾计，用之必败，去之。

计利以听，乃为之势，以佐其外。势者，因利而制权也。兵者，诡道也。故能而示之不能，用而示之不用，近而示之远，远而示之近。利而诱之，乱而取之，实而备之，强而避之，怒而挠之，卑而骄之，佚而劳之，亲而离之，攻其无备，出其不意。此兵家之胜，不可先传也。

夫未战而庙算胜者，得算多也；未战而庙算不胜者，得算少也。多算胜少算，而况于无算乎！吾以此观之，胜负见矣。

《谋攻篇》（三）

孙子曰：夫用兵之法，全国为上，破国次之；全军为上，破军次之；全旅为上，破旅次之；全卒为上，破卒次之；全伍为上，破伍次之。

是故百战百胜，非善之善也；不战而屈人之兵，善之善者也。故上兵伐谋，其次伐交，其次伐兵，其下攻城。攻城之法，为不得已。修橹轒辒，具器械，三月而后成；距堙，又三月而后已。将不胜其忿而蚁附之，杀士卒三分之一，而城不拔者，此攻之灾也。故善用兵者，屈人之兵而非战也，拔人之城而非攻也，毁人之国而非久也，必以全争于天下，故兵不顿而利可全，此谋攻之法也。

故用兵之法，十则围之，五则攻之，倍则分之，敌则能战之，少则能逃之，不若则能避之。故小敌之坚，大敌之擒也。

夫将者，国之辅也。辅周则国必强，辅隙则国必弱。故君之所以患于军者三：不知军之不可以进而谓之进，不知军之不可以退而谓之退，是谓縻军；不知三军之事而同三军之政，则军士惑矣；不知三军之权而同三军之任，则军士疑矣。三军既惑且疑，则诸侯之难至矣。是谓乱军引胜。

故知胜有五：知可以战与不可以战者胜，识众寡之用者胜，上下同欲者胜，以虞待不虞者胜，将能而君不御者胜。此五者，知胜之道也。故曰：知己知彼，百战不殆；不知彼而知己，一胜一负；不知彼不知己，每战必败。

《用间篇》（十三）

孙子曰：凡兴师十万，出征千里，百姓之费，公家之奉，日费千金，内外骚动，怠于道路，不得操事者，七十万家。相守数年，以争一日之胜，而爱爵禄百金，不知敌之情者，不仁之至也，非民之将也，非主之佐也，非胜之主也。故明君贤将所以动而胜人，成功出于众者，先知也。先知者，不可取于鬼神，不可象于事，不可验于度，必取于人，知敌之情者也。

故用间有五：有因间，有内间，有反间，有死间，有生间。五间俱起，莫知其道，是谓神纪，人君之宝也。乡间者，因其乡人而用之；内间者，因其官人而用之；反间者，因其敌间而用之；死间者，为诳事于外，令吾闻知之而传于敌间也；生间者，反报也。故三军之事，莫亲于间，赏莫厚于间，事莫密于间，非圣贤不能用间，非仁义不能使间，非微妙不能得间之实。微哉微哉！无所不用间也。间事未发而先闻者，间与所告者兼死。凡军之所欲击，城之所欲攻，人之所欲杀，必先知其守将、左右、谒者、门者、舍人之姓名，令吾间必索知之。敌间之来间我者，因而利之，导而舍之，故反间可得而用也；因是而知之，故乡间、内间可得而使也；因是而知之，故死间为诳事，可使告敌；因是而知之，故生间可使如期。五间之事，主必知之，知之必在于反间，故反间不可不厚也。

昔殷之兴也，伊挚在夏；周之兴也，吕牙在殷。故明君贤将，能以上智为间者，必成大功。此兵之要，三军之所恃而动也。

第 13 单元 《三国志》与《三国演义》

《三国志·出师表》（节选）

......

先帝创业未半而中道崩殂，今天下三分，益州疲弊，此诚危急存亡之秋也。然侍卫之臣不懈于内，忠志之士忘身于外者，盖追先帝之殊遇，欲报之于陛下也。诚宜开张圣听，以光先帝遗德，恢弘志士之气，不宜妄自菲薄，引喻失义，以塞忠谏之路也。宫中府中俱为一体，陟罚臧否，不宜异同。若有作奸犯科及为忠善者，宜付有司论其刑赏，以昭陛下平明之理，不宜偏私，使内外异法也。侍中、侍郎郭攸之、费祎、董允等，此皆良实，志虑忠纯，是以先帝简拔以遗陛下。愚以为宫中之事，事无大小，悉以咨之，然后施行，必能裨补阙漏，有所广益。将军向宠，性行淑均，晓畅军事，试用於昔日，先帝称之曰能，是以众议举宠为督。愚以为营中之事，悉以咨之，必能使行陈和睦，优劣得所。亲贤臣，远小人，此先汉所以兴隆也；亲小人，远贤臣，此后汉所以倾颓也。先帝在时，每与臣论此事，未尝不叹息痛恨於桓、灵也。侍中、尚书、长史、参军，此悉贞良死节之臣，愿陛下亲之信之，则汉室之隆，可计日而待也。

臣本布衣，躬耕於南阳，苟全性命于乱世，不求闻达于诸侯。先帝不以臣卑鄙，猥自枉屈，三顾臣于草庐之中，咨臣以当世之事，由是感激，遂许先帝以驱驰。后值倾覆，受任於败军之际，奉命於危难之间，尔来二十有一年矣。先帝知臣谨慎，故临崩寄臣以大事也。受命以来，夙夜忧叹，恐托付不效，以伤先帝之明，故五月渡泸，深入不毛。今南方已定，兵甲已足，当奖率三军，北定中原，庶竭驽钝，攘除奸凶，兴复汉室，还于旧都。此臣所以报先帝，而忠陛下之职分也。至于斟酌损益，进尽忠言，则攸之、祎、允之任也。愿陛下托臣以讨贼兴复之效；不效，则治臣之罪，以告先帝之灵。若无兴德之言，则责攸之、祎、允等之慢，以彰其咎。陛下亦宜自谋，以诹诹善道，察纳雅言，深追先帝遗诏。臣不胜受恩感激！

今当远离，临表涕零，不知所言。

《三国演义·开篇词》

滚滚长江东逝水，

浪花淘尽英雄。

是非成败转头空，

青山依旧在，

几度夕阳红。

白发渔樵江渚上，

惯看秋月春风。

一壶浊酒喜相逢，

古今多少事，

都付笑谈中。

《三国演义》第四十六回　用奇谋孔明借箭，献密计黄盖受刑（节选）

……

当夜五更时候，船已近曹操水寨。孔明教把船只头西尾东，一带摆开，就船上擂鼓呐喊。鲁肃惊曰："倘营兵齐出，如之奈何？"孔明笑曰："吾料曹操于重雾中必不敢出。吾等只顾酌酒取乐，待雾散便回。"

却说曹寨中，听得擂鼓呐喊，毛瑜、于禁二人慌忙飞报曹操。操传令曰："重雾迷江，彼军忽至，必有埋伏，切不可轻动。可拨水军弓弩手乱箭射之。"又差人往旱寨内唤张辽、徐晃各带弓弩军三千，火速到江边助射。比及号令到来，毛瑜、于禁怕南军抢入水寨，已差弓弩手在寨前放箭。少顷，旱寨内弓弩手亦到，约一万余人，尽皆向江中放箭，箭如雨发。

孔明教把船吊回，头东尾西，逼近水寨受箭，一面擂鼓呐喊。待至日高雾散，孔明令收船急回。二十只船两边束苇上，排满箭枝。孔明令各船上军士齐声叫曰："谢丞相箭！"比及曹军寨内报知曹操时，这里船轻水急，已放回二十余里，追之不及。曹操懊悔不已。

……

第 14 单元　《金刚经》

第三品《大乘正宗分》

佛告须菩提："诸菩萨摩诃萨应如是降伏其心！所有一切众生之类：若卵生、若胎生、若湿生、若化生；若有色、若无色；若有想、若无想、若非有想非无想，我皆令入无余涅盘而灭度之。如是灭度无量无数无边众生，实无众生得灭度者。何以故？须菩提！若菩萨有我相、人相、众生相、寿者相，即非菩萨。"

第四品《妙行无住分》

"复次，须菩提！菩萨于法，应无所住，行于布施，所谓不住色布施，不住声香味触法布施。须菩提！菩萨应如是布施，不住于相。何以故？若菩萨不住相布施，其福德不可思量。须菩提！于意云何？东方虚空可思量不？""不也，世尊！""须菩提！南西北方四维上下虚空可思量不？""不也，世尊！""须菩提！菩萨无住相布施，福德亦复如是不可思量。须菩提！菩萨但应如所教住。"

第十四品《离相寂灭分》

尔时，须菩提闻说是经，深解义趣，涕泪悲泣，而佛言："希有，世尊！佛说如是甚深经典，我从昔来所得慧眼，未曾得闻如是之经。世尊！若复有人得闻是经，信心清净，则生实相，当知是人，成就第一希有功德。世尊！是实相者，即是非相，是故如来说名实相。世尊！我今得闻如是经典，信解受持不足为难，若当来世，后五百岁，其有众生，得闻是经，信解受持，是人则为第一希有。

"何以故？此人无我相、人相、众生相、寿者相。所以者何？我相即是非相、人相、众生相、寿者相，即是非相。何以故？离一切诸相，则名诸佛。"佛告须菩提："如是！如是！若复有人得闻是经，不惊、不怖、不畏，当知是人甚为希有。何以故？须菩提！如来说第一波罗蜜，非第一波罗蜜，是名第一波罗蜜。须菩提！忍辱波罗蜜，如来说非忍辱波罗蜜，是名忍辱波罗蜜。何以故？须菩提！如我昔为歌利王割截身体，我于尔时，无我相、无人相、无众生相、无寿者相。何以故？

"我于往昔节节支解时，若有我相、人相、众生相、寿者相，应生嗔恨。须菩提！又念过去于五百世作忍辱仙人，于尔所世，无我相、无人相、无众生相、无寿者相。是故须菩提！菩萨应离一切相，发阿耨多罗三藐三菩提心，不应住色生心，不应住声香味触法生心，应生无所住心。若心有住，即为非住。是故佛说：'菩萨心不应住色布施。'须菩提！菩萨为利益一切众生，应如是布施。如来说：一切诸相，即是非相。又说：一切众生，即非众生。须菩提！如来是真语者、实语者、如语者、不诳语者、不异语者。须菩提！如来所得法，此法无实无虚。须菩提，若菩萨心住于法而行布施，如人入暗，即无所见。若菩萨心不住法而行布施，如人有目，日光明照，见种种色。须菩提！当来之世，若有善男子、善女人，能于此经受持读诵，则为如来以佛智慧，悉知是人，悉见是人，皆得成就无量无边功德。"

第三十二品《应化非真分》

"须菩提！若有人以满无量阿僧祇世界七宝持用布施，若有善男子、善女人，发菩提心者，持于此经，乃至四句偈等，受持读诵，为人演说，其福胜彼。云何为人演说，不取于相，如如不动。何以故？"

"一切有为法，如梦幻泡影，如露亦如电，应作如是观"

佛说是经已，长老须菩提及诸比丘、比丘尼、优婆塞、优婆夷，一切世间、天、人、阿修罗，闻佛所说，皆大欢喜，信受奉行。

第 15 单元　《黄帝内经·灵枢》

《淫邪发梦》第四十三

43.1 黄帝曰："愿闻淫邪泮衍，奈何？"

43.2 岐伯曰："正邪从外袭内，而未有定舍，反淫于脏，不得定处，与营卫俱行，而与魂魄飞扬，使人卧不得安而喜梦；气淫于腑，则有余于外，不足于内气淫于脏，则有余于内，不足于外。"

43.3 黄帝曰："有余不足，有形乎？"

43.4 岐伯曰："阴气盛，则梦涉大水而恐惧；阳气盛，则梦大火而燔灼；阴阳俱盛，则梦相杀。上盛则梦飞，下盛则梦堕；甚饥则梦取，甚饱则梦予肝气盛，则梦怒，肺气盛，则梦恐惧、哭泣、飞扬；心气盛，则梦善笑恐畏；脾气盛，则梦歌乐、身体重不举；肾气盛，则梦腰脊两解不属。凡此十二盛者，至而泻之，立已。"

"厥气客于心，则梦见丘山烟火；客于肺，则梦飞扬，见金铁之奇物客于肝，则梦山林树木；客于脾，则梦见丘陵大泽，坏屋风雨客于肾，则梦临渊，没居水中；客于膀胱，则梦游行；客于胃，则梦饮食；客于大肠，则梦田野；客于小肠，则梦聚邑冲衢；客于胆，则梦斗讼自刳嵋；客于阴器，则梦接内；客于项，则梦斩首；客于胫，则梦行走而不能前，及居深地布 苑中；客于股肱，则梦礼节拜起；客于胞膻，则梦溲便。凡此十五不足者，至而补之立已也。"

《五味》第六十二

62.1 黄帝问于少俞曰："五味入于口也，各有所走，各有所病。酸走筋，多食之，令人癃；咸走血，多食之，令人渴辛走气，多食之，令人洞心；苦走骨，多食之，令人变呕；甘走肉，多食之，令人悦心。余知其然也，不知其何由，愿闻其故。"

62.2 少俞答曰："酸入于胃，其气涩以收，上之两焦，弗能出入也。不出即留于胃中，胃中和温，则下注膀胱，膀胱之胞薄以懦，得酸则缩绻，约而不通，水道不行，故癃。阴者，积筋之所终也，故酸入而走筋矣。"

62.3 黄帝曰："咸走血，多食之，令人渴，何也？"

62.4 少俞曰："咸入于胃，其气上走中焦，注于脉，则血气走之，血与咸相得则凝，凝则胃中汁注之，注之则胃中竭，竭则咽路焦，故舌本千而善渴。血脉者，中焦之道也，故咸入而走血矣。"

62.5 黄帝曰："辛走气，多食之，令人洞心，何也？"

62.6 少俞曰："辛入于胃，其气走于上焦，上焦者，受气而营诸阳者也，姜韭之气熏之，营卫之气不时受之，久留心下，故洞心。辛与气俱行，故辛入而与汗俱出。"

62.7 黄帝曰："苦走骨，多食之，令人变呕，何也？"

62.8 少俞曰："苦入于胃，五谷之气，皆不能胜苦，苦入下脘，三焦之道皆闭而不通，故变呕。齿者，骨之所终也，故苦入而走骨，故入而复出，知其走骨也。"

62.9 黄帝曰："甘走肉，多食之，令人悦心，何也？"

62.10 少俞曰："甘入于胃，其气弱小，不能上至于上焦，而与谷留于胃中者，令人柔润者也，胃柔则缓，缓则虫动，虫动则令人挽心。其气外通于肉，故甘走肉。"

第 16 单元　《茶经》

《三之造》

凡采茶，在二月，三月，四月之间。

茶之笋者，笋烂石沃土，长四、五寸，若薇、蕨始抽，凌露采焉。茶之芽者，发于丛薄之上，有三枝、四枝、五枝者。选其中枝颖拔者采焉。

其日，有雨不采，晴有云不采；晴，采之、蒸之、捣之、焙之、穿之、封之、茶之干矣。

茶有千万状，卤莽而言，如胡人靴者，蹙缩然；犎牛臆者，廉襜然；浮云出山者，轮［口禾］然；轻飙拂水也。又如新治地者，遇暴雨流潦之所经；此皆茶之精腴。

有如竹箨者，枝干坚实，艰于蒸捣，故其形籭簁然；有如霜荷者，茎叶凋沮，易其状貌，故厥状委悴然；此皆茶之瘠老者也。

自采至于封，七经目。自胡靴至于霜荷，八等。或以光黑平正言佳者，斯鉴之下也。以皱黄坳垤言佳者，鉴之次也。

若皆言佳及皆言不佳者，鉴之上也。何者？出膏者光，含膏者皱宿制者则黑，日成者则黄；蒸压则平正，纵之则坳垤；此茶与草木叶一也。茶之否臧，存于口决。

《五之煮》

凡炙茶，慎勿于风烬间炙，熛焰如钻，使凉炎不均。特以逼火，屡其翻正，候炮出培塿（lóu）。状蟆背，然后去火五寸。卷而舒，则本其始，又炙之。若火干者，以气熟止；日干者，以柔止。

其始，若茶之至嫩者，蒸罢热捣，叶烂而芽笋存焉。假以力者，持千钧杵亦不之烂，如漆科珠，壮士接之，不能驻其指。及就，则似无穰骨也。炙之，则其节若倪倪如婴儿之臂耳。既而，承热用纸囊贮之，精华之气无所散越，候寒末之。（原注：末之上者，其屑如细米；末之下者，其屑如菱角。）

其火，用炭，次用劲薪（原注：谓桑、槐、桐、枥之类也）其炭曾经燔炙为膻腻所及，及膏木、败器，不用之。（原注：膏木，谓柏、松、桧也。败器，谓朽废器也。）古人有劳薪之味，信哉！

其水，用山水上，江水中，井水下。（原注：《荈赋》所谓"水则岷方之注，挹（yì），彼清流。"）其山水拣乳泉、石池漫流者上；其瀑涌湍漱，勿食之。久食，令人有颈疾。又水流于山谷者，澄浸不泄，自火天至霜郊以前，或潜龙蓄毒于其间，饮者可决之，以流其恶，使新泉涓涓然，酌之。其江水，取去人远者。井，取汲多者。

其沸，如鱼目，微有声，为一沸；缘边如涌泉连珠，为二沸；腾波鼓浪，为三沸；已上，水老，不可食也。

初沸，则水合量，调之以盐味，谓弃其啜余，（原注：啜，尝也，市税反，又市悦反。）无乃[卤舀][卤监]而钟其一味乎，（原注：[卤舀]，古暂反。[卤监]，吐滥反。无味也。）第二沸，出水一瓢，以竹环激汤心，则量末当中心而下。有顷，势若奔涛溅沫，以所出水止之，而育其华也。

凡酌，置诸碗，令沫饽均。（原注：字书并《本草》："沫、饽，均茗沫也。"饽，蒲笏反。）沫饽，汤之华也。华之薄者曰沫，厚者曰饽，轻细者曰花，花，如枣花漂漂然于环池之上；又如回潭曲渚青萍之始生；又如晴天爽朗，有浮云鳞然。其沫者，若绿钱浮于水湄；又如菊英堕于樽俎之中。饽者，以滓煮之，及沸，则重华累沫，皤皤（pó）。然若积雪耳。《荈赋》所谓"焕如积雪，烨若春敷"有之。

第一煮沸水，弃其沫，之上有水膜如黑云母，饮之则其味不正。其第一者为隽永，（原注：徐县、全县二反。至美者曰隽永。隽，味也。永，长也。史长曰隽永，《汉书》蒯通著《隽永》二十篇也。）或留熟盂以贮之，以备育华救沸之用，诸第一与第二、第三碗次之，第四、第五碗外，非渴甚莫之饮。

凡煮水一升，酌分五碗，（原注：碗数少至三，多至五；若人多至十，加两炉。）乘热连饮之。以重浊凝其下，精英浮其上。如冷，则精英随气而竭，饮啜不消亦然矣。

茶性俭，不宜广，广则其味黯澹。且如一满碗，啜半而味寡，况其广乎！

其色缃也，其馨也，其味甘，槚也；不甘而苦，荈也；啜苦咽甘，茶也。

Appendix 2
Bilingual Glossary of Chinese Culture
（常用中国文化专有术语
汉英对照精选）

一、历史与政治

新石器时代 the New Stone Age；the Neolithic Age

旧石器时代 the Old Stone Age（Paleolithic era）

炎黄子孙 descendents of Yandi and Huangdi

殷墟 Yin Ruins

夏商周三代 Three Dynasties：Xia，Shang and Western Zhou

南北朝 the Northern and Southern Dynasties

三国 Three Kingdoms

青铜时代 the Bronze Age

青铜铭文 bronze inscriptions

铁器时代 the Iron Age

宗法制度 patriarchal clan system

嫡长子继承制 the succession of the emperor by his legal wife's eldest son

礼乐制度 the system of rites and music

象形、指事、会意、形声 pictographic characters，self-explanatory characters，associative compounds and pictophonetic characters

青铜铭文 bronze inscriptions

春秋战国文化 the culture in the Spring and Autumn Period, and the Warring States

华夏民族 Huaxia nationality/Chinese nationality

战国七雄 seven powerful states of the Warring States Period

藩镇割据 separatist rule by military governors

五胡：匈奴、狄、羯、羌、鲜卑 Five Non-Han nationalities：Hun, Di, Jie, Qiang, Xianbei

匈奴满族 Huns and Manchus

大一统 great national unity

秦始皇 the First Emperor of Qin

秦始皇陵 Qinshihuang Mausoleum

西汉 the Western Han Dynasty

西域 the Western Regions

匈奴人 the Huns

河西走廊 the Hexi Corridor

中原 the Central Plains

三公九卿 highest-ranked official and ministers；dukes and Ministers

溥天之下，莫非王土；率土之滨，莫非王臣。The whole country belongs to the imperial court, and all the people are the emperor's subjects.

天子 Son of Heaven

司徒 Minister of Land and People

钦差大臣 imperial envoy

家天下 concept that regards the whole country as one's property

四海之内是一家 The whole country is one family

一则治，异则乱，一则安，异则危。When there is unity, there is order；when separation occurs, disorder will follow；when there is unity, there is peace；when separation occurs, danger will follow.

君权至上 supremacy of monarchical power

君权神授 Monarchical power is vested by divinity

天无二日，国无二君。As there is but one sun in the sky, there can be only one unrivalled ruler in one country.

君君，臣臣，父父，子子 the hierarchy of monarch and subject, father and son

陈胜吴广起义 Chen Sheng-Wu Guang Uprising

三国时代 The Three Kingdoms Period

围魏救赵 besiege the State of Wei to rescue the State of Zhao

贞观之治 the Golden Years of Zhenguan

开元盛世 Peace and Prosperity of the Kaiyuan Years

王安石变法 reform instituted by Wang Anshi

武则天 Empress Wu

《大唐西域记》 *Tang-dynasty Records of the Western Regions*

《旧唐书》 *Old Records of the Tang Dynasty/ Jiu Tangshu*

郑和下西洋 Zheng He's Voyages to the Western Seas

戚继光抗倭 Qi Jiguang suppressed the Wokou

戚家军 General Qi's Army

钦差大臣 imperial envoy

鸦片战争 the Opium War

洋务运动 the Westernization Movement

中学为体，西学为用 Chinese learning as base; western learning for application

江南制造局翻译馆 Translation Department under the South China Manufacturing Shop

甲午战争 the Sino-Japanese War of 1894 – 1895

二、思想与主张

黄老学派 philosophical school of the Huangdi and Lao Zi

诸子百家 various schools of thoughts and their exponents during the period from pre-Qin times to the early Han Dynasty

儒家学派 Confucian school

百家争鸣 contention of numerous schools of thought in the period of the Spring and

Autumn Period, and of the Warring States Period

"仁"与"礼" benevolence and rites

墨家 schools of Mohist

兵家 Military Strategists

道家 Taoist

法家 Logicians

阴阳家 Yin and Yang

纵横家 Political Strategists

重农抑商 giving priority to agriculture while curbing the industry and business

焚书坑儒 burning books and burying Confucian scholars alive

罢黜百家，独尊儒术 pay supreme tribute to Confucianism while banning all other schools of thought

程朱理学 the idealist philosophy of the Song and the Ming dynasties, the representatives being Cheng Yi and Zhu Xi

天理与人欲 heavenly principles and human carnal desires

存天理，灭人欲 keeping the heavenly principles and eliminating the carnal desires

内圣外王 supreme morality internalized as cultivation and externalized as governance of virtue

修身、齐家、治国、平天下 Cultivate yourself, put your family in order, run the local government well, and bring peace to the entire country.

三人行，必有吾师。When I walk along with two others, they may serve me as my teacher.

性善论 Theory of good by nature

天理杀人 killing people with the heavenly principles

天人合一 Man is an integral part of nature

天道自然 Heavenly laws are natural.

中庸之道 golden mean

三纲五常 the three cardinal guides and the five constant virtues

三纲：君为臣纲，父为子纲，夫为妇纲 the three cardinal guides：four guides subject，father guides son，and husband guides wife

五常：仁，义，礼，智，信 the five constant virtues：benevolence，righteousness，propriety，wisdom and fidelity

三从：未嫁从父，出嫁从夫，夫死从子 the three obediences（to father before marrige，to husband after marrige，and to son after the death of husband）

四德：妇德、妇言、妇容、妇功 the four virtues（morality，proper speech，modest manner and deligent needle-work）

四书 Four Books：

《大学》 *The Great Learning*

《中庸》 *The Doctrine of the Golden Mean*

《论语》 *The Analects of Confucius*

《孟子》 *Mencius*

五经 Five Classics：

《诗》 *The Book of Songs*

《书》 *Collection of Ancient Texts*

《礼》 *The Rites*

《易》 *The Book of Changes*

《春秋》 *The Spring and Autumn Annals*

兼听则明，偏听则暗。listen to both sides and you will be enlightened，and heed only one side you will be benighted/a clear head comes from an open-mind

经学 study of Confucian classics

玄学 Dark Learning

理学 Confucian school of idealist/philosophy of the Song and the Ming dynasty

考据学 a study of textual research

有无 existence and non-existence/Being and Not-Being

科举制 imperial civil examination system

进士 successful candidates in the highest imperial civil service examination， palace graduate

清朝翰林院 the Imperial Academy of the Qing Dynasty

国子监 Imperial College

京师大学堂 Metropolitan University

京师同文馆 Institute of Diplomatic Relations

有教无类 make no social distinctions in teaching/provide education for all people without discrimination

因材施教 to teach students in accordance with their aptitude

文字狱 Literary Inquisition

八股取士 selection of officials according to their performance in the stereotyped eight-part essay for imperial civil service examination

三、文化艺术

三晋文化 the culture of three Jin States

齐燕文化 the culture of Qi and Yan Counties

邹鲁文化 the culture of Zou and Lu Counties

齐鲁文化 the culture of Qi and Lu counties

宋词元曲 Poetry of the Song Dynasty and operas in the Yuan Dynasty

明清文化 the culture of Ming and the Qing Dynasties

彩陶文化 painted-pottery culture

黑陶文化 black-pottery culture

景德镇瓷器 Jingdezhen porcelain

雕版印刷 engraving printing

泥活字 clay movable letters

活字印刷术 movable-type printing

四大名著：four great novels

《三国演义》 *The Romance of the Three Kingdom*

《水浒传》 *Water Margin*

《西游记》 *Pilgrimage to the West*

《红楼梦》 *A Dream of Red Mansions*

《三字经》 *Three Character Textbook for Beginners*

《千字文》 *A Thousand Character Reader*

《孝经》 *Classic of Filial Piety*

天坛 the Temple of Heaven

紫禁城 the Forbidden City

祈年殿 the Hall of Prayer for Good Harvests

冬至 Winter Solstice

圜丘坛 the Circular Mound Altar

天神 Heavenly Deity

天帝 Heavenly Emperor

先农坛 the Temple for the Divine Cultivator

前门 the Front Gate

中华门 the China Gate

天安门 the Gate of Heavenly Peace

太庙 the Imperial Family Shrine

社稷坛 the Imperial State Shrine

端门 the Gate of Uprightness

午门 the Meridian Gate

神武门 the Gate of Divine Might

地安门 the Gate of Earthly Peace

太和殿 the Hall of Supereme Harmony

中和殿 the Hall of Central Harmony

保和殿 the Hall for Preserving Harmony

文华殿 the Hall of Literary Glory

武英殿 the Hall of Military Eminence

千佛殿 the One Thousand Buddha Hall

坤宁宫 the Hall of Earthly Tranquility

内金水桥 the Inner Golden River

汉字 Chinese Character

拼音文字 phonetic character

象形文字 pictographic character

象形字 hieroglyph

甲骨文 oracle-bone inscription

方块象形文字 the square-shaped pictographic character

毛笔 the writing brush

行草 Running-Cursive Script

一笔书 one-stroke character

篆文 seal character

大篆 dazhuan/greater seal/bronze inscription

小篆 xiaozhuan/lesser seal

丝绸之路 the Silk Road

敦煌石窟 the Dunhuang Grottoes

飞天 apsaras

兵马俑 the Terracotta Army

陶俑 terracotta warriors

云冈石窟 the Yungang Grottoes

莫高窟 the Mogao Grottoes

龙门石窟 the Longmen Grottoes

乐山大佛 Leshan Giant Buddha

大昭寺 Jokhang Temple

大昭孝寺 Great Temple to Glorfy Filial piety

布达拉宫 Historic Ensemble of the Potala Palace

壁画 mural

三教合一 integration of Confucianism, Taoism and Buddhism

千佛洞 the Cave of One Thousand Buddha Statues

观音菩萨 Guanyin/the Goddess of Mercy/the Bodhisattva

释迦牟尼 Sakyamuni

千手观音 Guanyin with 1,000 Hands

京剧 Peking Opera

京剧脸谱 Peking Opera mask

净角 jing/painted-face role

丑角 chou /clown

旦角 female role/dan

四大名旦 four famed Peking Opera female-role performers

名角 mingjue/famous actors or actresses

红脸 red face

黑脸 black face

白脸 white face

面人 dough figurine

泥人 clay figurine

福娃 Fuwa

曲调 aria

对白 dialog

身段 body movement

眼神 eye movement

独舞 solo dancing

群舞 group dancing

杂技 acrobatics

《霸王别姬》 *King Chu Bids Farewell to His Concubine*

《三岔口》 *At the Crossroad*

《贵妃醉酒》 *The Drunken Concubine*

《穆桂英挂帅》 *Woman General Mu Guiying*

昆曲 Kunqu Opera

河北梆子 Hebei Bangzi

评戏 Pingxi Opera

木偶戏 puppet shows

绸舞 silk dance

剑舞 sword dance

袖舞 sleeve dance

拂尘舞 duster dance

秧歌舞 yangko

腰鼓 waist drum

二胡 erhu

京胡 jinghu

景泰蓝 Cloisonne/Jingtaı blue

珐琅 enamel

掐丝 filigree

点蓝 stippling blue

打磨 burnishing

年画 New Year pictures

《连年有余》 *Surplus in Successive Years*

浮世绘 ukiyoe

铜板雕刻 bronze carvings

剪纸 papercut

刺绣/女红 embroidery/women's needlework

锦院 the Satin Academy

绣院 the Embroidery Academy

"百鸟朝凤" one Hundred Birds Worship the Phoenix

皮影戏 shadow play/shadow puppetry

木偶 shadow-play puppets

驴皮 donkey hide

《清明上河图》 *A Riverside Scene at Qingming Festival*

庙会 temple fair

大相国寺 Daxiangguo Temple

相声 crosstalk

口技 vocal minicry

京韵大鼓 Beijing musical storytelling accompanied by a small drum

生肖 Chinese Zodiac

四、饮食与茶道

涮羊肉 hotpot mutton

砂锅丸子 meatball hotpot

烩酸菜 braised preserved cabbage

扒鲍鱼 stewed abalone

溜鸡脯 stir-fried chicken

豌豆黄 pea-flour cake

窝窝头 corn-flour bun

肉末烧饼 cakes with meat fillings

扒糕 buckwheat cake

驴打滚 "donkey" roll

糖葫芦 sugar-coated haws on sticks

中秋月饼 Mid-Autumn mooncake

八大菜系 eight schools of cuisine

南甜北咸，西酸东辣 Sweet in the south, salty in the north, sour in the west, and spicy in the east

天府之国 Nature's Storehouse

花椒 Chinese prickly ash seed

豆瓣酱 fermented bean sauce

西湖醋鱼 West Lake Vinegar Fish

狗不理包子 Goubuli Steamed Buns

东坡肉 Dongpo Meat

睇跳墙 Buddha Jumping over the Wall

红烧狮子头 braised meat balls in brown sauce

坛烧八宝 Eight Treasures Stewed in a Pot

八宝烧全鸭 stuffed whole duck

福寿全 Blessing and Longevity

蚂蚁上树 Bean Vermicelli with Spicy Meat

清蒸鱼 steamed fish

青椒肉丝 Shredded Pork with Green Pepper

饺子 jiaozi/meat and vegetable dumplings

油条 deep-fried dough sticks

稀饭 gruel

馒头 mantow

刀削面 pared fresh noodles

四川担担面 Sichuan dandan noodles

全鸭宴 full-duck banquet

全家福 Stewed Assorted Meats.

二十四节气 solar terms

春分 Spring Equinox

夏至 Summer Equinox

立秋 Beginning of Autumn

冬至 Winter Solstice

春节 Lunar New Year/Chinese New Year/Spring Festival

元宵节 the Lantern Festival

元宵 yuanxiao/sweet dumplings made of glutinous rice flour

端午节 Duanwu Festival

粽子 zongzi/glutinous rice wrapped in a pyramid shape in reed leaves

重阳节 Double Ninth Festival

禅宗 Zen Buddhism

日本茶道 Japanese tea ceremony

广东早茶 Candon morning tea

茶具 tea set

茶圣 tea saint

绿茶 green tea

红茶 black Tea

乌龙茶 oolong tea

黑茶 dark tea

花茶 scented tea

龙井 Longjing

碧螺春 Biluochun

黄山毛峰 Huangshan Maofeng

六安瓜片 Liu'an Guapian

安徽祁门红茶 Qimen Black Tea of Anhui

云南滇红茶 Dian Black Tea of Yunnan

云南普洱茶 Pu'er Tea of Yunnan

菊花茶 chrysanthemum tea

茉莉花茶 jasmine tea

宜兴紫砂壶 boccaro teapot of Yi Xin

五、体育与养生

赛龙舟 dragon-boat race

相扑 sumo

摔跤 wrestling

马术 equestrianism

少林寺 the Shaolin Temple

武术 martial arts /wushu

李小龙 Bruce Lee

李连杰 Jet Li

成龙 Jackie Chan

剑术 swordplay

三节棍 three-section stick

长拳 long boxing

短拳 short boxing

刀术 knife play

少林童子功 Shaolin children's kung fu

童子拜观音 child worshiping Guanyin

童子拜佛 child worshiping Buddha

一指禅 One-finger Zen

八卦掌 Bagua

鹰爪拳 Eagle Claw

五形拳 Five Animals Claw

螳螂拳 Praying Mantis

白鹤拳（永春白鹤拳） White Crane

罗汉拳 arhat boxing

太极拳 taoi quan/shadow boxing/tai chi chuan

气功 qigong

八卦 Eight Trigrams

阴阳五行 Yin-Yang and Five Agents （mental，wood，water，fire and earth）

良药苦口利于病 good medicine tastes bitter，but beneficial to health

抽签 lots-drawing

算命 fortune-telling

符咒 spell

咒语 conjuration

中医 Traditional Chinese Medicine（TCM）

草药 herbal medicine

经络系统 Meridian system

针灸 acupuncture and moxibustion

阴盛阳衰 excessYin and Yang deficiency

阴阳失衡 imbalance between Yin and Yang

五脏学说 Zang-Fu organ theory

偏方 folk remedy

望闻问切 inspection，listening and smelling，inquiry and palpation examinations

脉搏 pulse

中医师 TCM practitioner

太医 palace physician

拔火罐 cupping

刮痧 skin-scrapping

药膳 medicated diet

Appendix 3
Booklists of "Library of Chinese Classics (Chinese-English)" (《大中华文库》(汉英对照) 部分书目)

《老子》亚瑟·韦利 英译

《庄子》汪榕培 英译

《论语》韦利 英译

《孟子》赵甄陶等 英译

《周易全二卷》卫礼贤 英译

《荀子》约翰·诺布洛克 英译

《管子》翟江月 英译

《列子》梁晓鹏 英译

《吕氏春秋》翟江月 英译

《史记选》杨宪益、戴乃迭 英译

《菜根谭》保罗·怀特 英译

《颜氏家训》宗福常 英译

《孙子兵法·孙膑兵法》林戊荪 英译

《三国演义》罗慕士 英译

《水浒传》沙博理 英译

《西游记》詹纳尔 英译

《红楼梦》杨宪益、戴乃迭 英译

《西厢记》许渊冲 英译

《牡丹亭》汪榕培 英译

《金瓶梅》克莱门特·厄杰顿 英译

《墨子》王宏 英译

《梦溪笔谈》王宏 英译

《浮生六记》Shirley M·Black 英译

《国语》王宏 英译

《明清小品文》王宏 英译

《山海经》王宏 英译

《儒林外史》杨宪益、戴乃迭 英译

《封神演义》顾执中 英译

《搜神记》丁往道 英译

《陶渊明集》汪榕培 英译

《长生殿》杨宪益、戴乃迭 英译

《儿女英雄传》贾致德 英译

《关汉卿杂剧选》杨宪益、戴乃迭 英译

《中国古代寓言选》杨宪益、戴乃迭 英译

《邯郸记》汪榕培 英译

《文心雕龙》杨国斌 英译

《镜花缘》林太乙 英译

《老残游记》哈罗德·沙迪克 英译

《吴子·司马法·尉缭子》潘家玢 英译

《六韬》聂送来 英译

《黄石公三路·唐太宗李卫公问对》何小东 英译

《黄帝内经·素问》李照国等 英译

《黄帝内经·灵枢》李照国 英译

《金匮要略》罗希文 英译

《伤寒论》罗希文 英译

《黄帝四经》余明光 英译

《茶经、续茶经》姜欣、姜怡 英译

《世说新语》刘尚慈 英译

《聊斋志异选》翟理斯 英译

《太平广记选》张光前 英译

《宋明评话选》杨宪益、戴乃迭 译

《汉魏六朝小说选》杨宪益、戴乃迭 译

《楚辞》陈器之 英译

《拍案惊奇》杨宪益、戴乃迭 译

《四元玉鉴》陈在新 英译

《唐诗三百首》许渊冲 英译

《宋词三百首》许渊冲 英译

《元曲三百首》许渊冲 英译

《新编千家诗》许渊冲 英译

《阮籍诗选》Grahaim Hartill 英译

《南柯记》张光前 英译

《商君书》戴闻达 英译

《人间词话》李又安 英译

References （参考文献）

一、外文著作

［1］ C. H. Brewitt-Taylor. *Romance of the Three Kingdoms*. Vermont：Tuttle Publishing，1990.

［2］ Daniel Kolak. *Lovers of Wisdom：An Introduction to Philosophy with Integrated Readings*. Beijing：Peking University Press，2002.

［3］ Evans, John C. *Tea in China：The History of China's National Drink*. New York：Greenwood Press. 1992.

［4］ Gunde，Richard. *Culture and Customs of China*. Westport：Greenwood Press，2002.

［5］ John Minford，Joseph S. M. Lau. *Classical Chinese Literature—An Anthology of Translations*（Vol.1：*From Antiquity to the Tang Dynasty*）. New York：Columbia University Press；Hong Kong：Chinese University Press，2000.

［6］ Mari，Victor H. *The Columbia Anthology of Traditional Chinese Literature*. New York：Columbia University Press，1994.

［7］ Moss Roberts. *The Columbia History of Chinese Literature*. Beijing：Foreign Languages Press，1995.

［8］ Wei，Francis C. M. *The Spirit of Chinese Culture*. New York：Charles Scribner's Sons，1947.

［9］ Wu，Dingbo & Murphy，Patrick（ed.）. *Handbook of Chinese Popular Culture*. Westport：Greenwood Press，1994.

［10］http：//en. wikipedia. org/wiki/Analects.

［11］http：//confucius. org/lunyu/Iange. htm.

［12］http：//www. gutenberg. org/browse/authors/I#a1114.

［13］Chinese Philosophy and Religion. http：//www. confuchina. com/

［14］Chinese Philosophy. http：//www. chinesephilosophv. net/.

［15］Chinese Religion. http：//www. religionfacts. com/chinese religion/index. htm.

［16］Traditional Chinese Medicine. http：//www. tcmpage. com/.

［17］Traditional Chinese Medicine. http：//www. pharnmet. com. cn.

二、中文著作

［1］王秀梅译注，《诗经》，北京：中华书局，2006 年版。

［2］刘毓庆、李蹊译注，《诗经》，北京：中华书局，2011 年版。

［3］樊东译注，《大学·中庸》，上海：上海三联书店，2013 年版。

［4］子思著，（英）理雅各译：《中庸》，北京：外语教学与研究出版社，2011 年版。

［5］蒙培元，重新解读孔子/任继愈：《文津演讲录》（之六），北京：北京图书馆出版社，2007 年版。

［6］张燕婴译注，《论语》，北京：中华书局，2006 年版。

［7］李泽厚，《论语今读》，合肥：安徽文艺出版社，1998 年版。

［8］万丽华、蓝旭译注，《孟子》，北京：中华书局，2006 年版。

［9］袁立，《易经》，武汉：武汉大学出版社，2011 年版。

［10］郭彧译注，《周易》，北京：中华书局，2006 年版。

［11］朱伯崑，《易学哲学史》，北京：昆仑出版社，2005 年版。

［12］刘大钧，《〈周易〉概论》，济南：齐鲁书社，1988 年版。

［13］朱谦之，《老子十三章》，北京：中华书局，1984 年版。

［14］流沙河，《庄子现代版》，上海：上海古籍出版社，1999 年版。

［15］张松如，《老子说解》，济南：齐鲁书社，1998 年版。

［16］陈鼓应、白奚，《老子评传》，南京：南京大学出版社，2001 年版。

［17］钱穆，《庄老通辨》，北京：生活·读书·新知三联书店，2005 年版。

［18］饶尚宽译注，《老子》，北京：中华书局，2006 年版。

［19］老子著，欧阳居士注译，《道德经》，北京：中国画报出版社，2012 年版。

［20］孙通海译注，《庄子》，北京：中华书局，2006 年版。

［21］（战国）庄子著，冯友兰译，《庄子》，北京：外语教学与研究出版社，2012 年版。

［22］周振甫，《〈文心雕龙〉二十二讲》，重庆：重庆大学出版社，2010 年版。

［23］周振甫，《〈文心雕龙〉今译》，北京：中华书局，1986 年版。

［24］缪文远译注，《战国策》，北京：中华书局，2012 年版。

［25］（西汉）司马迁著，韩兆琦评注，《史记》，长沙：岳麓书社，2012 年版。

［26］（西汉）司马迁著，王耀祖等注译：《史记》，北京：崇文书局，2007 年版。

［27］欧阳居士注释，《孙子兵法》，北京：中国画报出版社，2012 年版。

［28］黄朴民，《黄朴民解读孙子兵法》，长沙：岳麓书社，2011 年版。

［29］（晋）陈寿，《三国志》，北京：中华书局，2009 年版。

［30］［日］土岐秋子，［日］塩沢裕仁著，扈敏译，《图解三国志》，西安：陕西师范大学出版社，2012 年版。

［31］（明）罗贯中著，《三国演义》，北京：中国画报出版社，2012 年版。

［32］易中天著，《易中天品三国》，上海：上海文艺出版社，2006 年版。

［33］史东梅编著，《金刚经》，昆明：云南人民出版社，2011 年版。

［34］费勇，《不焦虑的活法：金刚经修心课》，上海：华东师范大学出版社，2013 年版。

［35］姚春鹏译注，《黄帝内经》，北京：中华书局，2010 年版。

［36］何平叔，《何平叔解读〈黄帝内经〉——古中医学的人体疾病观》，北京：人民军医出版社，2008 年版。

［37］（唐）陆羽著，钟强主编，《茶经》，哈尔滨：黑龙江科学技术出版社，2010 年版。

［38］（唐）陆羽著，紫图编绘，《图解茶经》，西安：陕西师范大学出版社，

2012 年版。

[39] 陈德生，《中医学入门》，台北：文光图书有限公司，1990 年版。

[40] 冯友兰，《中国哲学史新编（第一册）》，北京：人民出版社，1982 年版。

[41] 何满子，《中国酒文化》，上海：上海古籍出版社，2001 年版。

[42] 何其亮、张晔，《英译中国传统文化》，杭州：浙江大学出版社，2006 年版。

[43] 蒋雁峰，《中国酒文化研究》，长沙：湖南师范大学出版社，2006 年版。

[44] 姜欣、姜怡，《文化交流英语》，北京：高等教育出版社，2006 年版。

[45] 篱海波，《中国传统文化与中医》，北京：人民卫生出版社，2007 年版。

[46] 李霞，《英语畅谈中国文化 50 主题》，北京：外文出版社，2007 年版。

[47] 刘敦桢，《中国古代建筑史》，北京：中国建筑工业出版社，1984 年版。

[48] 刘勇强，《中国占代小说史叙论》，北京：北京大学出版社，2007 年版。

[49] 刘宝义，《明于阴阳 ——中医的概念与逻辑》，济南：山东大学出版社，2007 年版。

[50] 马国超，《中国传统体育》，北京：首都师范大学出版社，2007 年版。

[51] 马敏，《中国文化教程》，武汉：华中师范大学出版社，2007 年版。

[52] 任继愈，《中国哲学史》，北京：人民出版社，1979 年版。

[53] [美] 浦安迪，《明清小说四大奇书》，北京：生活·读书·新知三联书店，2006 年版。

[54] 宋莉，《风采中国——中国文化概况》（英文版），哈尔滨：哈尔滨工业大学出版社，2005 年版。

[55] 孙云焘，《烟酒茶与人生》，北京：商务印书馆，1935 年版。

[56] 王元化，《释中国》（共 4 卷），上海：上海译文出版社，1998 年版。

[57] 王宏印，《中国文化典籍译》，北京：外语教学与研究出版社，2009 年版。

[58] 王学泰，《中国饮食文化史》，桂林：广西师范大学出版社，2006 年版。

[59] 吴鼎民、郭龙，《中国文化概览》（英文版），南京：译林出版社，2010 年版。

[60] 徐城北，《京剧与中国文化》，北京：人民出版社，1999 年版。

［61］杨俊峰，《高级阅读——中国文化精粹》，长春：吉林音像出版社，2005年版。

［62］杨敏，《中国文化通览》，北京：高等教育出版社，2006年版。

［63］杨敏、王克奇等，《中国传统文化通览（英汉版）》，青岛：中国海洋大学出版社，2003年版。

［64］杨昆宁，《中国茶文化艺术论》，昆明：云南教育出版社，2006年版。

［65］叶朗、费振刚等，《中国文化导读》，北京：生活·读书·新知三联书店，2007年版。

［66］叶朗、朱良志，《中国文化读本》（英文版），北京：外语教学与研究出版社，2008年版。

［67］叶朗、朱良志等，《中国文化英语教程》，北京：外语教学与研究出版社，2008年版。

［68］余惠芬，《中国传统文化概论（英文版）》，广州：暨南大学出版社，2007年版。

［69］郑铁生、陈法春，《中国文化概览（英汉对照）》，天津：天津教育出版社，2010年版。

［70］周维权，《中国古典园林史》，北京：清华大学出版社，1999年版。

［71］朱一飞等，《中国文化寓言故事》（英文版），上海：上海外语教育出版社，2007年版。

［72］张缨，《中国人文经典翻译赏析》，西安：西安交通大学出版社，2010年版。

图书在版编目（CIP）数据

英译中国文化经典精读教程/陆道夫，粟孝君主编 . —广州：暨南大学出版社，2014.4
（21 世纪多维英语规划教材）
ISBN 978 - 7 - 5668 - 0881 - 3

Ⅰ.①英⋯　Ⅱ.①陆⋯②粟⋯　Ⅲ.①英语—高等学校—教材②中华文化—教材
Ⅳ.①H319.4

中国版本图书馆 CIP 数据核字（2013）第 293221 号

出版发行：暨南大学出版社

地　　址：	中国广州暨南大学
电　　话：	总编室（8620）85221601
	营销部（8620）85225284　85228291　85228292（邮购）
传　　真：	（8620）85221583（办公室）　85223774（营销部）
邮　　编：	510630
网　　址：	http：//www. jnupress. com　http：//press. jnu. edu. cn

策划编辑：杜小陆
责任编辑：杜小陆　高　洵
责任校对：王嘉涵　李雨锦

排　　版：弓设计
印　　刷：佛山市浩文彩色印刷有限公司

开　　本：	787mm×960mm　1/16
印　　张：	20.5
字　　数：	398 千
版　　次：	2014 年 4 月第 1 版
印　　次：	2014 年 4 月第 1 次
印　　数：	1—3000 册

定　　价：39.80 元